Shea L. Bradley-Farrell, Ph.D.

Last Warning to the West

Shea L. Bradley-Farrell, Ph.D.

Last Warning to the West

Hungary's Triumph Over Communism and the Woke Agenda

Shea L. Bradley-Farrell. 2023. Last Warning to the West.
Hungary's Triumph Over Communism and the Woke Agenda.

Copy editing: Sharon Higby
Typesetting: Sejla Almadi, Ph.D.
Cover: Attila Nagy

ALAPJOGOKÉRT KÖZPONT
CENTER FOR FUNDAMENTAL RIGHTS

JOGÁLLAM ÉS IGAZSÁG NONPROFIT KFT.
HU-1121 Budapest, Budakeszi út 36/c.
Publisher: dr. Miklós Géza Szánthó

ISBN (printed): 978-615-6476-16-6
ISBN (online): 978-615-6476-17-3

CONTENTS

For Chris, who always inspires me to be me.

Don't accept the EU propaganda version that we are celebrating the fall of the Berlin Wall as though 'freedom of movement' were all that it is about. We are celebrating the restoration of national sovereignty to people who had been absorbed and oppressed by a lawless empire. The fact that they are now absorbed by a lawful one does not alter the case.

—Sir Roger Scruton

FOREWORD

Kari Lake

You now have in your hands one of the last warnings we may ever get concerning the slow-motion collapse of America's democratic republic.

The warning comes through the insightful historical and political analysis of Dr. Shea L. Bradley-Farrell in this compelling study of Hungary—the vibrant, thriving, conservative success story in the very heart of Central Europe. Hungary's 1,000-year-long Christian history provides perspective that the West desperately needs today; it is a uniquely Magyar perspective, only gained through centuries of conquest, invasion, resistance, independence, subjugation, occupation, revolution, and finally freedom and national identity.

Dr. Bradley-Farrell has skillfully demonstrated the lessons of Hungary's success story to provide an American reading audience with a powerful analysis that illuminates the insidious dangers of contemporary America's flirtations with socialism. She provides not just a warning, but a context for understanding how we got here, and most importantly, a way out. We cannot begin the journey to restoring our constitutional republic without a clear understanding and expression of the problem. Dr. Bradley-Farrell takes us through all the points we need to know in an energetic, inspiring way, and then brings it home with crystal clear analysis and vision for a path forward.

In May 2023, the Center for Fundamental Rights in Budapest hosted the Conservative Political Action Conference (CPAC) in Hungary, where I had the opportunity to speak and meet so many amazing, dedicated, and dynamic people, including Dr. Bradley-Farrell. The enormously popular conference had doubled in participation since the inaugural event in 2022, during which the featured theme of the conference was "God, Homeland, Family!" There is rich irony in this unapologetic embrace of traditional Christian and national values that the former Soviet satellite—Hungary—provided to the increasingly 'Woke West' and the virulent cultural Marxism rampaging through Biden's America.

This book brings to life, like no other, how we can benefit today from the hard-learned lessons of Hungary's millennium-long history. The oppression imposed by the terror-filled Nazi and Soviet occupations of Hungary reveals the true face of socialism in both its fascist and communist forms. Modern-day European Union demands against Hungary's sovereign rights, as well as the undermining of Hungarian sovereignty by the current U.S. administration, show us the latest techniques of the self-anointed elites that seek only to consolidate power and dictate their rules to the compliant masses.

In contrast, Dr. Bradley-Farrell sheds light on the Magyar spirit of independence and resilience, showing us that the human spirit can never be fully crushed and assuring us of the hope and liberty guaranteed—under Divine Providence—in American and European founding documents. What follows here is an amazing story of a centuries-long struggle of a resilient nation and people that will inspire and educate our own continuing fight for freedom. The time to heed the warning is now.

REVIEW

Miklós Szánthó

"Let's learn from the past experiences of Hungary and the forty-seven years of darkness (under communist rule) – forty-seven years yearning for freedom, (...) We have to learn and to act, before we no longer have what makes our lives worth living," writes Dr. Shea, as she searches, as any good conservative should, for a way out of the institutional and moral crisis Western Civilization finds itself in. The book you are holding in your hands is the product of that search, months of painstaking research, dozens of interviews, and meticulous work, much of it conducted in what she discovered to be the last stronghold of traditional Occidental values: Hungary. Today, having recovered from leftist rule, the Hungarians have built a citadel of common sense and conservatism.

History loves irony, and there is no small measure of it in an American truth seeker coming to the Old World in hopes of finding solutions to a crisis in the United States. In the late 15th century, European explorers took to the sea in search of new trade routes as the Ottoman conquest spread east across the continent, cutting off our land-based access to global trade. Now, as many American conservatives search for ways to fight back against the virulent darkness that the Cult of Woke represents, Dr. Shea has returned to Central Europe to discover Hungarian conservatism, which may offer a recipe for a remedy that will cure America. An Age of Discovery in reverse, if you will.

The coming together of Hungarian and American conservatives is a match made in heaven in more ways than one. America's rich republican traditions provide a solid foundation for a free nation that has prospered for more than two centuries and served as a lodestar for all freedom-loving peoples of the world, including Hungarians. It is not surprising that the only enemy that could ever threaten this great country was one from within. The U.S. has been plunged into its deepest crisis since the Civil War by a domestic enemy: a scheming, postmodern version of Marxist socialism that has infiltrated every corner of American society, from kindergartens to the boardrooms of the tech giants.

For Americans, this is an unfamiliar conflict, but Hungarians know this enemy well. In our 1100-year history, we have fought many enemies with hegemonic ambitions, but we have outlasted them all. In the second half of the 20th century, we were captured by a Marxism that was little different from the version that has America in its grip today. We know how to fight this plague. Dr. Shea's book explores Hungarian history and identifies lessons that can be learned and applied to the American struggle against the postmodern, woke version of a dark ideology with ancient roots. Hungarian conservatives stand united with our American friends in this civilizational struggle. During the 40 years of communist captivity, America was a shining beacon of freedom for us, so it is only fair that we return the favor by serving as a lighthouse to common sense in your hour of need.

PREFACE

This Story: Arriving in Budapest

The first time I visited Hungary was in the fall of 2019 to speak at a conference. I flew into Budapest International Airport and took a black car to the city center. At first, traveling through the outskirts of the city, I was dismayed. Monolithic and gray buildings devoid of character, design, or personality first greeted me. Some were apartment buildings where one supposed the inhabitants, like the apartments—aligning row by row, all the same—were one just like the other, caught in a dreary existence. I knew Hungary had been occupied by the Soviet Union, and I guessed these buildings were Soviet era, a time when Hungarians were treated as resources and wards of the state. I, traveling throughout the world for work, am always excited to enjoy each country's unique and lovely architecture, but here I resigned myself to a depressing and uninspiring trip.

Almost like magic, upon entering Budapest proper, I was transported back to a beautiful and elegant time. Baroque, Gothic, Neoclassical, and other combinations of architectural wonder, most the result of the Austro-Hungarian monarchy and period of Hungary's golden era, fill the streets of Budapest. Grand, intricate, and theatrical, these buildings remind visitors that Budapest was a place of grandeur and prosperity less than two centuries ago. Today, Hungary has reclaimed this place of grandeur, with increased confidence, strength, and brilliance.

My first experience of Budapest, from the window of a car, gives insight into the account I will tell here. This study is a journey through the darkest days of Hungarian history and an exploration of how brave Hungarians fought for and secured the light and hope that shines in their culture today. The juxtaposition of Hungary's worst moments with the Hungarians' brave and intellectual spirit—and their will to survive—is in large part what makes Hungarians who they are today.

My research is based on information, data, and historical facts, but more importantly, on the thoughts of dozens of Hungarians who allowed me to interview them and catch a glimpse into their lives and hearts—from the youthful to the nonagenarian, from senior government officials to decorators, accountants, historians, bus drivers, firefighters, and students, I am very grateful for your time and help. I also wish to thank the Center for Fundamental Rights Director General, Miklós Szánthó, and Chief of Staff, Dóra Gulyás, for their true friendship and support throughout this very rewarding process.

Hungary is a place of wonder, and Hungarians are a unique and lovely people. I hope you will enjoy this story of their determination to embrace their culture, sovereignty, and national identity—no matter the cost.

Chapter 1

IMPERIALISTS, GLOBALISTS, AND THE U.S. ADMINISTRATION: CLAIMS AGAINST HUNGARY

Imperialism and nationalism are formidable and opposed ideals that have contended with one another in the past, and they have resumed their old conflict in our day.[1]

—Yoram Hazony,
The Virtue of Nationalism

[1] Hazony, Yoram (2018). *The Virtue of Nationalism*. New York, NY: Basic Books, 2018. p. 5.

Introduction:
Hungary and Its Relationship With Western Powers

How is it that Hungary, such a small country located in the heart of Europe and populated by less than ten million people, has been catapulted onto the world stage—as hated by 'woke' globalists as it is revered by American and European conservatives? And why is economically prosperous Hungary, an independent sovereign state and member of both the European Union (EU) and North Atlantic Treaty Organization (NATO), the focus of angry smear campaigns and the victim of lawfare, vitriol, and calculated sabotage, and, at the same time, praised as a global leader for freedom and as a model of conservative values?

Hungary has risen to global prominence with the mainstream media as both maligned and revered by reporters, opinion writers, and talking heads. Hungarian Prime Minister Viktor Orbán, an anti-communist revolutionary of the underground resistance during Hungary's Soviet occupation, has been called an ally by former U.S. President Donald J. Trump. Trump, who endorsed Orbán in Hungary's 2022 elections, also calls him "friend." Their alliance, and U.S.-Hungarian relations blossomed during Trump's four-year administration (2016 – 2020) and under the wise leadership of U.S. ambassador to Hungary, David Cornstein.

But Viktor Orbán, the freely and fairly elected leader of Hungary's republic with a multiparty parliamentary system, is arbitrarily and recklessly called 'authoritarian' and 'autocratic' by angry Leftists. These slurs are repeated as if they are irrefutable truth, in spite of the fact that in April 2022, for the fourth consecutive time, Hungarian voters placed their trust in both

Prime Minister Viktor Orbán and his Fidesz-led party alliance in a landslide victory; the conservative party list received more votes from the Hungarian electorate than any other party in Hungary's history.

Leftist international organizations routinely questioned Hungary's electoral integrity during the 2022 election. But other external organizations, including the American government-accountability watchdog Judicial Watch, have uncovered the bias and unquantifiable subjectivity of these rumors, and furthermore, observed and reported on the integrity of the elections.[2] Facts here don't seem to matter. U.S. President Joe Biden's persists in calling Orbán a totalitarian "thug" and denying Hungary an invitation to the U.S.-hosted Summit for Democracy for the past three years, essentially putting Hungary in the same category as communist-led China and authoritarian Russia.

In August 2022, Trump and Orbán met privately, just a few days before both were featured speakers at the Conservative Political Action Conference (CPAC) in Texas; both events instigated great excitement and controversy, as well as self-righteous, biased opining by the press.

Orbán's opening statement at CPAC 2022 hit a home run with his audience. He praised Texas, the Lone Star State, and Texans' historical love for independence, freedom, and sovereignty. Orbán noted the Hungarian's strong commonality with

---

[2] Judicial Watch (2022, April 12). Judicial Watch Election Monitoring Report: Firsthand Observations of the Hungarian National Elections of April 3, 2022.

Texans, calling Hungary the "Lone Star State of Europe," amidst great audience applause. The analogy was not entirely surprising, since earlier that year Hungary had become the first, and, at this time only, European host of a CPAC conference—a move that launched the country into the center of the conservative universe.

Hungary, a country that values family, Christian heritage, and traditional values—much like American conservatives—just does not fit into the contemporary progressive (read *extreme*) liberal agenda. Nor does Hungary wish to relinquish its rights as a sovereign nation. In July 2022, PM Orbán stood in the way of the European Union's adoption of a 15% global minimum tax on multinational corporations, a tax backed by the Biden administration but opposed by U.S. Republicans as a threat to U.S. competitiveness and sovereignty.[3] Shortly thereafter, the Biden administration announced the cancellation of a 43-year-old tax treaty with Hungary.[4] Coincidence? No—punishment.

Hungary's refusal to embrace a liberal social agenda—in particular, mass illegal immigration and LGBT ideology—has angered both the Biden administration and the EU. The EU Commission routinely takes legal action against Hungary, with-

[3] Stein, Jeff (2022, July 1). GOP Officials Back Hungary's Resistance to Global Tax Deal, Bucking Biden. *The Washington Post*. Web accessed at: https://www.washingtonpost.com/us-policy/2022/07/01/hungary-gop-tax-deal/

[4] Reuters (2022, July 9). U.S. Treasury To End 1979 Treaty With Global Minimum Tax Holdout Hungary. Europe. *Reuters*. Web accessed at: https://www.reuters.com/world/europe/us-treasury-end-1979-treaty-with-global-minimum-tax-holdout-hungary-2022-07-08/

holding critical funding in order to strong-arm Hungary into accepting both. David Pressman, U.S. ambassador to Hungary under Biden, energetically continues to undermine Hungary's sovereignty, even while being a guest in their country. Among many other things, Pressman has built a media and social-media smear campaign, labeling the Hungarian government as "anti-LGBT," "authoritarian," and in "democratic decline."

Perhaps what has angered the EU, NATO, and the U.S. the most is that Orbán blocked the West's energy sanctions against Russia by withholding his vote until Hungary was promised a waiver for the sanctions. Hungary, like most of Europe, has been reliant on Russian energy for decades and Orbán refused to sacrifice Hungary's economy. Although he has openly supported Ukraine's sovereignty and admission into the EU, and has allowed over three million Ukrainian refugees[5] through Hungary's border, Orbán will not send weapons to Ukraine. In addition, he and his administration are famous for steadfastly calling for peace negotiations and for criticizing the West's insistence on perpetuating the war. He has been proven right in that sanctions have not stopped the war—but have instead only strengthened relations between two top U.S. adversaries.

In spite of the controversy, Hungary continues to thrive as an economically and socially prosperous, independent, and free sovereign nation—how strange that these attributes are not celebrated by either the 'liberal' American or European ruling elite.

---

[5] UNHCR Operational Data Portal. Ukraine Refugee Situation. Countries Featured in the Refugee Response Plan. Hungary. Web accessed August 26, 2023 at: https://data.unhcr.org/en/situations/ukraine

Much like Trump, Prime Minister Orbán leads fearlessly and speaks truth plainly. He and his administration are undaunted by tyrannical powers. Hungary has been through centuries of tyranny, occupation, and bullying, but Hungarians still remain with a unique sense of their own national identity intact. As Hungarian Regent Miklós Horthy calmly told a screaming and irate Adolph Hitler in March 1944—the leader of a much younger "infant state"—he, Hitler, should remember that he was speaking to the head of *a thousand-year-old state*.[6]

Orbán's 'Illiberal' Democracy

In the era of Ronald Reagan and Margaret Thatcher, the idea of international 'liberalism' meant freedom, open trade, and prosperity; today, the concept of 'liberalism or 'extreme liberalism' is interpreted as 'progressivism'—which is not progressive at all. Instead, progressivism oppresses freedom and economic and social progress.

In 2014, Hungarian Prime Minister Viktor Orbán gave a speech in eastern Transylvania, Romania, the home of over one million ethnic Hungarians, that spoke of Hungary's desire to break with the previous "liberal democracy" in Hungary—one that protected neither Hungary's economy nor its national

[6] Montgomery, John F. (1947). *Hungary: The Unwilling Satellite*. The Devin-Adair Company. p. 35.

wealth, but had substantially increased its foreign debt. In addition, the political parties in power did not respect Hungary's foundational values, namely Christianity, freedom, and human rights. Because the liberals had failed, Orbán stated, Hungary would make itself independent from this failing system and search for the best way to create a globally competitive nation.[7]

The new state system that Orbán imagined—in contrast to the failed 'liberal' regime—was coined (facetiously) as an "illiberal" or "non-liberal" regime in his speech. The new system, he said, would be a state which "does not deny foundational values of liberalism, such as freedom," but would conduct its domestic and global affairs with a "nation first" attitude. This "illiberal democracy" would be "based on national sovereignty, national solidarity, and the principles of Christian democracy. One that creates a balance between the interests of the community and those of the individual."[8]

Orbán's speech stirred anger among his adversaries who quickly labeled it anti-democratic and illiberal. At the same time, it made Orbán one of the most visible leaders fighting against the power of the globalists, woke progressivists, and extreme liberalists of the world today.

---

[7] Orban, Viktor (26th July, 2014). XXV. Bálványos Free Summer University and Youth Camp, Băile Tuşnad (Tusnádfürdő).

[8] Schmidt, Mária (2021). *From Country to Nation: Thirty Years of Freedom.* (János Betlen, Trans.) Director General of the Public Foundation (Original work published 2020) p. 17.

Orbán is amused by the label *illiberal*. But he is also gratified. If the current political leaders waging war against the principles of freedom, family, national security, sovereignty, and religion are called *liberal*—well then, he wants nothing to do with them. Orbán explained this in an interview in 2022:

> Liberals now stand against freedom. They previously favored intellectual pluralism, but now they work for a hegemony of opinions and ideas. Today, I'm a freedom fighter against liberals! So, the question is, "what the hell am I fighting for?" I am fighting for an illiberal society, a freedom-based society. It's complicated, but it's true.[9]

The Western media-elite continue to feign shock at Viktor Orbán's illiberal democracy, or perhaps they are just that intellectually and culturally short-sighted. Either way, they refuse to understand his meaning. But, as is characteristic of Orbán, foremost in his mind is the preservation and protection of Hungary, and ... he just does not care.

The idea of breaking with Western liberalism may sound radical, but as we will discuss more fully in Chapter 10, the Hungarians believe the West has left them, and not the other way around.

---

[9] Pinto, Jaime N. (2022). Forged by History: The Hungarian Struggle for Nationhood. *The European Conservative*, Spring 2022, Issue 22, 30-37.

The European Union and Christian Democracy

Instead of an economic and political alliance of European Union member states, as was intended by the original treaties of the EU, today's leaders envision a federation—with the sovereign decision-making power of the nation-state firmly in their own hands.

And the Hungarians loathe the idea.

For a thousand years, Hungary has fought to maintain its freedom and unique Magyar identity. And while Americans have to reach back almost 250 years to remember the fight for independence, Hungarian memories of Soviet tanks, oppression, torture, and control are still extremely vivid—after 46 years of occupation, the Soviets only reluctantly withdrew in 1991.

> Having been enslaved and turned into a colony of the Soviet Union for more than 40 years, the nations of Eastern Europe understandably take their independence and sovereignty very seriously. That is why there is such striking contrast between the sovereigntist look of East Europe and the globalist impulse that dominates the world view of the leaders of the European Union.[10]

[10] Füredi, Frank. (2021). Foreword. In Schmidt, Mária (2021). *From Country to Nation: Thirty Years of Freedom*. (János Betlen, Trans.). Director General of the Public Foundation (Original work published 2020) pp. 9-13.

The Europe Union, founded after World War II upon a Christian Democratic tradition, once envisioned national sovereignty and the principles of religion, marriage, and family as the basis of a prosperous European community. In stark contrast, today's Eurocratic elite are determined to create a top-down political union, one with the European Commission, the executive body of the EU that proposes law and manages the budget, as the self-appointed dictator of 'progressive' social and political ideology for each of their 'colonies'.

In the early 2000s, heated debate began over whether or not the EU's new constitution would have any mention of Europe's Christian heritage. This debate brought to light the fact that religion-based values were fading in Europe, and that the EU believed it could now create its own rules and values. With a complex network of bureaucracy, the EU's elite autocrats went about building a "self-supporting structure of rights, laws, and institutions which could exist even without the source that had arguably given them life ... in the place of religion came the ever-inflating language of 'human rights' (itself a concept of Christian origin)."[11]

But the values of sovereignty, freedom, religion, and family, suppressed for decades in Eastern and Central Europe by the occupying regime of the Soviet Union, remained at the core of the democratic national resistance against the Soviets in underground networks and churches. These values were also the foundation for rebuilding constitutions and democracy after the Soviet regime collapsed in the latter part of the twentieth century.

[11] Murray, Douglas (2018). *The Strange Death of Europe. Immigration, Identity, Islam*. Bloomsbury Publishing. pp. 5-6.

Today Hungary, led by Prime Minister Viktor Orbán, is determined to maintain its hard-earned sovereignty. This determination—done skillfully, energetically, and even cheerfully, has caused Hungary and Orbán to emerge as a leading opponent of the globalist woke movement, and has also put them in serious conflict with the imperialist leadership of the European Union.

The EU has introduced selectively biased policies and a series of successive amendments to the governing treaties of the European Union that take more and more power away from the member states. With the EU increasing its controlling power, it is no longer clear what the line is between what the state should resolve and "what belongs to a joint bureaucratic machine ... ambiguity is in their interest."[12]

In 2007, the Lisbon Treaty gave the European Parliament (the body that approves or rejects legislation) more decision-making power and created the position of a long-term president for the European Commission. The Parliament, comprised of representatives in proportion to each state's population, were once called the representatives of the "peoples of the States." They have now been renamed the "representatives of the Union's citizens."[13]

Although the Lisbon Treaty did not officially legalize the supremacy of European Law over member state national legislation, this was its intent. The legal opinion of the Council of Min-

[12] Interview 1-February 20, 2023.

[13] European Parliament (2023, April). The Treaty of Lisbon. Fact Sheets on the European Union—2023. Web accessed at https://www.europarl.europa.eu/factsheets/en/sheet/5/the-treaty-of-lisbon

isters, attached to the Lisbon Treaty, states that "in accordance with well settled case law of the Court of Justice of the European Union, the Treaties and the law adopted by the Union ... have primacy over the law of Member States." Furthermore, the case law that this legal opinion is based on specifies that "the law stemming from the treaty, an independent source of law, could not, because of its special and original nature be overridden by domestic legal provisions, however framed, without being deprived of its character as Community law and without the legal basis of the Community itself being called into question."[14]

This intention has also been demonstrated in practice. In late 2021, the Polish Constitutional Tribunal decided that parts of EU law and decisions of the Court of Justice of the European Union (ECJ) were incompatible with their constitution and that in those cases, the Polish constitution would override EU law.

But the European Parliament, invoking the "rule of law" conditionality mechanism, threatened to punish Poland by withholding billions in funds and imposing daily financial penalties.[15] European media, entrenched in the progressivism of the EU, described Poland as "going rogue" or "democratic backsliding." Poland President Morawiecki was quoted as responding,

---

[14] Treaty of Lisbon (2007, December 17). Amending The Treaty on European Union and The Treaty Establishing the European Community. Declaration No. 17 Declaration Concerning Primacy.

[15] Moens, Gabriël (2021, October 18). Is it Time to Rethink 'Supremacy' of EU Law Over Member States? *The Epoch Times*. Web accessed at: https://www.theepochtimes.com/mkt_app/is-it-time-to-rethink-supremacy-of-eu-law-over-member-states_4054004.html?v=ul

"Brussels should concentrate on security, stopping terrorism, [and] economic collaboration with other countries."[16]

But successive treaties to the EU have also severely reduced the number of policy areas in which voting unanimity is required to adopt proposed legislation. The Council of the European Union (Council of Ministers) also has the power to approve or reject legislation. The latest amendment from the Lisbon Treaty limited the number of policy areas that require voting unanimity in the Council of Ministers to only a short list: taxation, social security, the accession of new EU member states, foreign policy, and police cooperation between member states. Additionally, a *passerelle* clause allows exceptions to the requirement for unanimity in these policy areas, which can be replaced with qualified majority voting.[17] More concerning is that an increasing number of politicians from the Western member states are calling for the complete abolition of unanimity and member-state vetoing-power.

On January 1, 2021, the European Parliament adopted the "rule of law conditionality" clause supposedly "designed to protect EU funds from being misused by EU governments who bend the rule of law."[18] Unfortunately, the EP's definition of rule of

---

[16] Reuters. (2021, October 12). Polish prime minister accuses opposition of lying about 'Polexit.' *Reuters*. https://www.reuters.com/world/europe/polish-prime-minister-accuses-opposition-lying-about-polexit-2021-10-12/

[17] EUR-Lex Access to European Union Law. Unanimity. Glossary of summaries. https://eur-lex.europa.eu/EN/legal-content/glossary/unanimity.html

[18] European Parliament (2021, 12-16). Parliament approves the "rule of law conditionality" for access to EU funds. News. https://www.europarl.europa.eu/news/en/press-room/20201211IPR93622/parliament-approves-the-rule-of-law-conditionality-for-access-to-eu-funds

law has been extremely far reaching, ambiguous, and strangely in sync with a politically progressive agenda. According to Polish Justice Minister Zbigniew Ziobro, the law is just a pretext: "It is really an institutional, political enslavement, a radical limitation of sovereignty."[19]

Poland and Hungary both challenged the conditionality clause, saying it was contrary to the EU Treaty and enabled the Commission to impose its own ideological agenda on the principles and national values of member states. But the ECJ ruled in favor of the EU and endorsed the conditionality clause.[20] Since then, the European Union has threatened and applied sanctions to Hungary, including for COVID-19 emergency relief funds and the cohesion funds earmarked by Hungary for education support for disadvantaged children and infrastructure.

According to the European Parliament, they "remain concerned" about democracy and fundamental rights in Hungary. However, they spell out their main areas of concern as the:

> constitutional and electoral system, the independence of the judiciary, corruption and conflicts of interest and freedom of expression, including media pluralism. Academic freedom, freedom of religion, freedom of association, the

[19] BBC (2020, November 16). EU budget blocked by Hungary and Poland over rule of law issue. *BBC News*. Web accessed at: https://www.bbc.com/news/world-europe-54964858

[20] European Parliament (2022, 10-03). Rule of Law conditionality: Commission must immediately initiate proceedings. https://www.europarl.europa.eu/news/en/press-room/20220304IPR24802/rule-of-law-conditionality-commission-must-immediately-initiate-proceedings

> right to equal treatment, including LGBTIQ rights, the rights of minorities, as well as those of migrants, asylum seekers and refugees, are also problematic.[21]

Hungary has sought to be accommodating and engage in negotiation with the parliament and its Committee on Budgetary Control. Where there were actual problems, Hungary has worked to meet the milestones set forth by the European Union. Yet, background materials, factual information, and actual data are often ignored by the parliament and its committees. Funds never come, more milestones are created, and parliament members actively threaten Hungary (and regularly on social media platforms) that funds will continue to be withheld unless they accept LGBT ideology, join in with Ukraine war mongering, and open their borders to illegal immigration.[22]

Sir Roger Scruton, one of the greatest conservative intellectuals of our time, described his growing disgust with the European Union twenty years ago in an article titled "Identity, Marriage, Family: Our Core Conservative Values Have Been Betrayed." The EU's policies, he observed, especially those centering around forced immigration and stolen sovereignty, led to Brexit in 2016.

---

[21] European Parliament (2022, 9-15). MEPs: Hungary can no longer be considered a full democracy. News. Web accessed at: https://www.europarl.europa.eu/news/en/press-room/20220909IPR40137/meps-hungary-can-no-longer-be-considered-a-full-democracy

[22] See for example, a Twitter post (2023, 6-16). https://twitter.com/daniel_freund/status/1638905750604107778 and Facebook, accessed at https://visegradpost.com/en/2023/06/16/eu-migration-pact-met-with-harsh-criticism-in-central-europe-poland-vows-not-to-comply/

> Instead of the common law of England we have the abstract idea of human rights, slapped on us by European courts whose judges care nothing for our unique social fabric. Instead of our inherited freedoms we have laws forbidding 'hate speech' and discrimination that can be used to control what we say and what we do in ever more intrusive ways. The primary institutions of civil society—marriage and the family—have no clear endorsement from our new political class. Most importantly, our parliament has, without consulting the people, handed over sovereignty to Europe, thereby losing control of our borders and our collective assets, the welfare state included.[23]

I have chosen to quote liberally from Sir Roger Scruton in this manuscript, not only because of his deep intellect and insight into the struggle between imperialism and nationalism, but also because he was a firsthand participant for a decade in the underground networks of the resistance in Czechoslovakia, Poland, and Hungary during Soviet occupation (at the cost of being arrested in Czechoslovakia in 1985). As we will discuss in the following chapters, the above paragraph of Scruton's description of EU policies could readily be applied to the philosophy and actions of communism—an authoritarian imposition of the ruling-class version of 'one truth'; the suppression of free speech; the negation of family, marriage, and other traditional

[23] Scruton, Roger (2013). Identity, Marriage, Family: Our Core Conservative Values Have Been Betrayed. *The Guardian*. In Dooley, Mark (Ed.), *Against the Tide*. Bloomsbury Publishing. pp 50-53.

values; the creation of laws and policies with the intention of gaining control; and a blurring of national lines in the pursuit of an empire.

The existence of the Comintern,[24] or the communist international—an association of communist parties established in 1919 (and purportedly disbanded in 1943) that envisioned sweeping communist or globalist control around the world—is denied fervently, but today we see its footprint throughout Europe and the United States. The sovereignty of member states contradicts this collective homogenous view. Scruton wrote:

> The resistance we have seen to the EU in Eastern Europe should be understood in this light. Although incomparably more benign than the Communist Party, European institutions involve imposing top-down government, unaccountable offices and a system of elaborate rewards for co-operation on a people who all associate such things with the Soviet past.[25]

The unchecked, increasing power of the EU does not correspond with the original intent of its founders and is concerning. In addition to policy changes encroaching upon sovereignty, international non-governmental organizations (NGOs) have

---

[24] Library of Congress. Research Guides. Communist International (Comintern). Archives at the Library of Congress. Web accessed at: https://guides.loc.gov/comintern-archives

[25] Scruton, Roger (2009). The Flame That Was Snuffed Out by Freedom. *The Times* In Dooley, Mark (Ed.) (2022). *Against the Tide*. Bloomsbury Publishing, pp. 19-22.

become political arms of the European Union. Many organizations, funded and supported by the EU, the George Soros' Open Society Foundations, and by the United States act as a voice for the EU's social and political ideology such as access to abortion and transgender 'rights'.

Although some nations may feel the need to compromise with richer Western ideologues in exchange for financial or political support,[26] promoting social values contrary to the religious or cultural traditions of the citizens in the nations undermines their sovereignty and amounts to "ideological colonization." This is especially true for the many nations around the world who respect the sanctity of life, honor the family and view marriage as a union between a man and a woman.[27]

Within its hyper-sensitive climate of rights-based "rule of law," the EU has erroneously labeled open borders and illegal immigration, LGBT cultural acceptance, and war propagation as human rights. The EU confuses the fundamental human rights of religious freedom, freedom of speech, and freedom of belief with government-given, or "positive rights." Positive rights are the sovereign choices each member state can make to give entitlements or "rights" to certain interest groups, according to the will of its society. But in creating new 'human rights', and demanding that each member state give up their sovereignty to

---

[26] As revealed to the author by a U.S. non-governmental organization working closely with UN delegates and by foreign delegates to the UN.

[27] Garrison, Shea (2019, February 15). How Trump's Conservative UN Social Policies Strengthen Foreign relations. *The Federalist*. Web accessed at: https://thefederalist.com/2019/02/15/trumps-conservative-un-social-policies-strengthen-foreign-relations/

adhere to these, the EU has given less freedom to its member states and their citizens, and not more. [28]

Love for national identity will always conflict with imperialism. Member states of the European Union that long for sovereignty believe in a world order that is most effective when nations are allowed to "chart their own independent course, cultivating their own traditions and pursuing their own interests without interference." In contrast, imperialists believe the most successful world order only comes by uniting people under one political regime, which "imposes its will on subject nations when its officials regard this as necessary."[29] Therein lies the problem for Hungary.

---

[28] Garrison, Shea (2019, September 30). How China is home to the worst human rights crisis of our time. *The Washington Times*. Web accessed at: https://www.washingtontimes.com/news/2019/sep/30/how-china-is-home-to-the-worst-human-rights-crises/

[29] Hazony, p. 3.

The United States of America and Ambassador David Pressman

As U.S. ambassador to Hungary under the Biden administration, David Pressman has cast himself as an energetic representative of both the LGBT community and the far Left, but not of the citizens of the United States of America.

In his U.S. Senate confirmation hearing statement on June 23, 2022, Pressman appeared to deliberately mischaracterize the state of human rights, media freedom, and the rule of law in Hungary. While extravagantly applauding the courage and bravery of Ukrainians in his introduction, he condemned Hungary's "deeply troubling trends" in democracy and liberty.[30]

Mr. Pressman's statements, though promoted by the Biden administration and its mainstream American media allies, are objectively not true. The majority of Hungary's media outlets are owned by private companies, about 55% of which are left-leaning and not ideologically aligned with the current government—but which operate freely and without government interference.[31] The real problem for Mr. Pressman and his leftist cronies is that conservative media outlets in Hungary are powerful, popular, and agree with the Orbán government's policies.

---

[30] Bradley-Farrell, Shea (2022, July 27). Joe Biden's pick for Hungary: Ambassador or Antagonist. *The European Conservative.* Web accessed at: https://europeanconservative.com/articles/commentary/joe-bidens-pick-for-hungary-ambassador-or-antagonist/

[31] Szilvay, Gergely (2022, April 5). Hungarian media freedom is alive and well. *Washington Examiner.* Web accessed at: https://www.washingtonexaminer.com/opinion/hungarian-media-freedom-is-alive-and-well

The exact opposite was true about ten years ago in 2010, when Orbán took leadership. Then, Hungarian media was mostly left-wing and 'progressive'.

Human rights are protected in Hungary by its constitution, its current government, and by the rule of law. Anyone who has walked the streets of Budapest today knows the freedom, safety, peace, and prosperity enjoyed by Hungarian citizens. But the Biden administration labels Hungary as a "human rights abuser" merely because of its traditional stance on the family, a stance the United States embraced not too long ago. In Hungary, marriage is defined as a union between a man and a woman, and the government recently prohibited gender theory and transitioning procedures from being promoted to minors publicly in schools or through media.

Could it be a coincidence then that the Biden administration chose for this appointment Mr. Pressman, a career leftist political operative who led the Obama administration's billion-dollar promotion of LGBTQ ideology around the world?[32] It certainly would be naïve to think so.

It is also not a coincidence that the three international organizations rating Hungary as 'undemocratic' are extreme left-leaning organizations and blatantly biased, which unfortunately leads them to make arbitrary, vague statements about Hungary's state of freedom—statements not backed up by facts

---

[32] Eddy, M. and Gladstone, R. (2012, February 20). A U.S. Ambassador Promises a Global Push to Decriminalize Homosexuality. *The New York Times*. Web accessed at: https://www.nytimes.com/2019/02/20/world/europe/grenell-homosexuality-decriminalize-.html

or data. These organizations do not measure freedom in Hungary by an internationally recognized standard of basic human rights, but rather base their definitions on their own political and social views. And all three of these NGOs—Freedom House, Amnesty International, and Human Rights Watch—are heavily funded by organizations connected with George Soros, including Soros's Open Society Foundations (OSF).

It is not a secret that George Soros actively opposes the conservative government of Hungary—now in power for over twelve years—nor that he is a main funder of the Left's ideological struggle against Hungary. Although born in Hungary, Soros is not well-liked there. His globalist agenda runs diametrically opposed to the Christian nationalist majority in Hungary: between 2018 and 2021, Soros' Open Society Foundations and its entities awarded Freedom House $3,574,980,[33] and Human Rights Watch, $3,425,000 ($3,000,000 of which was awarded in 2021 during the Biden administration).[34] Between 2016 and 2021, OSF and its entities awarded the amount of $12,477,089 to Amnesty International.[35]

---

33 Open Society Foundations Awarded Grants. Freedom House. Web accessed at: https://www.opensocietyfoundations.org/grants/past?filter_keyword=-freedom+house

34 Open Society Foundations Awarded Grants. Human Rights Watch. Web accessed at: https://www.opensocietyfoundations.org/grants/past?filter_keyword=human+rights+watch

35 Open Society Foundations Awarded Grants. Amnesty International. Web accessed at: https://www.opensocietyfoundations.org/grants/past?filter_keyword=amnesty+international

Amnesty International and others have applauded the Háttér Society as Hungary's "oldest and largest LGBTI organization," and the Human Rights Watch website posts a picture supposedly representing "thousands"[36] protesting Hungary's child protection laws. Rather than signs of disenfranchised people suffering under an oppressive government, these portrayals are evidence of a healthy country where 1. an LGBT community exists; 2. the LGBT community has the right to participate in civil society organizations; and 3. the LGBT community has the right to protest laws they do not agree with. That is the definition of democracy in action. Where were the police raids and attacks against these protestors? There were none, because Hungary is a free society with sound rule of law.

Why would the U.S. government mischaracterize a NATO ally in this way? The Biden administration's ill treatment of Hungary appears to have nothing to do with the reality of the state of affairs in Hungary, and everything to do with an attempt to bully a sovereign nation into compliance. Most people would have the grace to rethink the wisdom of antagonizing an allied nation, especially after taking up residence in the host nation as Pressman did. But Ambassador Pressman did not only reject diplomacy, he went much further.

While supposedly a diplomat intent on strengthening U.S.-Hungarian relations, Pressman built an ongoing media smear campaign instead, especially on Twitter, comparing

[36] Human Rights Watch. World Report 2022: Hungary. web accessed September 27, 2023 at: https://www.hrw.org/world-report/2022/country-chapters/hungary

Hungarian officials with Russian authoritarian dictators, and categorizing Hungary as anti-LGBT. He then used U.S. tax dollars to continue to undermine Hungarian sovereignty.

In April 2023, the U.S. embassy funded a nation-wide billboard campaign with U.S. tax dollars which undermined the Hungarian government's pro-peace position on the Russian-Ukraine war. This again was an attempt to shame Hungary into submission. The billboards drew parallels between the 1956 Hungarian Revolution against their former Soviet occupation and the Russian invasion into Ukraine. The billboards used an expression from the revolution "Russians, go home!" and declared "there can be peace in Ukraine when the Russian occupying army withdraws."[37]

The irony of the shame campaign is that the U.S., during the Hungarian 1956 revolution, turned a blind eye to the Hungarians. The U.S., believed to have encouraged the 1956 revolution, ignored Hungarian pleas for help as they died fighting Russia alone, (discussed at length in Chapter 9). Another fact is also ignored: Hungary has allowed entry to over three million Ukrainian refugees who, with Hungarian help and money, have either become permanent inhabitants or moved on to other EU countries.

---

[37] Losonczi, Márton (2023, April 18). The Many Faults in the U.S. Embassy's Billboard Campaign. *Hungarian Conservative*. Web accessed at: https://www.hungarianconservative.com/articles/current/us_embassy_billboard_campaign_hungary_many_faults/

In July 2023, after allowing seven million illegal immigrants to flood the U.S. southern border due to Biden's open border policies, the Biden administration put sharp restrictions on visa waivers for Hungarian citizens wishing to enter the U.S.[38] This, too, was seen in Hungary as just another politically-motivated action.

Administrator for the U.S. Agency for International Development Samantha Powers has also announced a USAID program in Central Europe to "protect the rule of law" and "strengthen democratic institutions, build independent media, and to promote and protect human rights."[39] Since Powers mainly met with liberal opposition in Hungary, including LGBT rights activists, her moves are considered preparatory for "a color revolution" in Hungary by the government and conservative media.

What is it about a successful, thriving, conservative, Christian, parliamentary democracy that the woke Left just cannot stand? And how does the Biden administration and David Pressman's repetition of false and misleading claims against the fifth-time, re-elected Orbán government strengthen U.S. relations with Hungary?

---

38 Bayer, Lili (2023, August 1). U.S. Limits Visa Waiver for Hungarians. *Politico*. Web accessed at: https://www.politico.eu/article/us-america-visa-waiver-program-esta-visa-waiver-hungary-tourism-viktor-orban

39 Power, Samantha (2023,February 9). @powerusaid on Twitter: https://twitter.com/PowerUSAID/status/1623788521369501696?lang=en

Conclusion: Human Dignity and Western Civilization

The Fundamental Law (national constitution) of Hungary states that “We hold that human existence is based on human dignity.”[40] The overriding theme of this book is simple: the importance of human dignity, the most basic of all human rights, to Hungary’s future and to the future of Western civilization. Human dignity is the right to be treated with value and with respect, ethically and morally.

It is important to understand and remember that different worldviews treat human dignity very differently. In 1998, in *America’s Thirty Years War: Who is Winning?,* Hungarian-born-turned-American-citizen Balint Vazsonyi explained that Anglo-American political philosophy, on which democracy and Western civilization are based, holds people as ultimately sovereign and the state serves the people. In contrast, Franco-Germanic political philosophy (speaking from a historical, not ethnic, perspective), from which communism and totalitarianism stem, places the state over individual rights and dignity, and the people derive their rights from the all-powerful state. Vazsonyi was speaking from firsthand experience of both types of worldview: he had escaped to America after the failure of the 1956 Hungarian revolution against Soviet occupation.

[40] Ministry of Justice (2021). The Fundamental Law of Hungary of 25 April 2011. Incorporating First -Ninth Amendments. National Avowal. p. 2.

Although human dignity should be the driving factor in creating a moral vision for society, too often throughout recent history and in this present age, the principle of human dignity is traded for the embrace of power, control, or for childish, selfish, evil desire.

The Hungarians established a sovereign, Christian, European nation over one thousand years ago. Since then, they've endured an almost constant battle against invading forces to retain sovereignty and the right to control their own destiny. In more recent history, Hungarians were the subjects of the Ottoman Turks and the Austrian Empire for almost four centuries, from 1526 to 1918, followed not long after—in 1945—by a short period under fascist dictatorial rule, followed by another forty-six years as a satellite-state of the brutal Communist dictators of the Soviet Union—years in which Hungarians longed to again have freedom and sovereignty.

Yet ironically, the EU still imposes another kind of dictatorial power over Hungary—acting as a colonizing force to push political and social ideology, one that badgers, maligns, and sanctions Hungary's traditional views and its right to national policy decision-making power. Scruton's warning is palpable:

> Don't accept the EU propaganda version that we are celebrating the fall of the Berlin Wall as though 'freedom of movement' were all that it is about. We are celebrating the restoration of national sovereignty to people who had been absorbed and oppressed by a lawless empire. The fact that they are now absorbed by a lawful one does not alter the case.[41]

---

[41] Scruton, Roger (2019, December 21). My 2019. *Spectator*. In Dooley, Mark (Ed.). *Against the Tide*. (2022). Bloomsbury Publishing. pp. 224-231.

And the United States is doing much the same as the European Union.

The sovereignty of nation states is one element that can work to preserve the human dignity of its citizens. Today, in the early part of the twenty-first century, we find ourselves battling for sovereignty as individuals, for free speech and freedom of belief. We also find ourselves battling against globalists who want to create bureaucratic empires and control national decision-making power. Hungary, as you will see in the next chapters, is well-experienced in this battle, and is a strong model for standing firm and holding fast to righteous belief, identity, and national values.

Chapter 2

WHO ARE THE MODERN MAGYARS?

In order to understand why we don't think nationalism is a bad word, it's because in our history, we always had to fight for our freedom. The nation was the key for our survival. Because what we could always trust, it was our own national tradition, our kings, our freedom fighters. For us historically there is no bad association with the word nation. On the contrary, it helped us to get rid of the communist internationally, from the Soviet era. It helped us to join the free nations of the West.[1]

—Judit Varga,
former Minister of Justice and MEP, Hungary

[1] Interview 2-February 20, 2023.

Introduction: Embracing National Identity

A young Hungarian law student recently explained to me, "Fighting for our sovereignty *is* our identity."[2] His words summarized quite a lot: how Hungarians overcame centuries of war and foreign occupation and how they have maintained a delicate balance—geographical, political, and economic—between two worlds and superpowers, the East and the West.

Today, in some circles, 'nationalism' has become a dirty word. But nationalism, the outcome of a nurtured national identity, is in its truest form an essential part of building and maintaining democracy; nationalism is based on common identity, common values, and the acceptance of a shared responsibility by the citizens of a nation. Sir Roger Scruton explained nationalism's relationship to democracy this way:

> Political wisdom, [Edmond] Burke argued, is not contained in a single head. It does not reside in the plans and schemes of the political class, and can never be reduced to a system ... It is a partnership ... a continuous trust that no generation can pillage for its own advantage.[3]

In this national partnership, the people run the state, not the other way around.

---

[2] Focus Group 1-May 25, 2023.

[3] Scruton, Roger (2013). Identity, Marriage, Family: Our Core Conservative Values Have Been Betrayed. *The Guardian*. In Dooley, Mark (Ed.). *Against the Tide*. (2022). Bloomsbury Publishing. pp. 50-53.

It is also within a nationalistic system that sovereign nations take an "independent course, cultivating their own traditions and pursuing their own interests without interference" within an international order.[4] We maintain loyalty to our heritage, common traditions, community, and country, because these all guide and inform how we make laws, shape the norms of religion and education, regulate our economies, and defend our nations.

Over the past decades, globalization has led to higher living standards, education, and human rights for disadvantaged people all over the world, but in many regards, globalists have taken international connectedness too far—pushing a concept of a one-world order that causes nations to lose their distinctiveness and autonomy, assuming many of the characteristics of communism in the end. For today's globalists, the rising nationalism of the early twenty-first century—in Hungary, the U.S., the United Kingdom, Italy, and Spain—clearly contradicts their pursuit of a homogenous, international order.

Communism and nationalism are incompatible. As Hungarian historian Mária Schmidt wrote, "nationalism is the Achilles heel of Communism."[5] So, in today's communist-like Leftist propaganda, national identity and sentiment have become code words for 'Nazi'.

---

[4] Hazony, Yoram (2018). *The Virtue of Nationalism.* New York, NY: Basic Books. p. 3

[5] Schmidt, Mária (2021). *From Country to Nation: Thirty Years of Freedom.* (János Betlen, Trans.) Director General of the Public Foundation (Original work published 2020). p. 57.

Globalization after WWII was not only a response to the necessity of rebuilding the global economy, but it was also a psychological reaction to the "toxic, aggressive, nationalism" that had arisen in Germany, Italy, and Japan that "combined a quest for world domination with vicious scapegoating that, in Germany's case, led to genocide."[6] It is certainly understandable that the perverted nationalism of Hitler's Nazi Germany has scared society and repelled us away from extreme nationalistic rhetoric. But we've thrown the baby out with the bathwater.

Like many other things, national sentiment can be exploited by bad actors and political movements. Nazism and ethnic cleansing are evil perversions of national sentiment, driven by a lust for power. Both Nazis and Communists used national sentiment for their own accumulation of power while they also suppressed the nationalist uprisings that did not suit their agenda in Central and Eastern Europe. But from the Baltics to the Black Sea, nationalist anti-communist movements persisted despite the Soviet oppression that killed, imprisoned, and displaced hundreds of thousands.

Remembering their national identity—their culture, families, religion, and beliefs—and keeping these alive in their thoughts supported Hungarians through the dark and dull days of the Soviet occupation. Remembering what was lost brought a reverence for its importance; in remembering what was lost, there came deep longing for its revival. British conservative intellec-

[6] Judis, John B. (2018). *The Nationalist Revival: Trade, Immigration, and the Revolt Against Globalization*. Columbia Global Reports. New York, NY. pp. 15-16.

tual Sir Roger Scruton, as we discussed, secretly supported the underground networks of the resistance during Soviet occupation in Czechoslovakia, Hungary, and Poland. He describes the occupied people and their longing:

> Nothing was of such importance to them as the survival of their national culture. Deprived of material and professional advancement, their days were filled with a forced meditation on their country and its past ... Their lives were an exercise in what Plato called anamnesis: the bringing to consciousness of forgotten things.[7]

Remembering their national identity—their culture, families, religion, and beliefs—and keeping these alive in their thoughts, also fortified Hungary's democratic and economic rebuild after occupation: "Marriage, family, and respect for the inviolability of innocent life were suppressed under Soviet Communism. They remained, however, the core of democratic and national resistance—the 'underground' and the 'domestic' church. They were also at the heart of rebuilding national values, democracy, and the social and economic policies that give substance to democracy."[8]

The conservative nationalistic or patriotic concepts in Hungary today are about "giving hope and a better future to all Hungarians—Gypsies, Jews, and Caucasian people ... those who are

[7] Scruton, Roger (2014). *How to be a Conservative.* Bloomsbury Publishing. London. p. 11.

[8] Kinsella, Ray (2023). A 'Captured and Colonised' EU Threatens Europe. *The European Conservative.* Spring (26). pp 12-17.

Christian or atheistic, agnostic, and so on. There is a very inclusive and very plural perspective of nationalism in Hungary in the conservative groups." There is a term in the Hungarian language which describes this 'inclusive nationalism': It is "az egész nemzetet," or "the whole nation."[9]

Government: From Soviet Model to Parliamentary Republic

During the fading years of the Soviet Union in the late 1980s, Prime Minister Viktor Orbán and other leaders of his Fidesz party were young adults and university students, but they were a critical part of the resistance that toppled the communist dictatorship in Hungary. In March 1988, Orbán co-founded the Alliance of Young Democrats (FIDESZ).[10] Fidesz was originally an anti-regime movement exclusively made up of youth—according to Orbán, "We were freedom fighters, not politicians!"—but in order to foment real change in the political system, Fidesz quickly became a political party. Fidesz envisioned a democratic Hungary based on the rule of law and a nation that provided freedom and security.

[9] Interview 3-February 20, 2023.

[10] Schmidt, Mária (2021). *From Country to Nation: Thirty Years of Freedom.* (János Betlen, Trans.) Director General of the Public Foundation (Original work published 2020). p. 71.

When the Communist puppet government dissolved in 1991, Hungary had a constitution established in 1949 on the Soviet model. This constitution, and the Communist party, had created an impoverished Hungary and a massive state debt.[11]

But in 2010, Viktor Orbán was elected prime minister with a supermajority of 68%, winning 263 parliament seats out of 386, an event which allowed his party to reject the 1949 constitution.[12] Finally, in 2011, the Fidesz parliamentary majority adopted the new Hungarian Fundamental Law based on the best traditions of Hungarian constitutional history, but with an eye toward meeting the challenges of the twenty-first century. Under a government-initiated National Consultation, more than one million Hungarian citizens proposed provisions for the new Fundamental Law. The final proposal, submitted to the Hungarian National Assembly (Parliament), incorporated the results of the National Consultation.[13]

The new Hungarian Fundamental Law declared: "We do not recognise the communist constitution of 1949, since it was the basis for tyrannical rule; we therefore proclaim it to be invalid." And furthermore, "We date the restoration of our country's self-determination, lost on the nineteenth day of March 1944,

---

[11] Minister of State. Ministry of Foreign Affairs of Hungary. The Fundamental Law. Official Document.

[12] National Election Office. (2010, April 25) Round 2 of the Parliamentary Election of 2010. Web accessed at: https://static.valasztas.hu//dyn/pv10/outroot/vdin2/en/l22.htm

[13] Minister of State. Ministry of Foreign Affairs of Hungary. The Fundamental Law. Official Document.

from the second day of May 1990, when the first freely elected organ of popular representation was formed. We shall consider this date to be the beginning of our country's new democracy and constitutional order."[14] The new Hungarian republic, after forty-six years of Soviet dictatorship, was solidified under a new democratic constitution.

Today, Hungary is a republic with a multiparty parliamentary system. In April 2022, for the fourth consecutive time, Hungarian voters placed their trust in both Prime Minister Viktor Orbán and his Fidesz-led party alliance. The coalition of Fidesz and the Christian Democratic People's Party (KDNP) won with 54% of the vote and a two-thirds parliamentary majority of 135 seats. The coalition of opposition parties, United for Hungary, took 57 seats and the 'far-right' Our Homeland (Mi Hazánk) won 6 seats.[15] That year, the conservative party list received more votes from the Hungarian electorate than any other party in Hungary's history.[16]

---

[14] Ministry of Justice (2021). The Fundamental Law of Hungary of 25 April 2011. Incorporating First -Ninth Amendments. National Avowal.

[15] Office for Democratic (2022, April 3). Institutions and Human Rights. Hungary. Parliamentary Elections and Referendum. Election Observation Mission Final Report. Web accessed at: https://www.valasztas.hu/web/national-election-office/parliamentary-elections-2022

[16] Schmidt, Mária (2021) *From Country to Nation: Thirty Years of Freedom.* (János Betlen, Trans.). Director General of the Public Foundation (Original work published 2020). p. 15.

Building Hungary's Economy, Post-USSR

In spite of the devastating human and material losses of the twentieth century—destruction of major cities, military defeat, the Nazi deportation of Hungarian Jews and the Communist deportation of the general public, as well as forced inflation from the Soviet occupation—in 2022, Hungary's Gross Domestic Product (GDP) growth rate of 4.6% was above the Central European average of 4.0 %[17] and well above the European Union average of 3.5%.[18]

Over the past several decades, with strategic economic alliances and focused fiscal policy, Hungary has overcome the poverty and instability of fifty years ago. The Warsaw Pact countries were many decades behind Western Europe in economic growth and development: immediately after the fall of the Soviet Union, Hungary's GDP annual growth had been -3.1% and -0.6% in 1992 and 1993, respectively.

Today, Hungary also has "very high human development," with an average life expectancy at birth of 74.5 years (2022), 15 expected years of schooling (2021), 12.2 mean years of actual schooling (2021) and decent living standards as demonstrated by a Gross National Income (GNI) per capita (or per person)

---

17 Includes the Baltic States.

18 The World Bank World Development Indicators Online. Web accessed August 2023 at: https://databank.worldbank.org/reports.aspx?source=2&series=SH.XPD.CHEX.GD.ZS&country=.

of $32,789 (2021).[19] After the fall of Communism, from the year 1990 to the year 2021, Hungary's life expectancy at birth increased by more than five years, expected years of schooling increased by almost four years, and Hungary's GNI per person increased by almost 80%.[20]

As a comparison to Hungary's development today, the average life expectancy in Central Europe is about 75 years, and about 80 years is the average for the entire European Union; GNI per capita in Central Europe is $32,680 and it is $49,175 in the European Union (2021).[21]

In 1991, the Visegrád Group (V3) was officially established to dissolve the Soviet institutions that had influenced Hungary, Poland, and Czechoslovakia (later split into Czechia and Slovakia). This group, which would later become the V4 with the split of Czechoslovakia, agreed to cooperate under three main pillars: "to overcome historical animosities among the signing countries; to join efforts ... [for] democracy and free-market capitalism ... and to advance common ideals." Their common vision was a supportive regional alliance of Central European

---

19 United Nations Human Development Reports. Human Development Index (HDI) Web accessed at: https://hdr.undp.org/data-center/human-development-index#/indicies/HDI. Chart downloaded on Hungary HDI. GNI per capita 2017 PPP.

20 United Nations Human Development Reports. Hungary. Data updates as of September 8, 2022. Web accessed at: https://hdr.undp.org/data-center/specific-country-data#/countries/HUN

21 United Nations Human Development Reports. Human Development Index (HDI) Web accessed at: https://hdr.undp.org/data-center/human-development-index#/indicies/HDI. Chart downloaded on Hungary HDI. GNI per capita 2017 PPP.

countries that could also help secure their successful integration into the European Union and the Euro-Atlantic alliance of NATO. An important economic alliance was CEFTA (Central European Free Trade Agreement), established a year later on December 21, 1992, which "served as a 'lobby' not only for them but for every other post-communist country to enter the EU in the future." CEFTA remains today, and has expanded to include many other countries in the region.[22]

After state-sponsored jobs and the Soviet central government's planned economy disappeared, there was a massive increase in unemployment. The most difficult time period in Hungary was between the Fall of 1990 and early 1993—the unemployment rate jumped dramatically from 1% to 12%. After 1993, the unemployment rate declined steadily until 2002, to about 5%, then gradually began to increase again at the time of the 2008 global economic crisis.[23]

Taking office in 2010, Prime Minister Viktor Orbán took an 'unorthodox' position and broke with neoliberal economic policies in order to bring Hungary out of the crisis. As part of the country's fiscal policy, Prime Minister Orbán set about decoupling Hungary from International Monetary Fund (IMF) loans and decreasing the national debt incurred under previous administrations.

---

[22] Orbán, Tamás (2021). Thirty Years of Visegrad Summits. In Bendarzsevszkij, Anton (Ed.). *30 Years of The V4*. Danube Institute. pp. 10-20, p. 11.

[23] Dövényi, Zoltán (2021). Economic Activity. In *National Atlas of Hungary Society* (Kocsis, Károlyl; Kovács, Zoltán; Nemerkényi, Zsombor; Gercsák, Gábor; Kincses, Áron; Tóth, Géza Eds.). Research Centre for Astronomy and Earth Sciences. Geographical Institute. Budapest. pp. 88-95.

Orbán also laid part of the burden of the crisis on the banks and big businesses that had benefited from the previous period of prosperity: he nationalized around $14 billion in assets from private pensions, imposed big taxes on corporations, and temporarily fixed the exchange rate (at a lower than market rate) on bank loans taken by individuals. The last move made it easier for people to pay their loans and forced banks to take big losses. Regarding this move that astounded global finance analysts, the critics said Hungary's "credibility suffers."[24]

However, Hungary had a period of steady growth for the next several years "the fruits of which were enjoyed by the population at large. By the second half of the 2010s, a fever of development and building projects swept through the country. Economic renewal followed both in the cities and in rural areas. Budapest began to be perceived once again as a global city and became one of the most popular tourist destinations."[25]

It is interesting to note that Orbán uses the profits of big businesses—not just from banking, but also from energy, insurance, communication sectors—to support Hungarian families and children through a demographic policy:

---

[24] Oprita, Antonia (2011, September 25). Investors Unnerved by Hungary's 'Unorthodox' Measures. *CNBC.* Web accessed at: https://www.cnbc.com/id/44639381

[25] Schmidt, Mária (2021). *From Country to Nation: Thirty Years of Freedom.* (János Betlen, Trans.). Director General of the Public Foundation (Original work published 2020). p. 16.

> We spend an enormous amount of money on the promotion of families, in the interest of a strong Hungary. The question is this: where does that money come from? The truth, Ladies and Gentlemen, is that we take this money from multinational companies... we then give the money to families raising children.[26]

The money is distributed to families and children in the form of family tax allowances for working people, free children's meals, holidays for children in need, free school textbooks, and housing allowances for parents raising children.

In 2012 unemployment hit a peak again at 11.1% leaving 472,000 people unemployed. But from 2014 onward unemployment sharply declined until it decreased to 3.5% or about 163,000 unemployed by 2019.[27] From 2016 to 2019, Hungary experienced strong economic growth with substantial increases in employment and real income, and the lowest unemployment rate in years.[28]

Historian Mária Schmidt describes the revival of the Hungarian economy and national pride, twenty years after the fall of the Soviet Eastern bloc:

---

[26] Orbán, Viktor (2014, July 26). Speech at XXV Bálványos Free Summer University and Youth Camp. Băile Tuşnad (Tusnádfürdő).

[27] Dövényi, Zoltán (2021). Economic Activity. In *National Atlas of Hungary Society* (Kocsis, Károlyl; Kovács, Zoltán; Nemerkényi, Zsombor; Gercsák, Gábor; Kincses, Áron; Tóth, Géza Eds.). Research Centre for Astronomy and Earth Sciences. Geographical Institute. Budapest. pp. 88-95.

[28] Organisation for Economic Co-operation and Development (OECD) (2021, July). Hungary. OECD Economic Surveys. Executive Summary.

During that decade, Orbán gave Hungarians back their self-esteem. He proved to them that they are capable of achieving great things. That it is worth working hard to improve their lives because, as a result of low taxation, they will be left with more money to spend on their families and their loved ones.[29]

2019-2023: Pandemic and War

The global COVID-19 pandemic interrupted Hungary's economic growth, and 4.9% GDP growth in 2019 quickly plummeted to -4.5% in 2020, as global economies shut down causing Hungary's external demand to decrease.[30] However, targeted fiscal policies and government 'relaunch programs' helped to rebalance the economy in 2021.

In response to the resulting higher cost of living from global inflation, the government increased public sector wages, exempted anyone under twenty-five years old from paying income tax, initiated a pension bonus and a thirteen-month pension payment, and gave new tax cuts to households and businesses.

---

[29] Schmidt, Mária (2021). *From Country to Nation: Thirty Years of Freedom.* (János Betlen, Trans.). Director General of the Public Foundation (Original work published 2020). p.16.

[30] Organisation for Economic Co-operation and Development (OECD) (2021, July). Hungary. OECD Economic Surveys. Executive Summary and also World Bank Data.

This was mainly financed by increasing taxes and lowering public spending in other areas.[31]

In 2021, following Russia's invasion of Ukraine, Western sanctions against Russia resulted in sky-rocketing energy prices, putting all of Europe in a financial strain. The Hungarian government responded by introducing price ceilings for petrol, diesel, and seven fundamental foodstuffs to combat inflation.

In 2021, Hungary's GDP growth rate returned to a strong 7.2%.[32] This number exceeded Hungary's pre-pandemic performance of 2019. In all three of these years—2019, 2021, and 2022—Hungary's GDP growth rate was above both the Central European[33] and the European Union average.[34]

Hungary experienced 4.3% GDP growth in 2022, despite the challenges of the unstable international environment: the next-door Ukraine-Russia war, energy sanctions and high prices, and the continuing pandemic. In May 2023, the economy's foundations were called "robust" with one of the lowest unemployment rates in the EU. The country's investment rate and export performance remained high. However, Hungary's inflation rate was the highest in the EU and within the Visegrad Group (V4), at 21.5% in May 2023. Other Visegrad countries and Baltic

---

31 Organisation of Economic Co-operation and Development (OECD) (2022, November). Economic Outlook, Preliminary Version (2), p.136.

32 The World Bank. Hungary. Web accessed August 2023 at: https://data.worldbank.org/country/HU

33 Includes the Baltic States.

34 The World Bank World Development Indicators Online Web accessed 2023 at: https://databank.worldbank.org/reports.aspx?source=2&series=SH.XPD.CHEX.GD.ZS&country=

states also had high inflation, as compared to the same month of the previous year.[35]

Due to the European Union's "rule of law" conditionality clause applied against Hungary, Hungary is yet to receive funding from the Resilience and Recovery Facility (RRF). In spite of this, Hungary's economic performance is still 4% above the level it was before the coronavirus pandemic, while the EU average hovers at only around 3% higher. According to the Hungarian government website: "Had Hungary been able to use the recovery funding it is entitled to, economic growth would have been above 5%. By withholding the funds, the European Commission hobbled our economic performance and competitiveness."[36]

The International Monetary Fund (IMF) and European Commission both report that Hungary will avoid recession in 2023 and return to "steep growth" in 2024. A temporary slowdown in 2023 reflects "persistently high inflation, the economic fallout of Russia's war of aggression in Ukraine, weaker external demand and negative confidence effects." In addition, the prime minister's office has reported that inflation will be in the single digits as early as October 2024.[37]

---

35 Interview-KSH. Hungary Central Statistical Office. Based on handout "Some General Indicators of Hungary, the European Union, and the V4."

36 About Hungary (2023, May 17). Finance Ministry: Hungary's economy to avoid a recession in 2023 and return to steep growth next year. Web accessed at: https://abouthungary.hu/news-in-brief/finance-ministry-hungarys-economy-to-avoid-a-recession-in-2023-and-return-to-steep-growth-next-year

37 About Hungary (2023, July 27). Gulyás Gergely: Any Kind of Migrant Distribution Mechanism is Unacceptable. Web accessed at: https://abouthungary.hu/blog/gulyas-gergely-any-kind-of-migrant-distribution-mechanism-is-unacceptable

Population Rising: A Nation Without Borders

Hungary's first female president, Katalin Novák, regularly tells audiences that she is proud to be a mother. Once, I heard her speak at length about her own family to an audience of international conservatives at a gala dinner held in the Royal Riding Hall in Budapest. She connected the importance of the family to Hungarian sovereignty saying, "The cradle of sovereignty is the family. A nation's unity starts in the family."[38]

After the withdrawal of the Soviet Union occupation in 1991, the fertility rate in Hungary began a steep decline until it evened out in the early 2000s. The years 2001 to 2005 were a historic low for births in Hungary, at a fertility rate around 1.3 (total births per woman), well below the population replacement rate of 2.1.[39] Prime Minister Viktor Orbán has responded to declining fertility rates by saying that Hungarians subscribe to the view that demographic problems must be solved "by relying on our own resources and mobilizing our own reserves, and ... by renewing ourselves spiritually."[40] This statement was meant to

---

38 Family Policy of Hungary. Official Brochure. Maria Kopp Institute for Demography and Families (KINCS).

39 The World Bank. Fertility rate, total (births per woman) Hungary. Web accessed at: https://data.worldbank.org/indicator/SP.DYN.TFRT.IN?locations=HU

40 Orbán, Viktor (2017, May 25). Prime Minister Viktor Orbán's opening speech at the Second Budapest World Congress of Families. Website of the Hungarian Government. Web accessed at: https://2015-2019.kormany.hu/en/the-prime-minister/the-prime-minister-s-speeches/prime-minister-viktor-orban-s-opening-speech-at-the-2nd-budapest-world-congress-of-families

contradict the "replacement migration" theories of the European Union—that declining population and demographic issues must be solved with migration.

Hungary's Family Policy, initiated in 2011, has greatly helped to boost the economy with family-based tax exemptions, subsidies, and refunds. This strategy, rolled out and developed over the last twelve or more years, has also resulted in a substantial increase in Hungary's fertility rate—from 1.2 in 2011 to 1.6 in 2021.[41]

In addition to increasing the fertility rate in Hungary, family policies have strengthened the family base: Since 2011, the number of marriages increased by 100% and divorce decreased, the number of abortions decreased by almost 50%, and the total fertility rate "climbed nearly 30%."[42] In 2020, Hungary had the highest marriage rate in the European Union with a divorce rate in the middle to middle-low range.[43] Educated women (high school or university graduates) are having more children too. And working mothers, or the employment rate of mothers with small children, "is constantly rising."[44]

---

[41] The World Bank. Fertility rate, total (births per woman) Hungary. Web accessed at: https://data.worldbank.org/indicator/SP.DYN.TFRT.IN?locations=HU

[42] Maria Kopp Institute for Demography and Families (KINCS). Family Policy of Hungary: Strong families make a strong nation. Source: Hungarian Statistical Office Budget Laws.

[43] Eurostat. An Official Website of the European Union. How many marriages and divorces took place. Web accessed at: https://ec.europa.eu/eurostat/web/products-eurostat-news/-/ddn-20220516-2

[44] Maria Kopp Institute for Demography and Families (KINCS) (2022, May 3). 10+1 Facts About Mothers Who Gave Birth in the 2010s. Source: Hungarian Central Statistical Office.

In spite of these efforts, Hungary has not yet reached a 'break-even' point. Until the replacement fertility rate is reached, "The Hungarian continues to be an endangered species."[45]

The Treaty of Trianon

It may surprise you to hear that "while Hungary has borders, the Hungarian nation does not."[46] After Hungary was defeated in World War I, the peace terms of the Treaty of Trianon, as dictated by the victors at Trianon Palace at Versailles in June 1920, divided the nation of Hungary into several parts, giving Hungarian territory to Romania and the newly formed nations of Czechoslovakia and Yugoslavia. All of Hungary's neighbors, in fact, received at least some Hungarian land.[47]

According to some historians, the Allies gathered at Trianon drafted the outline of the new borders with little or no respect for the historical, cultural, ethnic, geographic, economic, and

---

45 Gorondi, Pablo (2020, February 16). Hungary's Orban warns about the climate crisis, slow EU growth. *Associated Press*. Web accessed at https://apnews.com/article/28067d49c097ced2d2bda3b5f255c813

46 Gulyás, Gergely (2023). Minister Gulyás on the Hungarian Day of National Unity, as translated by and posted on Twitter by Secretary of State for International Communication and International spokesman for the Cabinet Office of the Prime Minister, Zoltán Kovács. Web accessed at: https://twitter.com/zoltanspox/status/1665399054585528320?s=20

47 Central Intelligence Agency (1987). The Tangled Web. Studies in Intelligence. Spring, 1987: 10-13-3 National Archives and Records Administration. RG263-Records of the CIA. P. 27.

strategic aspects of the region. Before the division, Hungary was a territory of about 109,000 square miles and about eighteen million people. After the division, Hungary lost about two thirds of its territory; the nation was reduced to about 36,000 square miles and eight million people. More than *three million* ethnic Hungarian citizens were lost to neighboring countries.[48]

The division at Trianon was a substantial loss of Hungarian territory and people, but it also weakened Hungary politically and made the country geographically vulnerable. Additionally, it had a profound emotional impact on Hungarians. The history of Trianon and its effects will be discussed in detail in Chapter 4, "Balancing Superpowers."

A decade ago, Orbán embraced the creed of former Hungarian Prime Minister József Antall, the first freely-elected Hungarian prime minister after the Soviet occupation, who insisted that the "Hungarian nation stands united regardless of the citizenship that some of them may have obtained in the thunderstorm of history."[49] Antall was not calling for Hungary to reclaim post-Trianon territory and population, but he spoke to the importance of the national identity of fifteen million ethnic Hungarians—even those that lived beyond Hungary's borders. In keeping with this sentiment, Orbán granted dual citizenship to the ethnic Hungarians outside the modern borders of Hungary. Today, there are more than one million transborder Hungarians who have also taken Hungarian citizenship.

---

[48] Cartledge, Bryan (2011). *The Will to Survive: A History of Hungary*. C. Hurst & Co. p. 326-327.

[49] Harden, Blaine (1990, April 11). 'Hungarian-ness' Back in Fashion. *The Washington Post*. Web accessed at: https://www.washingtonpost.com/archive/politics/1990/04/11/hungarian-ness-back-in-fashion/baa45b79-7cc6-454e-87a8-e3f28a608eed/

The Fidesz party encourages private investment in the trans-border areas—such as in Transylvania, Romania—and heavily invests in the schools. Children are taught in Hungarian, and subjects include Hungarian culture.[50] This policy is considered substantial progress in overcoming the devastating effects of the Treaty of Trianon and uniting Hungarians across state borders.

Conclusion: The Hungarian Journey

The Hungarians have succeeded in turning a Communist-occupied and exploited country, struggling for survival and autonomy, into an independent, prosperous, and modern nation. But that is only a small part of their story. The next few chapters tell the Hungarian journey from a nomadic tribal federation to a European Christian kingdom, to a country occupied by the multiple empires and superpowers of the Ottomans, Austrians, Germans, and Soviets—all while still remaining uniquely Hungarian. And the journey is fascinating: It is full of hope and despair, courage and fear, unbearable brutality and great, enduring humanity. The story of Hungary has much to teach us, if we are willing to learn.

[50] Schmidt, Mária (2021). *From Country to Nation: Thirty Years of Freedom.* (János Betlen, Trans.). Director General of the Public Foundation (Original work published 2020). p. 16.

Chapter 3

ORIGINS AND BATTLES: FIGHTING FOR HUNGARIAN IDENTITY

Finding themselves on a cultural island in the centre of Europe, speaking a language incomprehensible to their Slav or German neighbours, Hungarians are fascinated by the question of how they came to be there in the first place.[1]

—Sir Bryan Cartledge,
The Will to Survive

[1] Cartledge, Bryan (2011). *The Will to Survive: A History of Hungary*. C. Hurst & Co. pp. 3.

Introduction: It's Nothing New

Although egregious and potentially dangerous behavior, the empire-like maneuvers of today's globalist elites (bullying, sanctions, arrogant dictation) are nothing new: Hungarian sovereignty, nationalism, and identity have been threatened for over a thousand years.

Tribes, empires, and Nazi and Soviet superpowers rode into Hungary by horseback or by tank to destroy, dominate, and murder, but none have successfully squelched the Hungarian spirit or confidence in their own identity and abilities. Emperors, kings, Führer, and presidents have exploited, bullied, or just plain neglected Hungary, yet the Hungarian's determination to survive has never wavered.

These battles have, in fact, directly and profoundly shaped Hungarian culture and identity to help make them who they are today. Therefore, to have an authentic view of today's Hungary, knowledge of its history and thousand-year-long fight for freedom and sovereignty is critical. We'll discuss all—in this chapter and those proceeding.

Hungary's location—geographically, philosophically, and culturally—between the East and the West has made it a prime target for the predatory acquisition of resources, wealth, and political power. Mongols, Turks, Austrians, Russians, and Germans all successfully invaded and occupied Hungary at some point over the past centuries. Nestled in the heart of Central Europe, although its borders and territorial mass have shifted throughout the centuries, Hungary is now bordered by Austria and Slovenia to the west, Slovakia to the north, Ukraine and Romania to the East, and Croatia and Serbia to the South.

Hungary's geopolitical balance between East and West forces is also key in understanding its motives and relations today—one of the main goals of which has been survival. Hungarians were originally nomadic tribes from the East, yet they embraced Western culture and Christianity when they moved to the west of the Carpathian Mountains in Central Europe over one thousand years ago.

Origins:
Where Did They Come From?

The early origins of the Hungarians are blurry and the subject of contradiction, controversy, and sometimes myth and folklore. No one is fully sure of the roots of their language or people. Before approximately AD 1000, Hungarians had no written heritage, yet other civilizations wrote about them. Some believed them to be Huns or related to the Huns, but they were not. Though their origins are thought by some historians to be Turkic (from Central Asia), they are not a Turkic people. They are not Slavic either. They are 'Magyar,' their own unique people with a language that no one else in the world speaks. So, where did they come from? That question is hotly debated.

Sir Bryan Cartledge is a historian and the former British ambassador to Hungary from 1980 to 1983. To lay the foundation for our story about Hungarian identity and sovereignty, I rely upon his extensive work on Hungarian history. His book *The Will to Survive: A History of Hungary* (2011) has been called "the standard work on Hungary" and "the most detailed and balanced narrative of Hungarian history currently available in English."[2]

In *The Will to Survive,* Cartledge writes that the Finno-Ugrians, the ancestors of the Hungarians, most probably broke away from the Ugrians, a larger tribal federation in the central Urals[3] during the third millennium BC and gradually (over many centuries) moved west toward the Carpathian Basin. It is still debated whether or not these ancient Hungarians came from the western or the eastern slopes of the Urals,[4] though Cartledge places them in western Siberia on the eastern side.[5] Other tribal invaders that moved west, like the Ugrians, were eventually absorbed by the places they inhabited. It was only the Hungarians (as they later came to be known) who established their own kingdom, preserved their language, and assimilated the local Slavs into their own culture and communities.

After the initial break from the larger tribe, the Finno-Ugrians moved west beyond the Ural Mountains, forming their own language offshoot and calling themselves 'Magyars.' By the sixth century BC, the Magyars settled in the region between the Volga River and the Ural Mountains, (in an area today known as the Russian Republic of Bashkortostan or Bashkiria) "and em-

---

[2] Cover Reviews, Cartledge, Bryan (2011). *The Will to Survive: A History of Hungary*. C. Hurst & Co.

[3] The Urals or Ural Mountains are a mountain range that form a natural boundary between Europe and Asia running North-South through Russia to Northwestern Kazakhstan.

[4] Lendvai, Paul (2021). *The Hungarians: A Thousand Years of Victory in Defeat.* Princeton University Press. p. 13.

[5] Cartledge, Bryan (2011). *The Will to Survive: A History of Hungary*. C. Hurst & Co. pp. 3-4.

barked on their long history as an identifiably distinct ethnic and linguistic group."[6] The Magyars, though nomadic, undertook primitive farming and livestock production. It was here that their great skill for equestrianism and fighting on horseback was first developed, as they conducted raids on their neighbors to supplement supplies.

The late fourth to early fifth century AD marks the beginning of a period of tribal migration that drastically changed the ethnic and political landscape of Europe. Beginning with the arrival of the Huns and including the Germanic Vandals, Suevi, and Visigoths, tribes migrated into the Western Roman Empire from the Eastern European Plain and regions of the Carpathian Basin. Between AD 700 and about 830, the Magyars moved further westward, settling in a region of the north Caucasus, between the Rivers Donets and Dniester, north of the Black Sea, for about one hundred years. The first known leader of the Magyar tribes—Levedi—began the process of "welding the seven Magyar tribes into a tribal confederacy."[7]

Interestingly, some Magyars are purported to have remained in the Volga-Ural area instead of moving west. Around the year AD 1237, on the eve of the Mongol invasion, a pair of Hungarian Dominican friars traveled back to the Volga-Ural area, believing it to be the original home of the Magyars, and to find and convert their pagan kinsman to Christianity. Friar Julian found he could communicate with the ancestors of the Magyars who had remained there, in a (mostly) common language, in spite of the

---

6 *Ibid.*, pp. 3-4.

7 *Ibid.*, p. 4.

centuries between them. He named the area "Magna Hungaria" or "Great Hungary."[8]

In the late ninth century, most likely in pursuit of the wealth of Central Europe, the military commander Árpád led the tribal confederacy into the basin west of the Carpathian Mountains. The Carpathian basin at this time was sparsely populated (about 200,000 people) by a mixture of Avars, Bulgars, and other Slavs, over which the Magyars imposed their authority with little resistance.[9]

About 400,000 Magyars and their subordinate tribes settled in the area divided into two parts by the Danube River; there, the western region became known as 'Transdanubia,' and had been the former Roman province known as Pannonia. It is interesting to note that the occupying Magyars did not allow their language to be absorbed by the indigenous populations, but expected the Avars, Bulgars, and others to speak some Magyar.

Philip Longworth in *The Making of Eastern Europe* wrote that the arrival of the Magyars may not have been as significant if they had been

> absorbed linguistically by the peoples they conquered, as the Avars, Croats and Bulgars had been, rather than imposing their own language upon them; and their language Magyar, was outlandish ... it had very little in common with the languages which now surrounded it.

---

[8] Toynbee, Arnold (1973). *Constantine Porphyrogenitus and His World.* Oxford University Press. pp. 419-420.

[9] Cartledge, p. 7.

> In fact Magyar served as a linguistic wedge driven into the heart of Slavonic Europe, and speeded the process of linguistic differentiation among the Slavs.[10]

Sir Bryon Cartledge summed it up like this: "A linguistic island was thus created in the Germanic and Slavic Sea ... This single fact can be said largely to have determined the subsequent history of what was to become the Hungarian nation."[11]

By 895, the majority of the Magyar tribal confederacy, including women and children, had moved into the eastern half of the Carpathian Basin and it was here that the modern-day Magyars took their place to enter European history. Over the next fifty years, as the Magyars increased their control over the Carpathian Basin, they launched a series of terrorizing "predatory raids" into central, western, and southern Europe (into German lands, northern Italy, and parts of France). These raids were triggered by newly formed or broken political alliances, and the quest for sovereign territory and wealth.

The Magyar tribal federation had an incredible military culture of fierce, "bloodthirsty and heretical," warriors who were also expert horsemen using small, fast horses "unencumbered by the heavy armour favored by the European cavalry."[12] They were adaptive and clever, using riding techniques they learned from other tribes, such as iron stirrups that allowed them to turn and shoot arrows while feigning retreat from their enemies. Car-

---

[10] Longworth, Philip (1992). *The Making of Eastern Europe*. Palgrave Macmillan UK. p. 278.

[11] Cartledge, p. 8.

[12] Interview 17_February 21, 2023.

tledge observed that “a new prayer was inserted into the Christian liturgy: ‘O save and deliver us, Thine unworthy servants, from the arrows of the Hungarians’.”[13] Although the raids of the Magyars were certainly brutal, the chroniclers of their battles often confused them with the similarly brutal Huns.[14]

Breaking With the East and Embracing the West: King István

Chief Prince Géza, the great-grandson of Árpad, may have been the first Hungarian leader who dreamed of being the ruler of a civilized western nation, and “not a loose federation of eastern (pagan) tribes.” Geza passed his vision of Magyar westernization down to his son István (Stephen) and in this pursuit, educated István in Christianity and married him off to a Bavarian princess.[15]

---

[13] Cartledge, p. 8-9. Cartledge says this is a convenient point to begin to use the word “Hungarians” to describe the inhabitants of these geographical areas and reserve “Magyar” for the language spoken by Hungarians.

[14] Lendvai, p. 7. “The Old French Chanson de Roland describes the Magyars as “breeds of Satan” along with the Huns and Saracens, who left a trail of blood in their wake wherever they appeared. The chroniclers recount unimaginable atrocities, often confusing the Magyars—or Hungarians, as they were then called—with the Huns.”

[15] Montgomery, John F. (1947). *Hungary: The Unwilling Satellite.* The Devin-Adair Company. pp. 36-37.

In 997, István succeeded Geza; István believed that the only way Hungary could become a Western power was by fully embracing Christianity. However, István also wanted Hungary to remain an independent kingdom, free from the dictates of either the Holy Roman or Byzantine Empires.

At this time, it was only the three heads of state—the Holy Roman Emperor, the Pope, and the Emperor at Constantinople who had the right to crown a European king. In a bold move, Istvan asked the French head of the Roman Catholic Church—Pope Sylvester II (instead of one of the ruling emperors)—to establish him as king of Hungary. István wanted to align Hungary with the Holy Roman Empire but to avoid "political entanglements" with either the western (Holy Roman) or eastern (Byzantine) empires. King István's move (having the Pope ennoble him) also established Hungary as a kingdom and his household as royal—holding the crown "by the Grace of God," and not through an Emperor's concession.[16]

The Byzantine Empire was the eastern half of the Roman Empire, which had survived for a thousand years after the fall of Rome, when the western half had divided into various feudal kingdoms. The Byzantine Empire was Christian and Greek, both culturally and linguistically, while the Western Roman Empire spoke Latin. Church and state were tightly intertwined under the leadership of the emperor.

[16] *Ibid.*, pp. 36-37.

On Christmas day in the year 1000 (or some believe New Year's Day, 1001) István was crowned the first Christian king of Hungary under Pope Sylvester II, making Hungary the most eastern kingdom of the West. Even then, Hungary's monarchy had elements of a republic state. Former U.S. diplomat John Flournoy Montgomery, recalling the elevation of Miklós Horthy de Nagybánya from admiral to regent after World War I, remarked,

> Hungary, as contrasted with England and nearly every other kingdom, had always put the crown above its wearer: The king really served as a regent for the crown in which rested the sublime power carried down through the ages from the time of King Stephen ... Theoretically the king was elected and only became king when he was crowned by the nation. Actually, it was as regent for the crown that the nation bestowed upon him such royal powers as the right to confer nobility upon his subjects. At the same time the crown set limits to his rights. The territory was not his but the crown's –hence he could not alienate it ... by accepting the crown the king was bound to the constitution.[17]

Today, King István is the symbol of Hungarian statehood, having brought to Hungary its Western orientation, its church, and the organization of its state. After World War II, as the Soviet troops approached Hungary, his crown was given to the

---

[17] *Ibid.*, pp. 36-38.

United States Army for safe-keeping and held at Fort Knox until 1978. Today, the crown of King István is a national treasure, displayed in the Hungarian Parliament Building in Budapest.[18] King István was later canonized after his death and a national holiday is held in Hungary every August 20th in his remembrance.

For the four decades of István's reign, the Kingdom of Hungary was relatively peaceful, hugged between two empires. Hungary became a safe and welcoming bridge of passage between the Holy Roman Empire and Byzantium lands: István built hostels and a basilica in which the pilgrims could worship, which was also used as the royal chapel and burial place. Hungary's reputation for being a well-organized and Christian society brought merchants, travelers, and new settlers. István encouraged them, believing they would bring economic advancement and security to his newly formed kingdom—and increase his own power and prestige in Europe.

King István even instructed his young son Emeric: "A country that has only one language and only one tradition is weak and failing. I therefore urge you to welcome foreigners kindly and to hold them in honour, so that they prefer to stay with you rather than elsewhere."[19] It is interesting to note that over the centuries, Hungary has successfully assimilated other peoples, such as Jews and Chinese in modern-day history.

---

[18] Tour, Hungarian Parliament Building. February 2023.

[19] Vatican Archive. Admonition VI. Admonitions of St. Stephen, King of Hungary to his son Emeric. Based on translation from Message of John Paul II to the Hungarian Nation for the Millennium of St. Stephen Coronation. Vatican Archive. https://www.vatican.va/content/john-paul-ii/en/speeches/2000/jul-sep/documents/hf_jp-ii_spe_20000821_santo-stefano.pdf

During the reign of King István, religion was a formidable, formative influence in the world. As he expanded and solidified his power, Istvan's choice to turn to Rome and form a western Christian kingdom was the first clear separation of Hungary from the stern paganism[20] of their nomadic ancestors and from the Byzantine Empire brand of Eastern Orthodox Christianity. It also placed Hungary under the cultural influence of the Holy Roman Empire, and what came to be known as 'Western Civilization'. István established Hungary as both a European and Christian nation, only one hundred years after the Magyar's appearance in the Carpathian Basin.[21]

Today, critics of Prime Minister Orbán point out that Hungary's alliances with Russia and China contradict King István and his intentions for Hungary. This epitomizes a centuries-old debate among Hungarian politicians and historians: should Hungary, a country 'suspended' geographically between the East and West, choose eastern or western models to shape Hungarian political and economic systems, culture, and identity? Or, should Hungary create its own models of success? We'll debate that question in the last two chapters.

[20] Interview 17-February 21, 2023.
[21] Montgomery, pp. 129-130.

Mongol Invasion of 1241 —Death and Rebirth

In 1241, after existing as an independent kingdom for two hundred and forty years, Hungary was destroyed by the Mongols—a tribal people from Central Asia. The Mongols occupied Hungary for only a brief time, but their invasion devastated the Hungarian kingdom. The emperor at the time, Frederick II, wrote "That entire precious kingdom was depopulated, devastated and turned into a barren wasteland."[22] For graphic descriptions of the plundering Mongols, see *Lamentation for Hungary, after the Desolation of the Tatars:*

> Rachel weeps, her tears fall, no words to tell her pain, the wild Tartars, her sons' swift death, she sobs her endless grief. Even Judah and the Nile, where babes were slain of old, is surely now surpassed in this by our Pannonia.[23]

Following the Mongol occupation of 1241-1242, King Béla IV promoted the construction of stone castles and fortifications as an effective defense against the fearsome engines of the Mongol siege. He also reformed the Hungarian army, replacing light

---

[22] Lendvai, p. 49.

[23] *Planctus Destructionis Regni Hungariae Per Tartaros.* The Latin Library, http://www.thelatinlibrary.com/planctus.html Pannonia was a province of the Roman Empire corresponding with present-day western Hungary, parts of eastern Austria, and portions of Slovenia, Croatia, and Serbia.

cavalry with heavily armored knights, and encouraged the development of towns and cities for the defense of population centers and resources.[24]

As a result, the second Mongol invasion (1285-1286) was met by a better prepared and organized Hungarian army that successfully repelled the Mongol forces.

The Late Middle Ages were a time of growth and prosperity for Hungary—right until the invasions of the Ottomans and the terrible toll they took on the Magyar kingdom. The population of Hungary grew from about two million people in AD 1300 to three and a half million in AD 1500. Approximately 70% of the population was Hungarian and the remainder was German, Slovak, Croat, Romanian, Cuman, and Ruthenian.[25]

---

[24] Ertman, T. (2011). *Birth of the Leviathan: Building States and Regimes in Medieval and Early Modern Europe*. Cambridge University Press., p. 273.
[25] Cartledge, p. 47.

The Ottoman Empire: Divided and Conquered

Between 1521 and 1541, a wave of Ottoman invasions into Hungary was carried out by Sultan Suleiman the Magnificent, resulting in Hungary's annexation to the Ottoman Empire.

The Battle of Mohács on August 29, 1526, was a particularly devastating defeat. The Ottoman victory resulted in several centuries of territorial partitioning for Hungary, divided among the Ottoman Empire, the Habsburg monarchy, and the Principality of Transylvania. Hungary, the most eastern kingdom of Christian Western civilization, came under Turkish Muslim rule, an event that inspired—three hundred years later—the Hungarian poet János Arany to write: "Glinting atop Our Lady's tower, the crescent has replaced the cross."[26] North-western Hungary remained unconquered and was recognized (and controlled) by the House of Habsburg as "Royal Hungary."[27]

The one-hundred-fifty-year-long Ottoman occupation of Hungary fundamentally changed the fates of the peoples living in the Carpathian Basin. Half of the people were exterminated, and the majority of its structures were razed to the ground.

After the Battle of Mohács in 1526, Hungary descended into chaos and turned into a militarized zone. It became a buffer between two major powers, the Ottoman Turks and the Habsburg Empire, which controlled its western parts. The political and

---

[26] Semjén, Zsolt (2017). *In the Future of Europe: Hungary: Brave and Free.* Békés, Márton (Ed.). p. 121.

[27] Cartledge, p. 92-93.

religious elite fled to Habsburg (or Royal) Hungary, but life for Hungarian peasants, who were tied to the land, was miserable. Soldiers from both sides—Ottomans and Hungarians—regularly looted, overtaxed, and robbed the villages with impunity. The ultimate consequence for the Hungarian populace was that by the end of the seventeenth century, whole swaths of Ottoman Hungary were deserted.[28]

Following the Battle of Mohács and for the next twenty years, Hungary was divided for administrative purposes into Eyalets (provinces), which were further divided into Sanjaks (districts or counties).[29] Ownership of much of the land was distributed to Ottoman soldiers and officials, with about 20% of the territory being retained by the Ottoman state.

Even though Hungary was conquered and divided, in some ways Hungarian identity and self-governance were maintained. Since Hungary was a distant military frontier on the edge of their conquests, the Ottomans did not integrate most of Hungary into their empire. They meddled little in the internal affairs of smaller towns and villages in Hungary and largely left them to self-govern. In a handful of bigger cities, the Ottomans did settle in for the long term and establish administrative or religious institutions. The city of Buda—the hilly side of today's Budapest—was the center of the Ottoman provinces.[30]

---

[28] Pállfy, Géza (2001). "The Impact of the Ottoman Rule on Hungary," *Hungarian Studies Review,* Toronto, 26 (1-2). pp. 109–132.

[29] Detrez, Raymond; Segaert, Barbara (Eds.). (2008). Europe and the Historical Legacies in the Balkans. P.I.E-Peter Lang S.A., Éditions Scientifiques Internationales. p. 167.

[30] Ács, Pal (2019). *Reformations in Hungary in the Age of the Ottoman Conquest.* Brown, Christopher B., *et al.*, Editors, V&R Academic; Aufl. ed. Edition.

It is amazing that the Ottomans never succeeded in fully consolidating their power in Hungary during their one hundred and fifty-year occupation of the country. For example, neither the use of peaceful methods nor sheer force could make the religion of Islam victorious in Hungary. There were no mass conversions to the Muslim faith similar to those in the Balkans. Nor did forced Islamization take place.[31]

Hungary's eventual liberation from the Ottomans hinged on the Battle of Vienna on September 12, 1683, after the city had been besieged by the Ottoman Empire for two months. Ironically, it was a Hungarian—the Calvinist leader, Imre Thököly—who (for his own religio-political motives) appealed to the Ottoman Grand Vizier, Kara Mustafa, to attack the Habsburg capital. Capture of Vienna was a strategic goal of the Ottomans because of the city's control over the Danube River basin and ground trade routes to Germany and the Eastern Mediterranean. One hundred and fifty thousand Ottoman troops laid siege to Vienna, and succeeded in capturing the outer fortifications, and began to tunnel to the inner walls. The emperor at that time, Emperor Leopold fled the city.[32]

However, on the morning of September 12, 80,000 troops from the combined armies of Charles of Lorraine, Polish King Sobieski, the Electors of Saxony and Bavaria, and thirty additional German princes formed along the top of the Vienna hills

---

[31] Ágoston, Gábor. (1991) "Muslim Cultural Enclaves in Hungary Under Ottoman Rule." *Acta Orientalia Academiae Scientiarum Hungaricae*, 45 (2-3). pp. 181–204.

[32] Stoye, J. (2008). *The Siege of Vienna*. Pegasus. pp. 19, 55-59, 275.

and attacked and defeated the Ottomans.[33] After the Ottoman's defeat at the Battle of Vienna, the Hapsburgs assembled a large coalition of European powers known as the Holy League, which allowed them to fight the Ottomans and regain control over Hungary.

Holy League troops gradually expelled the Ottoman Turks from their strongholds in Hungary by 1689. Following the defeat of the Ottomans in the Great Turkish War, most of Ottoman Hungary was ceded to the Habsburgs under the Treaty of Karlowitz in 1699.

The Habsburg Dynasty

Under Habsburg Emperor Leopold, Royal Hungary became a part of the Habsburg monarchy, but had little influence in Vienna. Leopold directly controlled Royal Hungary's financial, military, and foreign affairs, and imperial troops guarded its borders. Even so, the eighteenth century was an era of rebuilding and gathering of forces for the Hungarian people.

Mid-eighteenth century military developments in Europe were characterized by Hungarian innovation and expertise that stretched back centuries. The military traditions and heritage of the Magyar tribal peoples—light cavalry formations and tactics, with roots in seventh century AD—had manifested themselves in a more sophisticated and coherent strategic presence across

33 *Ibid*, p. 352.

European armies of the fifteenth and sixteenth centuries. These cavalry units were named 'Hussars' in honor of their Hungarian origins—*huszár*—so-named for their shock tactics on horseback. By the eighteenth century, Hussar cavalrymen were dominant in irregular warfare, conducting raids, reconnaissance, and acting as a screening or covering force for larger, slower-moving, infantry formations. The Hussars had romanticized reputations as bold, dashing, adventurers. They enhanced that image with elaborate, distinctive uniforms and headgear.[34]

The eighteenth century also marks the beginning of Hungary's direct contributions to American revolutionary history. It may surprise you to know that the 'Father of the U.S. Calvary' was a Hungarian. Michael Kováts de Fabriczy (or simply 'Kováts'), was a Hungarian Hussar who fought in the American Revolutionary War and made the ultimate sacrifice for American independence.

Kováts began his military career under Maria Theresa, the Habsburg Empress and Queen of Hungary from 1740 to 1780, and the only female ruler of the Habsburg dominions. Kováts fought as a common hussar in the calvary regiment for the Habsburg Empire, but his growing belief in the self-determination of nations and the right to freedom, caused him to join the Prussian Army in 1756-1763 to fight against the Austrians. He was awarded the highest medal in the Prussian Army, *Pour le Mérite*.

[34] Muir, Rory (2008). Cavalry Combat. *Tactics and the Experience of Battle in the Age of Napoleon*, New Haven: Yale University Press. Also, Museum of Military History tour, Budapest, May 2023.

Later, Kováts wrote a letter to Benjamin Franklin, the then-American ambassador to Paris, to offer his service in the fight for independence in America. Kováts wrote to Franklin in Latin, as he had not yet learned English, saying: "I ... am also following the call of the Fathers of the Land, as the pioneers of freedom always did. I am a free man and a Hungarian ... raised from the lowest rank to the dignity of a Captain of the Hussars ... I am willing to sacrifice myself wholly and faithfully as it is expected of an honest soldier facing the hazards and great dangers of war ... for the freedom of your great Congress."[35]

Kováts made his way to America, joined the Continental Army and Brigadier General Casimir Pulaski's cavalry legion. Kováts was named Colonel Commandant of the legion on April 18, 1778. He was finally allowed to perform the task he had initially intended: to organize and train the Continental Army in hussar tactics. Sadly, Colonel Kováts letter to Mr. Franklin was prescient—he was killed-in-action leading the Continental Army cavalry he had trained, at the Siege of Charleston, South Carolina, during a battle on May 11, 1779. Kováts is memorialized in the U.S. at The Citadel military academy with a stone memorial and by his namesake, "Kováts Field." He is buried where he fell in Charleston.[36]

---

[35] Zemplényi, Lili (2022). Most Faithful unto Death. *Hungarian Conservative*, https://www.hungarianconservative.com/articles/culture_society/most-faithful-unto-death/

[36] VanBuren, Denise Doring (2022). Recalling the Life, Death and Courageous Example of Michael Kováts. *Daughters of the American Revolution.* https://tinyurl.com/3k39976j

The Hungarian Revolution of 1848 and the Dual Monarchy

The Hungarian Revolution of 1848 against the Austrian Empire was one of the many European revolutions of that same year. Like the Hungarian revolution against Soviet occupation a hundred years later, this one was also led by young intellectuals including Sándor Petőfi (1823-1849), a poet and liberal revolutionary. Petőfi played a leading role in the literary life of the pre-revolution era and is known for reciting his famous poem, *Nemzeti dal* (National Song), to a crowd on March 15, 1848, on the steps of the Hungarian National Museum. The *National Song* captured the spirit of Hungarian identity and its expression through the nationalist revolution[37]

Petöfi and his compatriots formulated the revolution's series of demands known as the 12 Points. The 12 Points included

> freedom of the press, a separate Hungarian government situated in Buda-Pest and responsible to an elected parliament, a National Guard, trial by jury, a national bank, a Hungarian national army, the removal of all "foreign" Habsburg troops, an amnesty for political prisoners, and union with Transylvania, hitherto administered as a separate Habsburg possession.[38]

[37] Clark, Christopher (2023). *Revolutionary Spring: Europe Aflame and the Fight for a New World: 1848-1849*. Crown, New York. p. 306-308.
[38] *Ibid.*, pp. 306-307.

The revolution was initially successful on March 15—in large part because the imperial household of Vienna was overwhelmed by many other nations and ethnicities revolting in 1848 against Habsburg rule. These included Czechs, Serbs, Slovaks, Croats, Romanians, Italians, Poles, and Germans. The Habsburgs allowed the Hungarians the illusion of victory for the opportunity to come back later and smash the revolution.

At this time, Lajos Batthyány (1806-1849), as a member of the committee that presented Hungarian demands for parliamentary reform to the Austrian imperial court on March 17, found himself appointed prime minister by the Emperor. But this was merely a ploy to buy time—to deal with the Hungarians at a later date, and under the terms and conditions that the Empire could manage. In the meantime, Hungarians believed they had achieved a revolutionary break with Vienna.[39]

Batthyány proved to be a patriotic leader, but he was also a devoted monarchist. Stuck in the middle of a clash between the Habsburg dynasty and the Hungarian separatists, he was in a very tough position. Batthyány was dependent on the support of a divided parliament, and this situation weakened his leadership position as prime minister. Batthyány's efforts to negotiate with the imperial power of Vienna, as well as minority ethnic groups seeking autonomy, was viewed as weakness. Pressure mounted on him because he was seen as too moderate and too conciliatory for the revolutionary environment. He tendered his resignation later that same year, in October 1848.[40]

---

[39] *Ibid.*, p. 309-310.
[40] *Ibid.*, p. 206.

A war between Austria and Hungary became increasingly unavoidable as it became apparent to the Hungarians that the Habsburg Emperor was not willing to grant them complete autonomy. Eventually, the Austrian army captured Battyhány in January 1849, and he and thirteen generals were executed on October 6, 1849.[41]

Another key leader of the 1848 Revolution and an iconic figure of enormous importance to Hungarians was Lajos Kossuth (1802-1894). Kossuth served as Minister of Finance in the revolutionary government. Kossuth was a more charismatic and uncompromisingly popular figure than Batthány. He presented the Hungarian Declaration of Independence to the National Assembly in closed session on April 13, 1849. The next day he was elected governor-president of Hungary by Parliament and served in that position until the Russian army was called in by the Habsburgs and destroyed all hope for a continued revolution.[42]

On August 11, 1849, the Russian army, operating in response to the call of the Austrian-Hungarian Emperor Franz Joseph, crushed the Hungarian revolution. Fearing "certain ruin" and that the order of the Empire had been imperiled by anarchy, Franz Joseph traveled to see Czar Nicholas I in Warsaw. Historian Christopher Clark tells us "the meeting opened with a gesture that confirmed the geopolitical reality of the moment:

---

[41] Székely, Tamás (2017). Leading Figures of Hungary's 1848-1849 Revolution and War for Independence. *Hungary Today*. https://hungarytoday.hu/thursday-top-ten-leading-figures-hungarys-1849-1849-revolution-war-independence-75376

[42] Clark, pp. 234-235, 312, 672-673.

Franz Joseph sank to his knees and kissed the Czar's hand."[43] By summer's end, the combined Austrian-Russian forces of 375,000 dominated the Hungarians who struggled to field only 170,000 soldiers. Hungary was placed under martial law. Governor-President Lajos Kossuth and many of his allies fled into exile in the United States.

After the defeat of the revolution in 1849, Emperor Franz Joseph instituted eighteen years of military dictatorship and absolutist rule over Hungary. However, Austria had been weakened by its defeat in the Austro-Prussian War of 1866, which eventually led to negotiations between Austria and Hungary and the Austro-Hungarian Compromise of 1867. The compromise established a dual monarchy between Austria and Hungary and restored the territorial integrity of the Kingdom of Hungary, putting an end to the military dictatorship and absolutist rule of Austria over Hungary.[44] The agreement also restored the old historic constitution of the Kingdom of Hungary, as being separate from and no longer subject to the Austrian Empire.

---

43 *Ibid.*, p. 674.

44 Frank, Tibor (2000). The Austro-Hungarian Compromise of 1867 and Its Contemporary Critics. *Hungarian Studies*. 14(2), Akadémiai Kiadó, Budapest.

Conclusion:
La Belle Époque

All in all, "The Hungarians proved to be increasingly troublesome subjects for the Hapsburgs, and, during the Dual Monarchy they were equally troublesome allies."[45]

After the Austro-Hungarian Compromise of 1867, Hungary enjoyed more real internal independence than it had in more than three hundred years, since the Battle of Mohács in 1526. Franz Joseph was received more sympathetically, but "Hungarian nationalists never forgave Franz Joseph for calling on Russians to help put down the Magyar Revolution of 1849."[46] His wife, Empress Elisabeth ("Sisi"), however, was beloved by the Hungarians for her overt sympathy for their national cause, her decision to become fluent in their language, and her deep affection for the country.

During the nineteenth century, Hungary underwent significant economic development—the country's infrastructure was modernized, and new industries were established. Budapest became known as a major European city, and monuments like the Opera House, the National Gallery, and Parliament were built. Despite lingering tensions with Vienna over customs duties and the administration of the Danube River, this was the *Belle Epoque,* or Golden Age, for Hungary, lasting until the outbreak of World War I.[47]

---

45 Central Intelligence Agency. The Tangled Web. *Studies in Intelligence.* (Spring, 1987): National Archives and Records Administration, RG 263—Records of the CIA, 10-913-3. p. 27.

46 Montgomery, p. 95

47 Gyöngyi Eri (1989). *A Golden Age: Art and Society in Hungary (1896-1914).* Barbican Art Gallery.

Chapter 4

BALANCING SUPERPOWERS

In foreign affairs, nothing is more alluring and more misleading than oversimplification. Not for a moment did the Hungarians renounce their right to make their own decisions—of course, within the limitations of a small, unarmed power.[1]

—John Flournoy Montgomery,
U.S. Ambassador to Hungary (1993-1941)

[1] Montgomery, p. 18.

Introduction: World War I, Defeat of the Central Powers of Germany and Austria-Hungary

The First World War was ignited by the assassination of the heir to the Habsburg throne, Archduke Franz Ferdinand, and his wife Sophie, Duchess of Hohenberg, at Sarajevo on June 28, 1914. Franz Ferdinand, who was the nephew of Emperor Franz Joseph, was assassinated by a Bosnian Serb student named Gavrilo Princip. That moment profoundly changed the course of Western Civilization in ways no one could have ever imagined on that summer day—the ramifications of which are still being realized today.

We will never know what impact the Archduke would have had on Hungary if he had become Emperor of the Austro-Hungarian empire. Franz Ferdinand loathed Hungary and Hungarians, commenting that "it was very bad taste of those gentlemen (the Magyars) ever to come to Europe at all."[2]

Franz Ferdinand referred to Hungarians contemptuously as "mustachioed Gypsies," and regarded the nature of the Empire's duality as the principal source of all of the problems of the Habsburg monarchy. In the 1890s, Franz Ferdinand ordered the General Staff to develop a contingency plan for an Austrian invasion of Hungary and a military occupation of Budapest—anticipating what Hitler would eventually execute in March 1944.[3]

---

[2] Seton-Watson, H. and C. (1981). *The Making of a New Europe*, London. p. 96.

[3] Cartledge, p. 534.

Nonetheless, Franz Ferdinand would never get to act upon his malice for Hungary.

Franz Ferdinand's murder resulted in the Austro-Hungarian Empire declaring war on Serbia and the start of the First World War. Austria-Hungary's declaration of war caused Russia to mobilize in support of Serbia, leading Germany to mobilize against Russia in support of Austria. The great irony of the entire tragic saga of the First World War was the seemingly inevitable domino effect that committed sophisticated European powers to primitive fratricide. Each of the great powers hurtled towards war recklessly—feeling compelled to act—dragging each other to destruction. For Hungary, the resolution of that brutal conflict would bring about the Treaty of Trianon—the most bitter and crushing defeat for Hungary since the Battle of Mohács in 1526.

We have the memoir of John Flournoy Montgomery, the U.S. Minister (Ambassador) to Hungary from 1933 to 1941, as our guide and interpreter for all things Magyar. I will quote liberally from Montgomery's book, *Hungary: The Unwilling Satellite*, over the next few chapters for two reasons: 1. As the U.S. ambassador to Hungary, he was an eyewitness or participant to many of the key moments discussed, and 2. His viewpoints, opinions, and narrative concerning the Hungarians are both frank, fair, and told in a manner that an American-reading audience can access and digest.

Furthermore, Montgomery's experience is instructive to our current-day diplomacy, since he routinely calls out the failures and negligence of the Allies in Central and Eastern Europe. As he notes, the Hungarians were always aware of "the two fires of German and Russian imperialism," though the Allies only focused on the German one. "Hungary's vision was far ahead of ours," he says. "Had we listened to Hungarian statesmen, we should perhaps have been able to limit Stalin's triumph in the hour of Hitler's fall."[4] Much of history agrees with this statement, as you will learn throughout this story.

Europe's "chain gang" style of compulsory war alliances were to continue and involve much more than just Central and Eastern Europe. As Montgomery reflected, "Germany was dragged in by Austria; England and France by Russia ... in other words ... respective allies were not given much choice."[5]

Count István Tisza de Borosjenő et Szeged (1861-1918) was Hungary's prime minister during Europe's 'July Crisis': the events following the death of Franz Ferdinand that churned Europe toward war. He alone counseled restraint to Emperor Franz Joseph at the Common Ministerial Council in Vienna, repeatedly and urgently cautioning against a course of action that would guarantee general mobilization and the path to war with Russia.[6] Tisza eventually came to realize that he could not win the argument, given the powers and forces stacked against him. Intransigence would have meant his dismissal by the emperor. Furthermore, desiring war, Vienna had put deliberately impossible political demands on Serbia, ones that Serbia could never adequately satisfy, thereby creating the circumstance for an inevitable war.[7]

There were differing views at home in Budapest. Some favored a hard line against Serbia, others sought alignment with Berlin—and then there was the uniquely Hungarian view expressed by Endre Ady in an article published just before the as-

---

[4] Montgomery, p. 11.
[5] *Ibid.*, p. 5.
[6] Cartledge, p. 293.
[7] *Ibid.*, p. 295.

sassination, in May 1914, where he wrote: "We like the civilized West, but we do not like and do not want the Germanic West, and we have better things to think of than Vienna, the junkers and Pomerania."[8]

Nonetheless, once war was declared, Hungary fell into line with Austria and Germany and was enthusiastic in the opening weeks with war fever. The optimism faded very quickly. Hungary was poorly prepared for the grim brutalities and realities of modern warfare. Resplendent hussar uniforms did nothing to defend against heavy caliber automatic weapons and massed artillery fire.[9] In less than one year at war, the Dual Monarchy tragically sustained losses of nearly two million men, with Hungary bearing 40% of those casualties.[10]

Off the battlefield, inflation ran rampant and food shortages resulted in street protests. Tisza responded aggressively, making no secret of his priority to place Hungarian interests first—economically and regarding food rations. This exacerbated the tension and friction between Vienna and Budapest. In 1916, a German observed the "inextinguishable hatred in Vienna against Hungary, and a similarly deep loathing in Budapest against Austria."[11]

Emperor Charles I succeeded to the throne of the Austria-Hungarian Empire in 1916, at the death of Franz Joseph. (Under the Dual Monarchy, he was also known as Charles IV, King of Hungary). He made attempts to take Austria-Hungary out of

---

[8] Galántai, J. (1989). *Hungary in the First World War*. Budapest. p. 23.
[9] Tour, National Military Museum. Budapest, Hungary, May 2023.
[10] Cartledge, p. 296.
[11] Vermes, G. (1989). *István Tisza*, in Bödy, P. (Ed.). *Hungarian Statesmen of Destiny, 1860 – 1960*. Boulder, CO. p. 328.

the war through secret overtures to the Allied powers—principally through his brother-in-law, Belgian Prince Sixtus. The effort failed and embittered Kaiser Wilhelm against Charles. Meanwhile, Tisza, having been emboldened by the defeats of Serbia and Romania, and by Russia's Bolshevik revolutionary collapse, became an advocate (ironically) for continuing the war and holding fast against peace initiatives. Eventually, Charles sought Tisza's resignation and he willingly complied.[12]

By 1918, the Hungarian position came down to two choices: whether to feed the Army or to feed the civilian populace. Crop failures had reduced annual harvest by 53%. The food crisis, combined with a large number of idle troops (on the comparatively small Italian or Balkan fronts) that had become inflamed by Bolshevik rhetoric they heard from prisoners of war released by Russia, posed a serious internal security threat to the country.[13]

The entire Austro-Hungarian Empire collapsed in the span of just one month—October 1918. Charles I declared Austria a federal state and devolved the army, sending soldiers and officers back to their own nations. No longer propped up by the crown, the aristocrats would gradually see their political influence dwindle and lose their most traditional profession, that of service in the armed forces. Hungary was allowed only a token army, and the proud Hussar regiments, which had covered themselves in military glory for five centuries, lay buried under the ruin of the old monarchy.[14]

---

[12] Cartledge, p. 300.
[13] *Ibid.*, p. 301.
[14] Montgomery, p. 25.

The Hungarian prime minister, who at this time was Sándor Wekerle, attempted to maintain Hungary's sovereign integrity in light of the emperor's move, and shortly thereafter sought an immediate armistice by letter to U.S. President Woodrow Wilson.[15]

Historian Charles L. Mee Jr. described the magnitude and impact at the end of the Great War in his book, *The End of Order: Versailles 1919*. The costs were horrific: "By November 11, 1918, when the armistice that marked the end of the war was signed, eight million soldiers lay dead, twenty million more were wounded, diseased, mutilated, or spitting blood from gas attacks. Twenty-two million civilians had been killed or wounded, and the survivors were living in villages blasted to splinters or rubble, on farms churned in mud, their cattle dead."[16]

The twists and turns of the diplomacy and statecraft of the Dual Monarchy, home of multi-ethnicities and nations with ancient history, are a complex web compared to the simplicity and ignorance of the American approach to World War I. In many ways, the Americans had a naïve understanding of the issues underlying the motives for the war.

As U.S. Minister John F. Montgomery noted: "To us, the first war appeared primarily as a conflict between Germany and our allies in Western Europe because it was there that our troops fought. .... We were not burdened with knowledge of Eastern European history and snatched gratefully the simple formulae

---

[15] Cartledge, p. 302.

[16] Mee, Charles L., Jr. (1980). *The End of Order: Versailles 1919*. New York: E.P. Dutton. p. xvii.

offered by foreign propagandists. Since Germany was the enemy, Germany was wrong, her Austrian-Hungarian ally was wrong, too. Since Russia was about to quit, why bother with her? France, Italy, England and Japan were certainly right. Am I exaggerating? I do not think so."[17]

That simplistic view of international relations and of one thousand years of European history would shape how inadequately Wilson sought to forge peace following WWI. We will see evidence of that with respect to Hungary, following in 1920.

Communist Revolution

At the end of World War I, the Social Democratic Republic of Hungary was "a weak and incompetent government."[18] It survived less than a year before being overthrown in March 1919 by a Communist revolt led by a brutal Leninist named Béla Kun. Kun formed an "outright Bolshevik government (based) on the Russian pattern" and maintained telegraphic contact with Lenin for advice and support.[19] His government fortunately collapsed after "a reign of 133 days of terror."[20]

---

[17] Montgomery, p. 5.
[18] *Ibid.*, p. 38.
[19] Borsanyi, Gyorgy (1993). *The Life of a Communist Revolutionary, Béla Kun*. Boulder, CO: Social Science Monographs. pp. 146–7.
[20] Montgomery, p. 38.

Interestingly, this was the first genuine instance of the Russian Bolsheviks exporting revolution outside of Russia. Vladimir Lenin, the head of government of Soviet Russia at this time, was determined to instigate a world socialist revolution—partly to fulfill the Communist Manifesto of 1848 and partly to secure the success of Bolshevism. In the aftermath of the German and Austro-Hungarian defeat, revolutions were igniting throughout eastern Europe.[21]

In early 1918, the Bolshevik Party began collecting non-Russian Communist sympathizers into a group called the Federation of Foreign Communist Groups. Hungarians inside of Moscow, most of whom were former prisoners of war, were pulled into this federation. In October 1918, they sent twenty of them back to Hungary, and on November 4, the Hungarian Workers' (Communist) Party was established in Budapest under the leadership of Béla Kun. *The Black Book of Communism* describes Kun's activities:

> Kun had been a prisoner of war (in Moscow) and had quickly rallied to the Bolshevik revolution, becoming president of the Federation of Foreign Communist Groups in April 1918. He arrived in Hungary in November, accompanied by 80 activists, and was immediately elected Party leader. It has been estimated that in late 1918 and early 1919 another 250 to 300 "agitators" and

[21] Courtois, S., Werth, N., Panné, J-L., Paczkowski, A., Bartošek, K., Margolin, J-L. (1999). *The Black Book of Communism: Crimes, Terror, Repression*, Harvard University Press. pp. 271-272.

> revolutionaries arrived in Hungary. With financial support provided by the Bolsheviks, the Hungarian Communists set about spreading propaganda, and their influence soon began to grow.[22]

The communist experience, however short-lived, scarred the Hungarian psyche. And as we will discuss in the coming chapters, the Hungarian Soviet Republic would certainly not be the last export of the Bolshevik revolution to the world.

At the same time, in 1919, the famous Hungarian dissident, Cardinal József Mindszenty, was imprisoned under a dictatorial regime for the first time (he would be arrested again under both the Nazis and the Soviet Union). Mindszenty—at the time a high school religion teacher and the founder of a local newspaper—was an outspoken critic against the Communist Revolution. People often quoted one of his sayings: "Remember, if power remains in the hands of the Communists, even your scythe and spade will be stamped: 'Government Property'!" The Communists in Hungary tried and failed to secure Mindszenty's collaboration and, realizing his great influence in Hungary, they arrested and imprisoned him. He was released after their government collapsed.[23]

---

[22] Courtois, pp. 271-272.

[23] Schlafly, Phyllis (1973, February 13). Mindszenty the Man. *The Phyllis Schlafly Report*. 6 (7). Section 1. Schlafly's report is referring to the biography of Cardinal József Mindszenty, written by Dr. Joseph Vecsey, his lifetime friend and personal secretary, and written again in English by Schlafly as related to her by Dr. Vecsey, to bring an understanding of Mindszenty's story to American readers.

In October of 1919, U.S.-Hungarian collaboration came again in the form of resistance against the Romanian army. As WWI victors, the French sought to impose its will on Hungary. France's more-than-willing surrogates for 'occupation' duty in Hungary were the Romanians, recently allied in November 1918. The Romanian army occupied large swaths of Hungary and actively resisted almost every effort of the Allied Military Mission in Budapest to restore order and move Hungary towards post-war recovery. Exploiting the nightmare scenario in Budapest, the Romanian army stripped the city bare of virtually all items of value, loading them up on trains bound for Bucharest.

On October 5, the Romanian Army tried to loot the Hungarian National Museum as well.[24] The Hungarian National Museum had been founded over a hundred years before, in 1802, and had collected many important and irreplaceable items of Hungarian history. The steps of the museum were where Sándor Petöfi had read his twelve points and spurred Hungarians on to the Revolution of 1848.[25]

But on October 5, 1919, U.S. Major General Harry Hill Bandholtz, the American representative to the Allied Military Mission, personally blocked the way of the marauding Romanians and sealed the entrances to the museum, reportedly 'armed' with only a riding crop. In doing so, General Bandholtz preserved Hungary's heritage and priceless historical pieces. A statue of General Bandholtz memorializing his brave actions stands

[24] Bandholtz, Harry Hill, Major General USA (1933). *An Undiplomatic Diary*, Kruger, Fitz-Conrad, Editor, New York: Columbia University Press.
[25] Visit to Hungarian National Museum, May 2023.

in Liberty Square (Szabadság Tér) in beautiful Budapest today, across from the United States embassy. Its inscription reads "I simply carried out the instructions of my Government, as I understood them, as an officer and a gentleman of the United States Army." A commemorative plaque to General Bandholtz was recently revealed in the garden of the Hungarian National Museum, and a few of his belongings, including his riding crop, were also displayed.

Admiral Miklós Horthy

At about the same time, Commander of the National Army Admiral Miklós (Nicholas) Horthy de Nagybánya (1868-1957) led army units from the west of Hungary into Budapest on November 16, 1919, mounted on a white horse, in a show of "liberation."[26] Horthy, who had been an aide-de-camp to Emperor Franz Joseph (from 1909-1914) and also Commander-in-Chief of the Austro-Hungarian Naval Fleet (until ordered to surrender by Charles IV), was hunting down communists and Kun collaborators and sympathizers.

In *The Iron Curtain*, Anne Applebaum writes about the influence of the communists in Hungary that lit the fire under Admiral Horthy. According to her account, Horthy

---

[26] Goldberger, Samuel (1998, February). *Goldberger on Sakmyster: Hungary's Admiral on Horseback: Miklos Horthy, 1918-1944.* H-Net Reviews in the Humanities and Social Sciences. Habsburg.

> persecuted the communist party because of its links with Soviet agents, because of the memory of the failed 1918 coup, and because of the brutality of Béla Kun's brief dictatorship. In the illegal underground, Hungarian communists hid from the law and developed what one veteran called "a severe, tough, hierarchical organization," one that tolerated very little internal democracy or dissent. Moreover, "this way of organization was idealized and admired."[27]

As Horthy and the National Army marched towards Budapest, Horthy's speeches at rallies in the towns of western Hungary were extremely nationalistic, ending usually with Horthy shouting "Long Live the Fatherland!" He even rode into each town on a white horse to link himself symbolically with Árpad, the tribal chief who in the ninth century had led the Magyars out of the Carpathian Mountains and into the Danubian Basin.[28]

The National Assembly of Hungary reestablished the Kingdom of Hungary on March 1, 1920, under the leadership of Admiral Miklós Horthy and consistent with a nationalist, Christian ideology. Due to pressure from the victorious Entente powers, the Assembly rejected a return of Charles IV to the Hungarian throne and decided to elect a regent to preside as Head of State. Admiral Horthy was already Minister of War as well as Commander of the National Army, and seemed a good choice.

---

[27] Applebaum, Anne. (2013) *Iron Curtain: The Crushing of Eastern Europe.* Knopf Doubleday Publishing. p. 53.
[28] Goldberger.

Upon being offered the Regency, Horthy pressed for increased powers, including "the general prerogatives of the King, with the exception of the right to name titles of nobility and of the patronage of the Church." Horthy wanted the power to appoint and dismiss prime ministers, to convene and dissolve parliament, and to command the armed forces. With those powers guaranteed, Horthy took the oath of office.[29] 'Regent,' in the Hungarian way of thinking, meant 'governor,' and contrasted with the notion of a ruling royal family.

We can rely upon the experience and excellent judgment of U.S. Ambassador John F. Montgomery in assessing Regent Horthy. Montgomery makes three broad points about Horthy in his thoughtful and insightful memoir. Montgomery explains Horthy as follows:

> Being an old sea dog, he was outspoken. It never occurred to him to dissemble and he would not have known how. If any correspondent asked him questions, he was liable to give answers which would involve Hungary in all sorts of trouble.[30]
>
> Was Horthy a good ruler? He was not brilliant, but it is questioned whether constitutional rulers should be brilliant. He had, however, an abundance of common sense, great patriotism, honesty and integrity. No one could truthfully deny that he did his best within the limits of his authority and according to his code.[31]

---

[29] Sakmyster, Thomas L. (1994). *Hungary's Admiral on Horseback: Miklós Horthy, 1918-1944.* East European Monographs. p. 56.

[30] Montgomery, pp. 41-42.

[31] *Ibid.*, pp. 41-42.

Hitler tried to convince the Regent to commit troops to the invasion of Slovakia. Horthy flatly replied, "You will get another world war and you will lose it, because you have no sea power." At this, Hitler began shouting and screaming, and according to the U.S. ambassador to Hungary, Horthy asked him not to forget that "he [Hitler], the leader of an infant state, was speaking to the head of a thousand-year old state; and told him that unless he was treated as such, he would leave at once!" Hitler calmed down. If Horthy was intimidated by Hitler, it did not show. The first time they met, Hitler bowed to Horthy who, in return, remained erect.[32]

The Losers of Self-Determination: The Treaty of Trianon

As Hungary worked through its domestic political crises, the Treaty of Versailles, formally ending WWI, was being written outside of Paris on June 28, 1919 and imposed upon the various warring parties. Between the summers of 1919 and 1920, a series of treaties redrew the political and national lines of Europe —purportedly according to Woodrow Wilson's "right of self-determination."

---

[32] Montgomery, pp. 35-36, wherein the author quotes de Kanya, then-foreign affairs chairman of the Upper House of Parliament and as told by Regent Horthy in August 1938.

The war's losers were reorganized, and empires were divided into republics and kingdoms. Various parties, who remained unaffected, of course, reveled in the broken shards of society and culture as if they were a glorious thing. Not everyone had the "right of self-determination"—a concept that was implemented in a very selective manner. When it came to the Hungarians, the Irish, and the American suffragists (among others)—it seemed their self-determination did not count. Wilsonian self-determination principles were naively simplistic, ignorant, hypocritical, and quasi-schizophrenic. They created confusion and resentment on a scale that guaranteed a Second World War.

On February 1918, Woodrow Wilson had told the world:

> There shall be no annexations, no contributions, no punitive damages. People are not to be handed about from one sovereignty to another by an international conference ... "Self-determination" is not a mere phrase ... Every territorial settlement involved in this war must be made in the interest and for the benefit of the population concerned, and not as part of any mere adjustment or compromise of claims amongst rival states.[33]

Hungary was brutally victimized by Trianon—in direct contravention to every syllable of Wilson's proclamation. The victors of WWI relocated most of the national boundaries of Europe—all Germany-allied nations were affected, but none

---

[33] Andelman, A. David (2007). *A Shattered Peace: Versailles 1919 and the Price We Pay Today*. Hoboken, NJ: John T. Wiley & Sons. p. 191.

more than Hungary.[34] The Hungarian delegation was officially invited to the Grand Trianon château in Versailles on December 1, 1919. However, the new borders of Hungary were nearly finalized without the presence or participation of the Hungarians.[35] So much for the much-vaunted American principle of "self-determination."

The proposed solution for boundary disputes was for the population to decide by free plebiscite to which country they wished to belong—but only one small consequential one happened in Hungary. According to some opinions, the Allies drafted the outline of the new borders with little or no regard to the historical, cultural, ethnic, geographic, economic, and strategic aspects of the region.[36]

The allies assigned territories of ethnic populations to states neighboring Hungary where these ethnicities had originated, but they also assigned sizable territories mainly inhabited by Hungarian-speaking populations. For instance, Romania gained all of Transylvania, which was home to 2,800,000 Romanians, but also contained a significant minority of 1,600,000 Hungarians and about 250,000 Germans.[37] Hungary's protests against losing their population to Romania were disregarded by the Allied representatives.

---

[34] Central Intelligence Agency (CIA) (1987). A Tangled Web. *Studies in Intelligence*, Spring, 1987: National Archives and Records Administration, 10-913-3 RG 263. Records of the CIA. p. 27.

[35] Mayer, Arno J. (1967). *Politics and Diplomacy of Peacemaking. Containment and Counterrevolution at Versailles, 1918–1919*. New York: Knopf. p. 369.

[36] *Ibid.*

[37] Cartographia, Kft. (1997). *Történelmi világatlasz* [*World Atlas of History*], Budapest.

U.S. Minister John Montgomery's analysis is harsh but on target: "The justification offered by the victors was that only by surgical separation could the declared war aim of national self-determination be achieved."[38] The bitter irony is that "in the name of national self-determination, more than three million Magyars had been put under Czech, Rumanian [sic] and Servian [sic] rule."[39]

The Treaty of Trianon was signed on June 4, 1920. The terms were brutal:

- Before, Hungary was a territory of about 109,000 square miles with 18.2 million people. Under the Treaty of Trianon, Hungary lost two thirds of its territory, which was reduced to less than 36,000 square miles and 7.9 million people. The nation lost more than 3 million ethnic Hungarian citizens.[40]
- The largest territory was given to Romania. The newly formed nations of Czechoslovakia and Yugoslavia benefited also.[41]

'Trianon', the shorthand expression common to Hungarians, left the country "isolated politically, disarmed, encircled by hostile countries, (and as such) Hungary became one of Central Europe's weakest, most vulnerable states." The revision of their territory by peaceful means to reinstate historical boundaries

---

[38] Montgomery, p. 49.
[39] *Ibid.*, p. 22.
[40] Cartledge, p. 326-327.
[41] CIA. p. 27

then became the focus of Hungary's domestic and foreign policy. The neighboring states viewed Hungarians as "their principal external and internal enemies (and) the millions of Hungarians forced into minority status were subjected to hitherto unsurpassed oppression."[42]

The ink was barely dry at Trianon when the Hungarians began their quest to recover their territories lost at Trianon. "Historic Hungary" is the term that describes their irredentist drive. Irredentism is a political ideology that advocates for the recovery of territory considered to belong to a nation based on history, tradition, or ethnic grounds. The irredentists of Hungary had two things in common: "a desire for a common frontier with Poland and the return of Transylvania to Hungary."[43]

The natural barrier of the Carpathian Mountains had, for many centuries, been of great psychological importance for the Hungarians. Montgomery says that "every Magyar had inherited the subconscious conviction that the Carpathian Mountains were the God-given wall against the East, against barbarism, against Asia, Europe's eternal menace." [44] But when the Romanians "stepped across the Carpathians, it was as though the natural wall against Asia had crumbled ... Rumania treated the Magyars as subjects with minor rights, paying back in kind, they said, what Hungary had done to Romanians."[45]

---

[42] Schmidt, Mária (Ed.). (2019). *Terror Háza*, Public Foundation for Research on Central and Eastern European History and Society, Budapest. p. 6.
[43] Montgomery, p. 53.
[44] *Ibid.*, pp. 55 and 130.
[45] *Ibid.*, p. 131.

Because of King István, the Hungarian nation had developed under the cultural influence of the Holy Roman Empire and Western Civilization. But, Romania,

> facing the East and under Turkish domination for centuries, was different in outlook and way of living, so Hungary became and remained the most eastern outpost of Western civilization. The standard of living, especially of the working class, was very much higher in Hungary than in Rumania, and it was considered a great humiliation by Hungarians that so many Magyars were put under Rumanian rule by the transfer of Transylvania to Rumania.[46]

Steven Béla Várdy's book *Hungary in the Age of Total War* helps us to understand how the loss at Trianon affected the development of the Hungarian psyche. The depth and magnitude of the psychological shock and scarring of the national psyche by the Treaty of Trianon was "so pervasive and keenly felt that the syndrome it produced can only be compared to a malignant national disease."[47] Montgomery also explains the Hungarian position in terms Americans can relate to:

---

46 *Ibid.*, pp. 129-130.

47 Várdy, Steven Béla (1998). The Impact of Trianon upon the Hungarian Mind: Irredentism and Hungary's Path to War. In Dreisziger, Nándor (Ed.). *Hungary in the Age of Total War*. New York: Columbia University Press. pp. 27-48; p. 28.

> No one could be in Hungary very long without knowing that "nem, nem, soha" meant "no, no, never" and that it referred to the boundaries fixed by the Treaty of Trianon. If Japan had defeated us and made Canada and Mexico her satellites and given Texas to the latter and most of New England to the former, and had annexed California and Oregon, something similar to nem, nem, soha would probably appeared in our flower beds, on our mountain slopes and would have burned in our hearts. It is very hard for one not intimately acquainted with the history of Hungary to understand what revision meant to Hungarians, but if we would think of it in terms of our own country [...] [48]

The shock of Trianon and the initial irredentism for "Historic Hungary" manifested itself in a false hope for boundary adjustments under the provisions of Article 19 of the Covenant of the League of Nations. Hungarians were led to believe (by a letter delivering peace terms to them by French President Alexandre Millerand) that the boundaries of Trianon would be reconsidered by the League of Nations, referencing Article 19.[49] But nothing ever came of it. The Hungarians felt wronged, cheated, and tricked.

---

48 Montgomery, p. 47.

49 *Ibid.*, pp. 50-52.

Conclusion:
The Inter-War Years

Hungary's foreign policy in the interwar period was largely influenced by the goal of 'correcting' the injustice of Trianon[50] which fueled a strong irredentist movement, as well as by post-war economic and political challenges of inflation, unemployment, social unrest, and reparations to the victorious allies. Hungary also had to cope with the rise of fascism in Italy and Germany, and the rise of Communism in Soviet Russia, as well as the changing alliances and interests of the major powers.

In 1927, Hungary signed The Treaty of Rome, which recognized Hungary's territorial claims and promised them Italian support. This began a move in international relations that later carried Hungary into the Berlin-Rome Axis and accelerated "after 1938 when the Western Allies rejected Hungarian claims against Czechoslovakia." The First Vienna Award in 1938 granted Hungary parts of southern Slovakia and Carpathian Ruthenia from Czechoslovakia.

The Second Vienna Award in 1940 granted Hungary northern Transylvania from Romania.[51] Hungary would lose these territories again after Soviet occupation.

While seeking opportunities to regain lost territories, or at least improve the situation for the Hungarian minorities living in them, Hungary tried also to balance its relations with Germa-

---

[50] Pritz, Pál (2003). *Hungarian Foreign Policy in the Interwar Period*, Hungarian Academy of Sciences, Budapest, 2003.
[51] CIA, p. 27.

ny, Italy, France, Britain, and the Soviet Union. As Montgomery had noted, Hungary was always aware of the "two fires of German and Russian imperialism."[52] If we had only paid attention.

From the mid-thirties onward, Hungary found herself in the buffer zone between the increasingly more aggressive Nazi Germany and the Soviet Union, who had, by the end of the decade, once again became a power to reckon with. Allied with one another, and subsequently locked in a life-and-death battle, the two totalitarian dictatorships strove for a new order that had no place for an independent Hungary.

The secret Hitler-Stalin Pact (or Molotov-Ribbentrop Pact) of August 23, 1939, brought Hungary's deepest fears to fruition. German and Soviet Foreign Ministers Molotov and Ribbentrop signed a nonaggression pact in Moscow, to which was attached a secret protocol between the two countries that divided central and eastern Europe between the German Reich and the USSR.[53] Hitler would get western Poland and be allowed to exert influence over Hungary and Romania without Soviet interference. Stalin would acquire eastern Poland, the Baltic States, and northern Romania. More about the impact of this on Hungary and Eastern and Central Europe will be discussed in Chapter 7: "'Liberating' Eastern Europe."

Hungary's foreign policy of the interwar period ultimately proved disastrous for the country. In seeking to advance its own interests and recover lost lands and population, it maneuvered itself into a position firmly within the vise grip pressures of Nazi Germany and Soviet Russia.

52 Montgomery, p. 11.
53 *Ibid.*, p. 180.

Chapter 5

HITLER AND STALIN'S VISE GRIP

Foreign Minister of Hungary Mr. de Kanya "felt, quite rightly, that whosoever won, Hungary would lose.... he said he would not mind living under British hegemony, but he would rather be dead than to live under German."[1]

—John Flournoy Montgomery,
U.S. Ambassador to Hungary (1993-1941),
quoting Kálmán de Kánya,
former Hungarian Foreign Minister (1933-1938)

[1] Montgomery, p. 77.

Introduction:
World War II, Aligning With Hitler

Hungary's intentions in World War II have been the matter of great debate and discussion. Some historians, deemed by many to be reputable, expound that Hungary's leader, Admiral Miklós Horthy, was an authoritarian dictator and had much in common with Adolph Hitler.

The uncomfortable reality is that Hungary, ideologically *not* fascist, aligned itself with fascist, dictatorial Germany. But the *truth* is much more complicated. The truth is not a cartoonishly simplistic "good guys vs. bad guys" scenario homogenized for consumption by official propagandists. The truth is, again, understood in the context of Hungary's necessity to balance itself between East and West (both politically and geographically) for survival.

I believe Hungary's position in World War II was ultimately shaped by the Hungarians' attempt to balance many competing threats—compounded by the reality of the situation of Hungary after Trianon. As we have discussed, Hungary was drastically weakened by Trianon—in direct contravention to every syllable of Wilson's proclamation of self-determination. With severely diminished post-Trianon borders and population, Hungary desperately fought for survival and to retain its own national identity and objectives, all while surrounded by two superpowers who had *already* determined, according to the secret Hitler-Stalin Pact, to carve up Eastern and Central Europe (see the end of Chapter 4).

Four of the main threats to Hungary were as follows:

- One: Hungary, whose location and resources were desired by Hitler, was ultimately at the mercy of the German army and Hitler's whims.
- Two: Hungary believed that the Soviet air force, at that time on the side of the Western allies, had on June 26, 1941, attacked and bombed three areas of Hungary—Kassa, Munkács, and Raho[2]—inflicting substantial destruction and death. And, having survived a brief and brutal experiment with Communism in 1919, they wanted nothing to do with the Communists or the Soviets.
- Three: the Arrow Cross, the Hungarian National Socialist party, had grown in political influence.
- Four: Hungary's cry for help and attempt at an armistice with Western allies were ultimately ignored.

The notion that Hungary had to pursue its own best interests, when surrounded and threatened by the larger, more aggressive military powers of Fascism and Communism, should not surprise anyone when examining the international situation on the cusp of WWII.

The Nazis were a formidable force in Central Europe. For contemporary context, we need only look to the words of Sir Neville Henderson, GCMG, who served as the UK ambassador

[2] Schmidt, Mária (Ed.). (2019). *Terror Háza*, Public Foundation for Research on Central and Eastern European History and Society, Budapest, p. 7. At the time the bombs were thought to be dropped by the Soviet air force but the truth is not clear, even today.

to Germany from 1937 to 1939. The Nazis had taken control of Prague on March 15, 1939, and had continued to spread their power. Writing in his 1940 memoir, *Failure of a Mission*, Henderson reflects:

> After Prague, no nation in Europe could feel itself secure from some new adaptation of Nazi racial superiority and jungle law. In 12 months, Germany had swallowed up Austria, the Sudeten lands, and Czechoslovakia. Verbal protests were so much wastepaper; and the firm stand had to be taken somewhere and force opposed by force; otherwise, in the course of the intoxication of success, Hitler, in the course of another 12 months, would continue the process with Poland, Hungary, and Romania. The principles of nationalism and self-determination, which had served Hitler to create Greater Germany ... had been cynically thrown overboard at Prague and world dominion had supplanted them.[3]

Wilhelm Höttl (1915-1999), member of the *Sicherheitsdienst* (intelligence arm of the SS) and chief of intelligence for Central and Southeast Europe, gives us the German perspective. In *The Secret Front: Nazi Political Espionage 1938-1945*, Höttl describes Hungary's desperate attempt to rebuild their nation, including making alliances with Italy and with Germany. Hungary had a flirtation with Mussolini's Italy to install an Italian prince on the vacant Hungarian throne, and Hungary had also

[3] Henderson, Sir Neville (1940). *Failure of a Mission*. New York: G.P. Putnam's Sons. pp. 225-226.

cultivated a friendship with Germany which had resulted in the recovery of Trianon-lost lands through the Vienna Arbitration Awards of 1939 and 1940. We defer to Höttl to see the Hungarian position more clearly:

> Hitler agreed to the territorial gains of Hungary between 1938 and 1941. This was based purely on tactical grounds. He undoubtedly had a strong leaning towards Hungarians, in whom he saw the descendants of those brave Asiatic horsemen who had been the terror of Central Europe and had later become the foremost defenders of the West against the menace from the East. He admired equally their glorious history, their resistance to the Peace Treaty of Trianon, their overthrow of the Communist Government in 1919 and the strong anti-Bolshevist policy of the "Protectors of the Race" movement [outlawed in 1924 by Hungary's conservative government of István Bethlen] of Prime Minister Gömbös.
>
> In spite of this, Hitler was conscious of a feeling of profound distrust towards the Regent Horthy. He regarded him as a fossilized, old, Austrian Admiral, completely in the hands of his Anglophile and Jewish entourage and imbued with a strong aversion to National Socialism and the person of its Führer. When Gömbös died prematurely in 1936, Hitler could see no successor as Prime Minister on whom he could rely, and he watched developments in Hungary with some concern.[4]

[4] Höttl, Wilhelm (1954). *The Secret Front: Nazi Political Espionage 1938-45*. New York: Enigma Books. pp. 177-178.

World War II Begins and the Rise of Arrow Cross

World War II began with the German invasion of Poland on September 1, 1939—one week after the signing of the Hitler-Stalin Pact. Two days later, Britain and France declared war. The Soviets then engaged in their own act of war and unprovoked aggression, invading Poland just fourteen days later.

The secret Hitler-Stalin pact had enabled Germany to invade Poland without fear of Soviet intervention. The pact had assigned Hungary to the German sphere of influence, meaning that Hungary, at least in the minds of both Hitler and Stalin, must follow German influence and support German political and military interests in Eastern Europe. It also meant that Hungary would have to accept Germany's mediation and arbitration in its territorial disputes.The secret protocol would also put Hungary on the side of Axis powers in the war against the Soviet Union in 1941, which proved to be a fatal mistake for Hungary, as it faced heavy losses on the eastern front and became a target of Allied bombing raids.

After the Germans invaded Poland in 1939, Poles fled into Hungary seeking refugee status. Hungarians set up 141 military camps in the southwest of the country, but that number dwindled rapidly to twenty-one, as Polish men went on to France with the goal of joining the Polish Legion and fighting the Germans there. Nonetheless, the Hungarians eventually established twenty-seven Polish-language elementary schools, as well as middle schools. Upwards of 15,000 Polish Jews were granted refugee sanctuary. The Germans viewed all of this as "unfriendly acts" and applied severe pressure to the Hungarian government.[5]

Horthy worked hard to resist German pressure and keep his country a nonbelligerent in the war. Some cold, realistic analysis from U.S. Ambassador Montgomery illustrates Hungary's position: "To become dependent on Germany would be a hard fate. Yet, since Germany seemed to be invincible, they could not court complete disaster by openly opposing her."[6]

Yet at the same time, Horthy "felt the need to placate influential parties within his own country and protect his nation from Soviet domination."[7]

Hungary at this time was ruled by an elected, legitimate parliament and government, with "representatives of active opposition parties sitting in the chambers. Freedom of the press was upheld ... [and] Hungarian citizens lived a better and freer life than their neighbours."[8]

Although Hungary was ideologically not fascist, it did have weak right-wing elements at play in its politics, including the philosophically Nazi-aligned Hungarian National Socialists. The Hungarian National Socialist Party specifically designed what was called an 'Arrow Cross' as their emblem—because in 1933 the Hungarian government specifically forbade them to wear the German swastika or to use it with the Hungarian flag.[9]

---

5 Cornelius, Deborah S. (2011). *Hungary in World War II: Caught in the Cauldron*, New York: Fordham University Press. pp. 116-118.

6 Montgomery, pp. 19-20.

7 History.com Editors (2019, December 30). Hungary Declares War on Germany. *A&E Television Network*, https://www.history.com/this-day-in-history/hungary-declares-war-on-germany

8 Schmidt, Mária (Ed.). (2019). p. 6.

9 Tour at Terror Háza. June 1, 2023.

However, in the Hungarian parliamentary elections of 1939, a group that became known as 'Arrow Cross' had become the second strongest political party, with more than 300,000 members, and supported by close to a million voters. In the working-class districts of Budapest, they had received one out of every three votes.[10] The dynamic of the new parliament shifted dramatically to the right. The parliamentary diary "noted an unprecedented number of incidents of verbal aggression, representatives shouting out at the speaker during debate especially against the Social Democrats. From that time on, actual opposition to government policies came not from the Left but from the Right."[11]

In 1940, the Arrow Cross party united with other far right groups under the Hungarian National Socialist Party. The Communist Party of Hungary, which was actually illegal in Hungary, was also aggressively pursuing influence, though at the time it was a relatively small group.[12] The Communist Party had been operating since 1919 and only had a few hundred members with a handful of activists.

Arrow Cross had much in common with Hitler and his Nazis, yet it had a more pro-Hungarian focus. Ferenc Szálasi led the Arrow Cross Party from 1939 until his execution on March 12, 1946, by hanging, on order of the People's Tribunal, a court established by the Soviet-backed provisional government.[13] Szála-

[10] Schmidt, Mária (Ed.). (2019). p. 15.
[11] Cornelius, p. 111.
[12] Vazsonyi, p. 7.
[13] Cornelius, p. 392.

si saw himself as the savior of Hungary; his vision was to lead a federation made of Hungary and its lost historical territories that would expel all Jews and Communists. He, like the Nazis, had a twisted sense of nationalistic pride. He was described as a "burning patriot," and was considered mentally unbalanced. His gnostic self-regard is captured in one of his speeches:

> It is my conviction that the whole ordering of Europe can be affected only by that little people (the Hungarians), despised of the Germans, the Hungarian people, on the Hungarist basic principles evolved through me. He who does not identify himself with my doctrine, who does not recognize me unreservedly as leader and will not agree that I have been selected by a higher Divine authority to redeem the Magyar people—he who does not understand me or loses confidence—let him go! At most, I shall remain alone, but even alone I shall create the Hungarist State with the help of the secret force that is within me.[14]

14 Macartney, C.A. (1956). *October Fifteenth, A History of Modern Hungary 1929-1945*. Part I, Edinburgh University Press. pp. 160-1.

Hitler Attacks the USSR

On June 22, 1941, Hitler surprised the world. Hitler's attack on the Soviet Union changed the nature of the Second World War fundamentally and the political landscape of Europe for decades. Hitler wanted to expand Germany's territory and create *lebensraum,* or 'living space', for the German people. His attack was also an action based on his racial theories against Slavic people and his hatred of 'Jewish Bolshevism'. Hitler also suspected that Stalin would have no hesitancy in attacking him—and he wanted to strike first. Lastly, he was overconfident and believed he would sweep through the Soviet Union in the same way he had conquered France.

Until that point in the war, Hungary had experienced a wartime boom, and general economic and industrial growth. The Horthy regency was at its peak of popularity.[15] Because of Hitler's successes across Europe, it would have been easy just to ride in the wake of Germany but "Hungarians were horrified by his (Hitler's) methods."[16] As we shall see, that was a driving force in the Hungarian government's initiatives to find a way out from under German control.

During 'Operation Barbarossa', when Germany invaded the Soviet Union, Hitler demanded that Hungary also mobilize its military against the Soviets. About 250,000 Hungarian soldiers were sent to fight on the Eastern Front against the Soviet Union.

---

15 Cornelius, pp. 146-147.

16 Montgomery, p. 170.

On June 26, three areas of Hungary—Kassa, Munkács, and Raho—were attacked by bombs, which at the time were thought to be dropped by the Soviet Air Force—an assertion still disputed today.[17] On June 27, less than a week after Germany's invasion, Hungary declared war on the USSR, making Hungary an adversary of the U.S. and its allies.[18]

Hungary was now in a vise grip, squeezed between two superpowers once again—Germany and the Soviet Union.

The Hungarian declaration of war against the USSR, combined with the deployment of the Second Army to the Russian Front, caused Admiral Horthy to reevaluate strategic and political positions. He decided that with these radical new developments threatening Hungary, "what he needed was a 'real Hungarian'—a man that would be able to stand up to the Germans, neutralize the noisy right-wing extremists, and protect the country's interests in wartime."[19]

Horthy chose Miklós (Nicholas) Kállay, to whom he had hinted months earlier that the premiership was in his future, during a shooting party in January 1942 with German Foreign Minister Ribbentrop. Horthy had been impressed with Kállay's facility for deftly insulting Ribbentrop during the outing. In early March 1942, Kállay was summoned to the Royal Castle where Horthy offered Kállay the position of prime minister, with almost no strings attached, and a promise of long-term appointment. And, should parliamentary challenges face Kállay, Horthy vowed to

---

[17] Schmidt, Mária (Ed.). (2019). p. 7 and Cornelius, p. 149 *et seq.*
[18] Cornelius, pp. 148-151.
[19] *Ibid.*, p. 198.

dissolve the parliament and move for new elections rather than fire his new prime minister.[20]

Kállay respectfully declined Horthy's offer, noting the inherent opposition in Parliament and German hostility toward the idea of Kállay in power. But Horthy persisted and eventually, after a few days, won. Horthy embraced Kállay with tears in his eyes and thanked him for accepting the position. As Kállay was leaving the Royal Castle, he came upon Horthy's son and Hungary's vice regent, István Horthy, who exclaimed, "Now everything is all right [sic]; everything will be all right!"[21]

---

[20] *Ibid.*, p. 199.

[21] Kállay, Nicholas (1954). *Hungarian Premier.* New York: Columbia University Press. p. 12.

Conclusion: Hungary's Failed Quest for Peace

As soon as he took office, Kállay and his operatives put out multiple 'peace-feelers' in an effort to attract the attention of the British or Americans. Messages and emissaries were dispatched to all of the key neutral cities: Stockholm, Lisbon, Berne, The Vatican, and Istanbul. Unfortunately, Hungary's multi-pronged effort—across at least five major cities—to make contact and broker an exit from the war actually created confusion and distrust. Allied intelligence officers, getting wind of the Hungarian overtures, did not know which Hungarian or surrogate was legitimate and whether they were being played by an agent provocateur.[22]

As efforts to extract Hungary from the Axis were underway, Kállay also sought to both minimize combat losses with the Soviets and avoid German military occupation, knowing the later would lead to mass extermination of Jews and anti-Nazi Hungarians.[23] His was an increasingly pressured situation, and time was of the essence.

It is interesting to note that President Franklin D. Roosevelt believed that the small satellite countries of Germany, like Hungary, had been forced by Hitler to declare war on the Soviet Union, and therefore he was inclined to ignore them. FDR ac-

---

[22] Petersen, Neal H. (Ed.). (1996). *From Hitler's Doorstep:The Wartime Intelligence Reports of Allen Dulles,* University Park, PA: Pennsylvania State University Press. pp. 45-46; 79-80; 82; 96-97; 129-130; 137-39; 170; 203; 569.
[23] Montgomery, p. 161.

tually dismissed their war declarations saying: "I realized that those three governments (Romania, Bulgaria, Hungary) took that action not upon their own initiative or in response to the wishes of their own peoples, but as instruments of Hitler."[24] If only this keen insight into their position had been applied to the peace terms that went on at the Yalta Conference.

Nonetheless, having been on the losing side of the last world war, Horthy and Kállay desperately wished to extract themselves from Nazi alliance and sue for a separate peace with the Allies. And Kállay was aware of a ticking time-bomb: he believed the British and Americans would reach the Hungarian frontier by the beginning of 1944 or earlier; at that point it would be impossible for Hungary to join the alliance against Germany, like the Italians had been able to do on October 13, 1943, one month after their surrender to the Allies.[25]

Kállay's policies and directives—to dial back support for Germany and seek peace with the Allies—resulted in Hungary's increased resistance to Germany and corresponding intense pressure from the Germans back against the Kállay government for further industrial, economic, and military support.[26]

In 1943, Hungary suffered huge losses at the hand of the Red Army.[27] In the Battle of Voronezh in Russia, in January of 1943, Hungary's entire Second Army was decimated by the Soviets, making Hungary militarily impotent.[28]

---

[24] *Ibid.*, pp. 153-4.
[25] CIA, p. 27.
[26] Montgomery, pp. 188-9.
[27] Schmidt, Mária (Ed.). (2019). p. 7 and Cornelius, p. 209-210.
[28] Cornelius, p. 225.

With pressure mounting, in August 1943, Kállay sent Ladislas Veress, press secretary of the Foreign Ministry, to Istanbul to establish direct contact with the British and offer them Hungary's unconditional surrender and military collaboration. It took Veress two trips to Istanbul, but he was eventually successful. On September 9, 1943, Veress—acting on behalf of the Kingdom of Hungary—signed a secret agreement for Hungary's surrender aboard the yacht of British Ambassador Sir Hugh Knatchbull-Hugesson, anchored in the Sea of Marmara.[29] The agreement with the British for Hungary's unconditional surrender was to be effective as determined by the Allies. It was never made public.

While the Hungarians continued to play for time and look hopefully for a Western (British or American) Allied intervention that would save them from German occupation or Soviet rape, the Allies provided nothing but frustration. The only British or American military operations that had been planned or carried out in Hungary were small-scale unconventional warfare missions. Most of these missions frustrated the Hungarians because in trying to attack the Germans, the Allies targeted Hungarian infrastructure. The British were only interested in parachuting small teams of Special Operations Executive (SOE) operatives to organize underground activities and to engage in sabotage operations.[30] These were largely unproductive.

---

[29] Kállay, p. 373.

[30] Cornelius, p. 268.

The British representative advised Hungary (via Veress) not to do anything to provoke German military occupation.[31] Perhaps that was intended as sincere advice, but the Germans—from Hitler, to his military, to his security services—all knew what the Hungarians were attempting. Hungary's efforts to extract itself from the Axis was, in a sense, one of the worst kept secrets of WWII. In September 1943, Russel Hill of the *New York Herald Tribune* reported:

> It is in Hungary that opposition to the German war is best organized and most articulate. The Hungarians have prepared well for the day when Allied troops arrive ... There are in Hungary today eleven anti-Nazi newspapers, of which the leading one is the liberal daily Magyar Nemzet ... But even the parties that support Premier Kállay's government have given the Germans only minimum co-operation. There have never been more than four divisions at the Russian Front. The Germans have not been allowed to control Hungary militarily as they have Romania and Bulgaria. They have been restricted to railroad stations and airfields, and German troops are not seen in Budapest or other Hungarian cities. Undoubtedly, the Germans could have forcibly denied the Hungarians their relatively free press, their parliamentary institutions and their independent national existence.[32]

31 Montgomery, p. 161.
32 *Ibid.*, p. 165.

Only a month later, Swedish journalist K.G. Bolander, wrote a piece carried in the *London Times* observing:

> The greatest surprise was to see how widespread and marked the anti-German feeling was and how openly expressed. The Hungarians are well aware that they are in the wrong box, but also know that attempts to get disentangled from Germany may lead to German countermeasures resulting in complete annihilation, and the possibility of the Germans letting loose neighboring people on Hungary.[33]

By the time the Tehran Conference concluded in November 1943—wherein Roosevelt and Churchill collapsed before Stalin's demands for control over Eastern and Central Europe—the British were urging Kállay to make contact to negotiate with the Soviets before the Red Army breached Hungary's borders and began their rampage.

The decisions made at Tehran also concluded that no Allied attack would occur through the Balkans. The Hungarians had long hoped for (and heard stories about) a powerful amphibious assault somewhere along the Adriatic coast that would then drive east and north, liberating Budapest and seizing control of the Danube River basin, from Vienna to Belgrade. There was, in fact, an Allied plan to do exactly what the Hungarians wanted. The plan was code-named "Operation Zeppelin," but it was

---

[33] *Ibid.*, pp. 166-167.

only a deception operation, one of a number of red herrings dreamed-up to deflect attention away from the Normandy invasion.[34] The Hungarians' hope evaporated. The Nazi-Soviet vise grip on Hungary would not be broken. Ambassador Montgomery wrote:

> It is surprising therefore that the Hungarians sympathized with the cause of the Allies to such a great extent as they did. It is undeniable that they did not receive encouragement from the democracies. We did not promise them anything—we only threatened. Yet with stout hearts and great political wisdom, they clung to the traditions of belonging to the Christian civilization of the Occident although they seemed to be destined for the un-Christian civilization of the Orient.[35]

By March 1944, German pressure on Hungary was at the breaking point. The Germans would request passage for troops across Hungarian territory, but Kállay would flatly refuse them.

Horthy, lured away to Klessheim Castle in Austria at the same time, would be "diplomatically held" by Hitler while Germany invaded Hungary. Horthy would never see a truly sovereign Hungary again.

---

34 Brown, Anthony Cave (1975). *Bodyguard of Lies*, Guilford CT: The Lyon's Press. pp. 434, 461.

35 Montgomery, p. 20.

Hungary had made desperate attempts with the British and the U.S. to maintain—albeit limited—elbow room and to avert the worst scenario: German occupation. But the realization of Franz Ferdinand's Austrian contingency plan would be finally carried out by Hitler—the former "Austrian Corporal." At the same time the Red Army marched ever closer to the Hungarian borders.

Chapter 6

NAZI OCCUPATION AND THE ARROW CROSS

Hopeless or not, humanity has to assert itself for its own sake. The worst thing the Germans could do is to dehumanize other people and silence the voices that protest against cruelty and injustice. If they stifle moral indignation, they destroy more than cities or nation; they win their war against the spirit of man.[1]

—Anne O'Hare McCormick

[1] McCormick, Anne O'Hare (1944, July 15). As Nazi Desperation Grows. *New York Times.*

Introduction:
House of Terror

If you wish to fully understand the events and history that have shaped modern Hungary, a visit to the museum of the House of Terror in Budapest, at 60 Andrássy út (Andrassy Road), is a must. The House of Terror, or *Terror Háza*, is the former headquarters of both the Nazi– (1944) and Soviet-led (1945) occupying dictatorial regimes. While the Nazis occupied Hungary for less than a year, the Soviets remained for four and a half decades.

Terror Háza is both fascinating and despicable, dark and hopeful; it is a tribute to the Hungarian spirit and will to survive the worst and most impossible circumstances: the dark and monstrous Soviet tank that first greets visitors; the imposing uniforms of the Arrow Cross and the Red Army; the propaganda posters and films designed to brainwash Hungarians into submission; and the cramped, damp, underground chambers where hundreds of Hungarians were interrogated, imprisoned, tortured, and killed—by both regimes. All are needful reminders of what the loss of freedom can look like. And I can assure you, it is indeed a 'house of terror'.

As the Soviets marched ever closer toward Central Europe, Nazi desperation began to grow. *The New York Times* reported: "The looming threat of the arrival of Russia on the doorstep of Germany was an 'outrage' that evokes the note of hysterical panic never heard before in broadcast from Berlin ...The current broadcasts sound like the bellow of a beast at bay." Seeing their defeat on the horizon, the Nazis threatened to take Europe down with them and "turn this Continent into a maelstrom of destruction where only one cry is heard—the cry of blood." [2]

Anne O'Hare McCormick, Pulitzer Prize-winning foreign correspondent, wrote in *The New York Times* on July 15, 1944:

> It is hard to imagine that the Nazis, in their desperation, would wreak more death and destruction—in the lands outside Germany, of course—than they have already wrought. Millions of human beings have perished at their will, not in battle alone but before firing squads, in prison camps, in hundreds of murdered villages ...in the ghettos, box cars and slaughter houses where the Jews were hunted to death. Even the ruin of German cities is on their head. What worse can they do? In the Nazi hierarchy and the Gestapo, we are dealing with reckless and cornered men, aware that they are doomed. For them military defeat is not just unconditional surrender: it is death.[3]

In March 1944, Hungarian sovereignty would be lost again and Hungarian Jews would become targeted victims. Hungary had desperately tried to keep German forces from attacking—by balancing appeasement of the Germans with a deft refusal to cooperate. But Hitler believed securing full control over Hungary's material and human resources could help him attain the final victory.[4]

The American Jewish Committee has published the American Jewish Yearbook, its prestigious annual publication, from

---

[2] *Ibid.*
[3] *Ibid.*
[4] Schmidt, Mária (Ed.). (2019). p. 7.

1899 to the present; it is the premier publication for leading academics and a major resource for institutions, media, and university libraries on topics of interest to the Jewish community. *The American Jewish Yearbook 1944-1945* review of the year wrote:

> On March 19, 1944, Hitler wiped out the last vestige of a distinction between those nations which indulged in the illusion of being his allies, and those which he had subjugated by force. On that day, his legions started and, within a few days completed, the military occupation of Hungary. Since then, eight hundred thousand native Jews, and large numbers of Jewish refugees from Nazi-dominated neighbor lands, the last large and physically intact Jewish population in Europe, together with many so-called 'non-Aryans,' are under absolute Nazi subjugation.[5]

Until 1944, Hungary had been "the only European country east of the Pyrenees where the lives of Jews could be considered as secure." Besides the almost one million Hungarian Jews, Hungary had offered safety and shelter for sixty to seventy thousand foreign Jews—Slovakian, Austrian, German, Romanian and Polish—all fleeing extermination by Hitler. In fact, Hitler's wrath against Hungary was, in large part, because so many Jews had escaped his death sentence by fleeing to Hungary.[6]

---

[5] Hevesi, Eugene (1944-1945). Review of the Year. IV. Southern Europe, Hungary, *American Jewish Yearbook*. American Jewish Committee. pp. 254-261.
[6] Montgomery, p. 99.

Out of all Hitler's war collaborators in Central Europe—including the Czechs, Slovaks, and Romanians—Hungary had held out the longest against German demands and especially against Hitler's "Jewish Solution."[7]

Hitler required that Anti-Jewish legislation be enacted in Axis nations as a basic tenet of his foreign policy and as a very visible measure of allegiance to Germany. But Hugo Csergo, secretary of the Jewish community of Budapest declared in a public address in January 1944, that "Hungary has lived for two centuries in the liberal spirit, and the transitory period we are now living through cannot deflect us from our proper course."[8]

The American Jewish Yearbook noted in 1945 that it was the public popular sentiment in Hungary which was "overwhelmingly anti-Nazi and largely decent toward the Jews" that gave the government the support it needed to avoid or delay taking the anti-Jewish measures that Hitler required.[9] In order to appease the Germans, Hungary had enacted Jewish Laws in 1938, 1939, and 1941,[10] but these were rarely or never fully applied, rather they were used to keep the Germans at bay by appearing to fall in line with their demands.

Horthy was strongly opposed to antisemitism, a position which was backed by Cardinal Serédi—the Prince Primate of Hungary—and by Hungary's Christian churches.[11] U.S. Ambassador to Hungary (from 1933-1941) John F. Montgomery wrote:

---

[7] *Ibid.*, p. 21.
[8] Hevesi, p. 257.
[9] *Ibid.*, p. 256.
[10] Schmidt, Mária (Ed.). (2019). p. 7.
[11] Montgomery, p. 103.

"It is obvious, and proved by history, that conservative regimes offer Jews the best opportunities, and of this Hungary was an outstanding example. Conservative Magyars were, as a rule, loyal to the Christian faith, and all churches in Hungary condemned anti-Semitism. Conservatives, especially people of title, are generally immune to racial nationalism. ... The Hungary of my day was in religious and racial matters much more liberal than any other country with which I am familiar."[12]

At that time, 70%, or six and a half million people in Hungary, were of the Roman Catholic faith. The Church played a major role in shaping national culture and identity with a "network of education, social, cultural and devotional institutions" located throughout the entire country.[13]

In the fall of 1943, the Smallholders Party of Hungary had announced a new party platform which included a demand for the abolition of anti-Jewish laws, a demand backed by many Catholic and Protestant clergymen who were close to the peasant movement for agrarian land reform. The Peasant League also demanded that "all legislation" that discriminated against any Hungarian citizen be abolished. In December of the same year, the Smallholders Party introduced a resolution to Parliament demanding the revocation of the "Jew Law," calling it a "disgrace for Hungary," and the American Jewish Yearbook wrote that "all liberal and socialist members of parliament backed the resolution."[14]

---

[12] *Ibid.*, pp. 21, 104.

[13] Schmidt, Mária (Ed.). (2019). p. 52.

[14] Hevesi, p. 256.

Nazi Terror Begins: The Hungarian Jews

In late February 1944, Germany requested that Hungary allow three thousand German military trucks, carrying about 100,000 soldiers[15] and war materials, to cross Hungarian territory to Romania and Bulgaria. Prime Minister Kállay refused.

On March 17, Admiral Horthy was lured to Austria by an urgent invitation from Hitler, under the pretext of discussing the withdrawal of Hungarian troops from Russia and their repatriation into Hungary—a desire Horthy had expressed to Hitler in February.[16] Before leaving, Horthy messaged to Hungarian embassies overseas that in the event of a potential German occupation of Hungary, they must not recognize any government that might be formed.[17]

Horthy arrived at Schloss Klessheim, a grand palace in Austria belonging to a friend of Hitler's, along with Horthy's foreign minister, minister of defense, and chief of staff, on the morning of March 18. According to Horthy, Hitler was "very ill at ease" and began conversation by accusing the Hungarian government of planning to switch sides and join the Allies. Excitedly, Hitler told Horthy that he would not tolerate another

---

[15] Kertesz, Stephen D. (1953). *Diplomacy in a Whirlpool: Hungary between Nazi Germany and Soviet Russia.* University of Notre Dame Press. pp. 76-77.
[16] *Ibid.*, 76.
[17] Montgomery, pp. 191-2.

betrayal like Italy's alignment with the Allies, and that he, Hitler, "must take precautionary measures."[18]

The conversation grew more heated, and Horthy responded: I do not know what you mean by "taking precautionary measures". If by that phrase you mean military measures, or in other words the occupation of an independent and sovereign state which has made many sacrifices on Germany's behalf, that would be an unspeakable crime.[19]

Later that day, swearing he would never interfere with Hungary's sovereignty, that he *loved* Hungary,[20] Hitler gave Horthy several ultimatums: Hungary must completely mobilize against Russia; Kállay's government must be replaced with a quisling government that would assure full and unconditional economic and military cooperation between Germany and Hungary; there must be German military occupation in Hungary, with Germany controlling waterways and railways; Hungarian press and radio "must change their tune," from their anti-Nazi rhetoric; Hungarian workers would be supplied for German factories, and there would be the "strict application of Nuremberg laws against 1 million Jews in Hungary."[21] Horthy flatly refused all, vowing to resign if a German occupation happened in Hungary.[22]

---

[18] Horthy, Nicholas (1957). *A Life for Hungary: Memoirs of Admiral Nicholas Horthy, Regent of Hungary*. Robert Speller & Sons. p. 212.
[19] *Ibid.*
[20] *Ibid.*, p. 214.
[21] Montgomery, pp. 191-2.
[22] Kertesz, p. 76.

Hitler had expected this: German forces of eight divisions began to cross into Hungary from Austria, Yugoslavia, and Poland on March 18. The forces, with motorized guns and Tiger tanks, reached Budapest at 4:00 a.m. on March 19.[23] Kállay was warned by telegram from Field Marshal Keitel, the German Chief of Staff, that any Hungarian resistance would be reason for the Germans to involve the armies of surrounding countries in the invasion against Hungary.[24]

According to Kállay, news of the invasion was continuously transmitted in code by the secret Hungarian broadcasting station to the British in Istanbul. No reply or advice (from the Allies) was received.[25] *Sicherheitsdeinst* Intelligence Chief Wilhelm Höttl discussed the Hungarian peace-feeler efforts in his memoir and concludes that an American Office of Strategic Services (the OSS, the precursor of the CIA) colonel had finally been dispatched to Hungary to coordinate Hungary's *volte face* (position reversal) in the middle of March 1944 (remember Hungary had agreed to unconditional surrender in September 1943), only to be preempted by the Nazi invasion and occupation of Hungary.[26]

At the time, Horthy did not know that Hitler's "precautionary measures" had already been put into motion, but he did recognize that calm discussion and negotiation were no longer possible—Hitler had made up his mind. Horthy tried to return

[23] Montgomery, pp. 191-2.
[24] Cartledge, p. 396.
[25] Montgomery, p. 192.
[26] Höttl, pp. 180-181.

to Hungary immediately, but various pretexts were created to delay and prevent his departure: a fake air raid was staged to prevent Horthy's train from departing, alarms sounded and a smoke screen hovered over the palace. Horthy and his men were told telephone lines were "badly hit" by bombing and that communication outside had been severed.[27, 28]

March 19 is considered "a tragic day" in Hungarian history—a day when Hungary's relative peace and calm abruptly ended and chaotic destruction began. The German military took over Budapest, including all communications[29] and important railways and airfields. In addition, Allied bombing started. Dr. Stephen D. Kertesz, who served in the Hungarian Foreign Ministry at that time, described that "the looming shadow of the Nazi dictator became a cruel reality ... The Hungarian people began to feel the full impact of war and occupation."[30]

Hungary was now under the occupation of the armed forces of the Third Reich, which were determined to crush the will of the Hungarian people to fight back. Horthy and his delegation finally arrived back in Budapest to find that his minister of interior, along with many prominent citizens and members of Parliament, had been arrested by German secret police. The Germans had also seized police headquarters[31] and Hungari-

---

27 Kertesz, pp. 76-77.
28 Horthy, p. 214.
29 Cartledge, p. 396.
30 Kertesz, p. 78. Dr. Kertesz served in the ministry during the war and post war years, and was part of the group of officials who tried to keep Hungary out of the war and in contact with Western powers to reach an armistice.
31 Horthy, p. 216.

an patriots had been jailed or forced underground. The Social Democrat and Smallholder parties had been banned and their leadership either interned or executed.[32]

Horthy was forced to accept the appointment of Döme Sztójay[33] as prime minister; Sztójay had been a former army officer and Hungary's envoy to Germany. He now presided over a state cabinet of right-wingers from the Government Party and the Party of Hungarian Revival. Members of the Arrow Cross were not accepted in the cabinet by Hitler at this time because they were thought not to be sufficiently "pro-German."[34] Horthy was also forced to accept the roundup and liquidation of thousands of Hungarian Jews. To ensure his compliance to all Hitler's demands, Hitler had Horthy's son Miklós Jr. kidnapped and held hostage.[35]

Hitler's promises to withdraw his troops once a new government was formed and to cease interfering in the Hungarian government's affairs were not kept. Prime Minister Miklós Kállay urged Horthy to abdicate as a retaliation against the Germans, as well as for his own good, and to withdraw to the countryside. Kállay wrote:

> They had promised that if I resigned and a pro-German, non-hostile government came in my place, Hungary's independence and internal liberties should remain unimpaired. Since the occupation, however, Hungary had

---

32 Vazsonyi, p. 7.
33 Cartledge, p. 396.
34 *Ibid.*
35 CIA, p. 33.

> ceased to be a constitutional state. Any measure of his [Horthy's], sanctioned by a parliament meeting under the shadows of bayonets, would not be constitutional. The principle of popular sovereignty had ceased to operate. Henceforward all the Regent's actions would be taken on his own individual responsibility.[36]

Kállay pleaded to Horthy that if he remained it would appear that Horthy validated the actions of the Nazis and assumed responsibility. Horthy refused to resign, saying: "I am still an admiral. The captain cannot leave his sinking ship; he must remain on the bridge to the last ...Who will defend the honorable men and women in this country who have trusted me blindly? Who will defend the Jews or our refugees if I leave my post? I may not be able to defend everything, but I believe that I can still be of great, very great, help to our people. I can do more than anyone else could.[37]

The next few months in Hungary were tragic. The Nazis, upon arriving, had forced Hungarian Jews to wear a yellow star for identification and in mid-April they were rounded up *en masse* and concentrated in ghettos and camps. The large number of Jews in these zones, some of which were just small towns or communities, made living conditions unbearable.[38] This was carried out by the Germans and their main Hungarian accomplices—State Secretaries László Endre and Lászlo Baky from the Ministry of Interior.[39]

---

36 Kállay, p. 432.
37 Kállay, p. 433.
38 Kertesz, p. 79.
39 *Ibid.*

May 15, 1944, marks a day of utmost sadness, tragedy, and loss that lives on in the memories of Hungarians today. The evacuation of Jews from Hungary to death and labor camps began, zone by zone, as directed by German SS Colonel Adolf Eichmann—one of the architects of the Nazi genocide, responsible for the persecution and murder of millions of Jews.[40] Horthy was unable to stop the deportations from happening, except from the Hungarian capital of Budapest.[41]

Within two months, almost 440,000 Hungarian Jews from the countryside were deported under the authority of the Third Reich. The majority were sent to the largest Nazi concentration camp in Auschwitz, Poland.[42] Children under the ages of twelve to fourteen, adults over fifty, the disabled, and those unfit to work (as classified by an on-site SS doctor) were immediately sent to the gas chambers.[43] In July 1944, Hungarian Jews were being 'liquidated' at a rate of 12,000 people per day.[44] If the on-site crematorium could not keep up with the large numbers of people, they were thrown into pits and covered with quicklime.[45]

Anne O'Hare McCormick wrote in *The New York Times* on July 15, 1944:

---

[40] Schmidt, Mária (Ed.). (2019). p. 10.
[41] Kertesz, p. 79.
[42] Schmidt, Mária (Ed.). (2019). pp. 7-9.
[43] Kertesz, p. 79.
[44] International Military Tribunal (1945). *Trial of the Major War Criminals before the International Military Tribunal,* "Blue Series" (3). [Periodical] Retrieved from the Library of Congress, https://www.loc.gov/item/2011525338_NT_Vol-III/. p. 567. (Also as found in Kertesz, p. 213).
[45] Kertesz, p. 79.

> It must count in the score of Hungary that until the Germans took control, it was the last refuge in Central Europe for the Jews able to escape from Germany, Austria, Poland and Rumania. Now these hapless people are exposed to the same ruthless policy of deportation and extermination that was carried out in Poland. But as long as they exercised any authority in their own house, the Hungarians tried to protect the Jews.[46]

The churches in Hungary, which were mainly Christian, strongly condemned antisemitism and their clergy and parishioners put faith into action. That year, the American Jewish Committee reported:

> While there is a segment in Hungarian society which seeks profit from this tragedy, the program of extermination has generally met with passionate popular condemnation and opposition. Tens of thousands of Christian Hungarians are known to have rushed to the aid of Jews in distress, trying to shield and hide them, to take over their homes and valuables for safekeeping, and to help them in their futile attempts to escape. When the confinement of Jews in camps and ghettos started, in many places masses of towns-folk swarmed to the places of confinement, carrying food and clothing for the inmates.[47]

---

[46] McCormick.

[47] Hevesi, p. 259.

"Tens of thousands" of Christian Hungarians put their own safety in serious jeopardy to protect the Jews or to openly protest on their behalf, and many protected Jewish property and businesses when the Jews were deported, actions which often resulted in arrest:

> Many Hungarians have been prosecuted for wearing the yellow badge in protest against the shocking persecutions, and young Christian girls have frequently been parading the streets of cities and towns arm-in-arm with young Jews wearing the Star of David. ... On May 9,1944, the government threatened with severe punishment, including internment, any Hungarians who aided or sheltered Jews. But despite these warnings and the appeals of the Nazi-controlled press, hundreds of people were arrested for hiding Jews and helping them to escape.[48]

Ilés Golopencza was one of the many Hungarians who came to the aid of the Jews. An unassuming harbor master, he risked his life to save one hundred and fifty people from certain death under the Arrow Cross regime. In autumn of 1944, Golopencza was elected the air-raid commander of a Yellow Star house in a Jewish ghetto in Budapest. Instead of enforcing the anti-Jewish laws of the Nazis, he sabotaged their enforcement.

When Arrow Cross squads came in search of Jews for 'work' and a sure march to death camps, Golopencza lied and said the only people left in his building were the sick and elder-

48 *Ibid.*

ly; he helped Jews secretly leave the building to get passports issued by foreign embassies; he hid a young boy from Arrow Cross gunmen; he led and helped establish a Red Cross on the ground floor of the building which became a shelter for Jewish doctors and health workers. Although Golopencza kept the fact to himself that he had risked his life to save so many people, the one hundred and fifty later signed a certificate detailing his actions.[49]

According to the American Jewish Committee at that time:

Both Catholic and Protestant clergymen issued thousands of spurious birth certificates, in the vain hope of saving their bearers from persecution. In one small community, the rabbi and all four Christian clergymen were arrested for connivance in such measures.[50] Firebrand and fearless, Cardinal József Mindszenty (see Chapter 4) who was at the time Bishop of Veszprém, protested strongly against the treatment of the Jews. Mindszenty was possibly "the most vigorous and vocal" of Hungary's Christian leaders, and certainly one of the bravest. He called antisemitism "the basest tool of Nazi propaganda—a tool which seeks to undermine the very foundations of Christian civilization." We have Cardinal Mindszenty's very detailed and provocative biography *Mindszenty the Man* as it was related to American conservative activist Phyllis Schlafly, by Mindszenty's personal secretary, Dr. Joseph Vecsey:

---

49 Czókos, Gergely; Kiss, Réka; Máthé, Áron; Szalai, Zoltán, Eds. (2021). *Heroes Among Us. 50 True Stories of Brave Hungarians in the 20th Century.* Trans. Thomas Cooper. *Committee of National Remembrance.* Open Books Publish, Budapest. pp. 91-94.

50 Hevesi, p. 259.

> As Bishop, he turned every religious house under his jurisdiction into a sanctuary for Jews hiding from the Gestapo. Even though the Nazis threatened death as punishment for concealing Jews, Bishop Mindszenty ordered every Catholic monastery, convent, seminary, rectory, cloister, and church to open its doors to the Jews and hide them from the Gestapo. He told his fellow Catholics: "If today we do not keep sacred and inviolable the Jew's personal freedom, his common and civil rights, tomorrow we may find that we have lost our own."[51]

On November 27, 1944, Mindszenty was arrested by the Nazis and named "a dangerous enemy of the Government." He spent four and a half months in prison until the Nazi occupation collapsed.[52]

The Hungarians, despite the Nazi terror regime, were still a people full of spirit and hope, the determination to set wrong to right, and the desire to secure their own sovereignty and independence. Unfortunately, Hungary's independence at this time was completely at the mercy of the Nazis.

[51] Schlafly.
[52] *Ibid.*

The Arrow Cross Takes Power

By the end of the summer of 1944, it was clear that Germany had lost the war. The Allies were squeezing the Axis countries from both the west and the east. On August 27, 1944, the Soviet Red Army crossed the Hungarian border and Hungary became the major battlefield in the fight between the superpowers—two former 'allies' now turned mortal enemies.

Emboldened by having led a successful halt to the deportations of Hungarian Jews in Budapest, on August 29, 1944, Horthy dared to replace the government led by Döme Sztójay and Sztójay's right-wing pro-German cabinet. In its place, he installed a new government led by his faithful confidant Géza Lakatos and other trusted senior army officers, and gave this new government the task of withdrawing Hungary from the war. A secret armistice delegation traveled to Moscow in order to arrange the terms of Hungary's surrender.[53]

Bulgaria and Romania, both of which were experiencing German withdrawal, proclaimed their defection from Hitler at almost the same time. But unlike Bulgaria and Romania, Hungary was still firmly under German occupation and was taking a great and terrible risk.[54]

At the same time, the threat of the Red Army came ever closer. The Hungarian cities of Debrecen and Szeged—east of Budapest—were now occupied by the Soviet forces. The battle against

[53] Cartledge, pp. 396-400.

[54] Montgomery, p. 198.

the Red Army had advanced to the east of the Tisza River when on October 15, 1944, the Nazis decided to turn authority and power over to the Arrow Cross Party led by Ferenc Szálasi.[55]

That day, Horthy courageously sealed his own fate. Over a radio broadcast to the nation, he reviewed Hungary's case against the Nazis and announced that Hungary had already asked the Allies for a ceasefire.[56] He explained that he had tried to make the best situation for Hungary under impossible German pressure—pressure which had forced Hungarian soldiers to fight outside of Hungary against the Allies. He declared:

> Hungary was forced into war against the Allies by German pressure, which weighed upon us owing to our geographical situation. But even so we were not guided by any ambition to increase our own power and had no intention to snatch as much as a square meter of territory from anybody.[57]

Under German military occupation, and threat of being attacked by neighboring countries, Horthy had finally agreed to set up a new government acceptable to Hitler. In return, Hitler had promised not to interfere with Hungarian sovereignty, but the Germans had repeatedly broken their word and most egregiously "tackled the Jewish question in a manner incompatible with the demands of humanity." And this, Horthy said, is why:

---

[55] Schmidt, Mária (Ed.). (2019). p. 10.
[56] Montgomery, p. 198.
[57] *Ibid.*, pp. 236 -237. Appendix II.

> Conscious of my historic responsibility, I have the obligation to undertake every step directed to avoiding further unnecessary bloodshed. A nation that would allow the soil inherited from its forefathers to be turned into a theater of rearguard actions in an already lost war, defending alien interests out of a serf-like spirit, would lose the esteem of public opinion throughout the world ... I informed a representative of the German Reich that we were about to conclude a military armistice with our previous enemies and to cease all hostilities against them.[58]

The Nazis acted quickly—even before Horthy finished his speech—and attacked the radio station, killing most of the student guards who were guarding the entrance. Horthy evaded them and reached his palace, but the majority of his palace guards were also killed. Horthy was seized, and he and his wife, daughter-in-law, and grandson were deported to Germany.

The Germans then established the Arrow Cross Party as the official government.[59] Major Ferenc Szálasi, leader of Arrow Cross, named himself regent and made a subsequent broadcast to the nation in his "best national socialist style."[60] Szálasi's "Report to the Nation" broadcast gave clear understanding to anyone listening of his objectives: "Anyone who sabotages the population's endeavours in any shape or form, anyone who un-

---

58 *Ibid.*

59 Schmidt, Mária (Ed.). (2019). p. 7.

60 Montgomery, p. 198.

dermines stability, leaves his workplace, does not perform his job with the utmost responsibility thereby impeding the attainment of our goals, shall forfeit his life."[61] No. 60 Andrássy Road was Arrow Cross headquarters at that time and had been named by Szálasi, "The House of Loyalty."[62] Backed by Hitler's Nazis, Szálasi had finally reached his life-long ambition to be dictator and national leader of Hungary.

Szálasi wanted the total mobilization of Hungarian resources in the attempt to secure Hitler's victory in Europe; Hitler had promised "miracle weapons" in the fight against the Soviets that would give Germany the advantage to win the war.[63]

Former Prime Minister Kállay reported that Arrow Cross rule "was worse than the German domination in that it was baser and more immoral. Szálasi was a madman; his followers were the dregs of the people. The Germans knew this ... Their adoption of him was simply an action of revenge against Hungary."[64]

The more than 200,000 Hungarian Jews in Budapest that Horthy had managed to protect were no longer safe. Shortly after Arrow Cross took over, Adolf Eichmann had 60,000 force-marched to the Austrian border to dig trenches.[65] Seventy thousand remaining in Budapest were concentrated into a ghetto. Many Jews were looted, shot, and dumped into the Danube River. Near the Hungarian Parliament building today, there are sixty iron replicas of the shoes of the Jews who were shot and

---

61 Schmidt, Mária (Ed.). (2019). p. 9.
62 *Ibid.*, p. 5.
63 *Ibid.*, p. 10.
64 Kállay, p. 471.
65 Schmidt, Mária (Ed.).(2019). p. 9.

dumped, as a memorial to those who lost their lives senselessly at the hand of the Nazis. The Jews shoes—men's, women's, and children's—were sometimes removed at the command of the Nazis who would sell or use them.

Conclusion: Waiting for the Red Army

Szálasi and his Arrow Cross members were Nazi puppets who relied upon German control for their political and physical power.[66] Without German support, Arrow Cross could never have become the controlling political party. Kállay wrote that Szálasi believed it was only:

> the Germans he had to reckon with, accommodate himself to, and share the power with. That belief was an illusion, however, for there soon came into being another power in the country—that of the advancing Russian hosts, who had planted their feet in Hungarian soil in late September.[67]

And, as we shall discuss, the actions of Western powers would do much to help solidify the planting of the Soviets in Eastern Europe.

---

66 Kállay, pp. 470-471.
67 *Ibid.*, pp. 470-471.

Chapter 7

'LIBERATING' EASTERN EUROPE

The idea that we are just now on the threshold of a better era is refuted by the fact that the second World War has immensely increased the power of the most perfectly totalitarian nation.[1]

— John Flournoy Montgomery,
U.S. Ambassador to Hungary (1993-1941)

[1] Montgomery, p. 2.

Introduction: The Hitler-Stalin Pact and Western Denial of Soviet Aggression

Germany's war of aggression, by invading Poland and thus precipitating WWII, was condemned by the United Nations in 1950 at the Nuremberg Tribunal as a crime punishable under international law. Conspicuously absent from that legal finding of fact against Germany was any mention of the Soviet Union's criminal conduct by its unprovoked invasion of Poland.

As we discussed briefly in Chapter 4 "Balancing Superpowers" and Chapter 5 "Hitler and Stalin's Vise Grip," it was not known publicly at the time, though reference was later made to it at the tribunal, that a secret pact had been made between Hitler and Stalin in August 1939 and attached to their nonaggression pact signed in Moscow. The secret Hitler-Stalin Pact divided central and eastern Europe between the German Reich and the USSR. Hitler would get western Poland and be allowed to exert influence over Hungary and Romania without Soviet interference; Stalin would acquire eastern Poland, the Baltic States, and northern Romania.[2]

As planned, Hitler invaded Poland on September 1, 1939, and Russia followed by invading Poland on September 17, partitioning Poland according to their agreement. But in 1941, the Soviet Union turned against Germany (after the German invasion) and fought alongside the Western Allies.

---

[2] Applebaum, Anne (2013). p. 55.

The existence of the secret pact was first discovered during the re-examination of a witness for the defense of Rudolph Hess in the Nuremberg Trials on May 21,[3] 1946.[4, 5] The very next day, the *St. Louis Post-Dispatch* ran an article in the United States which detailed the text of the secret protocol, called "Secret Soviet-Nazi Pacts on Eastern Europe Aired."

Ambassador Montgomery wrote in 1947 that the U.S. State Department had copies of the secret protocol. Given that, plus the fact that news of the secret protocol had been published in U.S. newspapers several times and the protocol was a definite factor in precipitating the war, it was strange that no official statement from the U.S. was made concerning the protocol.[6]

As the trials continued, the Soviets avoided scrutiny. Instead of standing trial at Nuremberg for waging a war of aggression like the Germans, they were allowed to place a judge on the tribunal to judge the Nazis,[7] and, at the insistence of the Russian representatives at the tribunal, the text of the secret treaty was kept out of official Nuremberg records[8] by the Allies. Neither

---

3 International Military Tribunal, Nuremberg (1949). Re-examination of Witness Weizsäcker. 21 May 1946. XIV. 228-286. *Trial of the Major War Criminals Before the International Military Tribunal, Nuremberg, 14 November 1945 - 1 October 1946 in 42 Volumes,* Nuremberg, Germany. p. 46.

4 See Marrus, Michael (2018). Crimes Against Peace. *The Nuremberg War Crimes Trial,* 1945-1946. Bedford/St. Martin's. p. 37. Also see Alfred Seidl's questioning of Ernst von Weizäcker on the secret protocol. Seidl interviewed Weizäcker formally on "his recollection of" the secret protocol on May 31, 1946, also in Marrus, p. 165.

5 Montgomery, pp. 180-1.

6 *Ibid.*, pp. 182-3.

7 Farrell, Christopher J. (2021). *Exiled Emissary: George H. Earle III. Soldier, Sailor, Diplomat, Governor, Spy.* Academica Press. p. 131.

8 Montgomery, p. 180-1.

were the Soviets held responsible for the Katyn Forest Massacre, the massacre of twenty-two thousand Poles.

> Even to participate in these trials, the Western Allies had to overlook Stalin's crimes and pretend they had not taken place within the timeline of the war whose very outbreak was precipitated by the infamous 1939 Nazi-Soviet nonaggression pact ... after all, the Nazis and Soviets had begun World War II together as allies with the invasion of Poland. The Germans invaded Poland from the west on September 1, 1939—a well-known date—and the Red Army invaded from the east on September 17, 1939. Not a well-known date. Why?[9]

When the Hitler-Stalin Pact was first publicly disclosed at Nuremberg, it must have been an embarrassment for the Western Allies to have been aligned with one of the countries that began World War II. What was worse, in 1945 the allies had in essence sanctioned the secret pact by accepting Soviet occupation in Central and Eastern Europe and allowing the USSR to occupy the very territories in Central Europe that the secret pact (and Hitler) had promised them. The fate for these territories was to be handed over to Soviet domination and 'Sovietized' by communist ideology and oppression for decades after.

Mária Schmidt writes: "From that moment on, the Western side also became interested in covering up the true nature of the Soviet regime" in an attempt to maintain a moral supe-

[9] West, Diana (2013). *American Betrayal. The Secret Assault on our Nation's Character*. St. Martin's Press. p. 54.

riority based on the narrative that the West fought WWII for "democracy and freedom."[10] Schmidt asserts that this began a decades-long love affair between Western leftist liberals and Russia, where the true nature of the Soviet Union and its communism was routinely hidden and ignored, while at the same time Nazism was deemed repugnant. But, as we shall discuss in repeated examples, Nazism and Communism are "opposite sides of the same coin."

Schmidt's assertion is backed up by the actions of the Western allies during and immediately after the war, and for decades after. In January 1943, George H. Earle III, U.S. presidential emissary, war hero, and former Pennsylvania governor, delivered a message to U.S. President Franklin Delano Roosevelt (FDR) that could have abruptly ended World War II, but that the U.S. president flatly rejected. At that time, Earle was the assistant U.S. naval attaché in Istanbul, Turkey, a thin cover for his clandestine activities on behalf of the U.S. in a neutral city during wartime.

In January 1943, Earle told FDR that the German Resistance or *Widerstand*—made up of intelligence, diplomatic, and military leaders—offered to give Hitler and his 'inner circle' to the Western Allies—but only in exchange for an Armistice and an attack on the Russian forces now moving west toward Central Europe. This history is little known, but official U.S. archived documents prove it true.[11] Chris Farrell's *Exiled Emissary: George H. Earle III Soldier, Sailor, Diplomat, Governor, Spy*

---

10 Schmidt, Mária (2021). p. 21.

11 Farrell, pp. 3-5, 86-87.

is the most exhaustive treatment of the resistance overtures by Admiral Wilhelm Canaris, Chief of the *Abwehr* (the German military intelligence), directly to a presidential emissary. In *Exiled Emissary*, Farrell discloses previously top-secret documents he obtained from the U.S. National Archives.

In response to George Earle's message, rather than taking the opportunity to stop the war, and move against Soviet forces, FDR rejected their offer and continued to demand the unconditional surrender of the Germans.

In May 1944, George H. Earle III personally delivered a chilling message at the White House to U.S. President Roosevelt about the Soviets, which the president also flatly rejected. Earle revealed that the Soviets were responsible for the massacre of the almost twenty-two thousand Poles in the Katyn Forest in April and May of 1940, and not the Germans, as was being claimed. In an effort to decapitate the strength and leadership of Polish society and make Poland weak to Soviet rule, the Soviet secret police had murdered thousands of Polish priests, business owners, military leaders, government officials, academics, lawyers, and others, dumping them in mass graves in the Katyn Forest. And Earle had the photos, affidavits, International Committee of the Red Cross reports, personal interviews, and autopsies to prove it. But FDR rejected Earle's evidence and called it German propaganda.[12]

The Soviets had laid the blame of Katyn on the Nazis and later "even sought to have themselves whitewashed by the International Military Court during the Nuremberg trials ... they

[12] *Ibid.*, pp. 4-5, 130.

silenced, persecuted or killed anyone who put their lies in doubt or threatened to debunk them."[13]

Earle had routinely informed FDR about the Soviet threat, warning that America was "giving its life blood to exchange one bunch of gangsters for another as masters of Europe, and as a world menace."[14] But another year passed, and FDR gave no heed. Becoming increasingly concerned about the Soviet threat, Earle felt compelled to make his knowledge public. But his desire to do so would eventually lead to FDR firing him as emissary, and in March 1945 Earle, 55 years old, was transferred to the far side of the Pacific to the island of Samoa into a war zone.[15]

Earle, and many others watching events unfold in Europe, saw Soviet Communism as the real and long-term threat to Western Civilization. But FDR's administration was well-infiltrated by Communist sympathizers, many of whom were on official U.S. payrolls working on behalf of Russia.[16] Staff, like the American-turned-Soviet spy Alger Hiss, Soviet sympathizer Harry Hopkins, and many others, influenced and guided the administration. FDR himself pushed back against the official investigations that were probing into the Communist infiltration of the U.S. government.[17]

John Foster Dulles, U.S. Secretary of State under Dwight D. Eisenhower (1953-59), is quoted as saying as early as 1946 that

---

[13] Schmidt (2021). pp. 23-24.

[14] Farrell, p. 108.

[15] *Ibid.*, pp. 137-141.

[16] See Evans, M. Stanton (2013). *Stalin's Secret Agents: The Subversion of Roosevelt's Government*. Threshold Editions.

[17] West, p. 16.

the Soviet Union had achieved global psychological dominance. "Few men in political life anywhere act without first thinking whether they will please or displease the leaders of the Soviet Union. Never in history have a few men in a single country achieved such worldwide influence." The ingredients they used to achieve influence were "fears, guilt, neuroses, lack of willpower, and disoriented minds for the democracies, and fearlessness and resoluteness for a Communist elite acting with firm discipline and according to one doctrine."[18]

Allen Dulles, then the Berne Station Chief of the Office of Strategic Services (OSS),[19] wrote in an April 1944 cable to OSS headquarters in Washington, D.C., that the "principal motive" of the German resistance in stopping Soviet encroachment upon the West was to "prevent Central Europe from coming ideologically and factually under the control of Russia." The Germans "are convinced," Dulles wrote, "that in such an event Christian culture and democracy and all that goes with it would disappear in Europe and that the present dictatorship of the Nazis would be exchanged for a new dictatorship."[20]

And that is exactly what happened, in very short order.

---

[18] Sanders, Ralph & Brown, Fred R., Eds. (1961). *National Security Management: Global Psychological Conflict*, Industrial College of the Armed Forces, Washington, D.C., p. 59.

[19] The first independent U.S. intelligence agency.

[20] Dulles, Allen (1947). *Germany's Underground: The Plots to Kill Hilter and End the War*. Eumenes Publishing. p. 165. Originally published in 1947 by Macmillan Company, N.Y.

The Siege of Budapest

Soviet and Romanian forces encircled Budapest and the siege of the Hungarian capital began on Christmas Eve, 1944, and lasted until February 12, 1945. The capture of Budapest was strategically important to Stalin, without which Russian advancement to Vienna would not be possible. Aided by the Romanian soldiers, the Soviets advanced against the Germans and their Hungarian allies. Montgomery comments, "the Soviets regarded Hitler as the icebreaker who would destroy Hungarian democracy, prosperity and freedom to their final advantage."[21]

The siege of Budapest is considered one of the bloodiest battles of the war, where German and Hungarian armies defended Budapest with prolonged and bitter fighting and utmost devastation. Ten percent of the population perished.[22] Hitler had declared Budapest to be a *Festung*, meaning 'Fortress'—his command meant the city was to be defended to the last man.[23] Besides the psychological pressures of the Fuehrer's order and the warrior ethos of the German officer corps, commanders like SS General Karl Pfeffer-Wildenbruch also greatly feared Siberia and the Soviets.[24]

---

[21] Montgomery, p. 19.

[22] Schmidt, Mária (Ed.). (2019). p.16.

[23] Cartledge, p. 409.

[24] Ungváry, Krisztián (1995). The 'Second Stalingrad': The Destruction of Axis Forces at Budapest (February, 1945). In Dreisziger, Nandor (Ed.). *Hungary in the Age of Total War (1938-1948).* (1998) Columbia University Press. p. 152.

Military scholars compare the intensity of the battle of Budapest to the brutal battles of Leningrad, Stalingrad, and Warsaw.[25] Budapest had not been evacuated, and during the siege about 38,000 civilians died through starvation and military action. About the same number of Hungarian and German soldiers died as well. At the point of surrender, German and Hungarian forces had lost all combat effectiveness, and in some cases whole divisions had been destroyed. The dead soldiers of the Red Army totaled about 80,000.[26]

Soldiers surrendering to the Red Army were simply shot. Wounded were also shot by Red Army soldiers "accidentally," presumably because they would be nothing but a burden to the Soviets. Ethnic Russian and Ukrainian soldiers serving in the German Army were instantly shot by the Soviets.[27]

In addition, all the bridges on the Danube River had been destroyed and 80% of the city's buildings were damaged or demolished. Budapest was in ruins. The Swiss Delegation to Budapest, leaving the city in March and April of 1945 reported:

> It is estimated that more than half of the city of Budapest is destroyed. The commercial district and the hills of Buda (the Fortress and the Rozsadomb) have suffered most. The Quays on the Danube and especially the Elizabeth Bridge and the Chain bridge have been almost completely destroyed. In the Fortress there is almost no house standing. The Royal Palace was burned down. The

[25] Cornelius, p. 365.
[26] Cartledge, p. 409.
[27] Ungváry, p. 164.

> Coronation Church collapsed. The Parliament Building is severely damaged, but its skyline has remained intact. The hotels ... are all in ruins. The Vaczi-utca has suffered very much.[28]

Montgomery's observation also reveals the extent of the devastation: "Today the outlook from the Fisherman's Bastion is not fascinating but saddening. The Royal Palace ... is in shambles, the Coronation Church is gutted. All six bridges have gone, and with them the lovely Széchenyi Chain Bridge. Margaret Island is devastated and the Corso, scene of mirth, grace and elegance, is no more. Eleven weeks of fighting, preceded by air bombardments, transformed many districts, rich and poor, into deserts of wreckage and rubble. Worst of all, hunger still stalks the capital of an agricultural country in which, before the Russians looted it, not even the destitute had lacked for daily bread."[29]

The Russian troops looted Budapest by entering the homes of both the poor and wealthy, freely taking food supplies, clothes, and other valuables. Larger objects of art or furniture were destroyed, and homes destroyed by fire.[30] Many Hungarians, weary from Nazi occupation and caught between the warring armies, had believed the Russians had come to liberate them from the Germans. But Russia considered Hungary to be enemy territory, and the Hungarians soon found that they had traded one dictator for another.

[28] Swiss Legation Report of the Russian Invasion of Hungary in the Spring of 1945, Appendix III. In Montgomery, p. 239.
[29] Montgomery, p. 16.
[30] Swiss Legation Report of 1945.

Two Hungarian men, both of whom were children at the time, recount hiding in a cellar with their families in the Buda Castle District for six weeks as the district was heavily bombed, packed in with other people with no running water, no heat and little food. The families of these men, along with many others, had fled the countryside to Budapest from the advancing Red Army, believing it to be a safe haven and that there would be no fighting in Budapest. Both of them recount that their introduction to Soviet troops were that the soldiers went down to the cellars and raped the women in front of everyone there.[31]

Women were constantly and indiscriminately raped—from the ages of ten to seventy years—few women escaped this brutality. Many were kept for hours or days at the mercy of Russian soldiers in their own homes. The Swiss delegation to Budapest report of 1945 notes: "Many women prefer to commit suicide in order to escape monstrosities."[32] The two Hungarian men, as well as many other eyewitnesses to the days of the siege, said that the "ladies put carbon [coal] on their faces to appear unattractive to the soldiers and avoid being raped."[33]

The initial siege on Budapest was immediately followed by "a period of calculated destruction" according to the usual method of Soviet occupation. It is interesting to note the deception the Soviets used—not in order to deceive the Hungarians, but in order to deceive their own troops. After a well-equipped and disciplined group of Russian troops destroyed any remaining

[31] Interview 17-June 6, 2023 and Focus Group 2-June 8, 2023.

[32] Swiss Legation Report of 1945.

[33] Interview 17 and Focus Group 2.

opposition, "propaganda shock troops" arrived next to destroy any evidence of living standards that were beyond those that Russians had in the Soviet Union. This was "necessitated by the differences between the East and West in standards of living." Details from the Swiss delegation report:

> Propaganda plays the supreme role in the Russian army. For instance, the castle of Seregelyes, belonging to Count Gela Hadik—the Russian shock troops removed all the furniture and destroyed all the installations within the castle, poured gasoline over the mass of things and ignited it. The castle was then refurnished by the Russian soldiers with straw beds in order to prove to the troops following them in what misery even the bourgeoisie were living. The same procedure was followed in the villages and in the peasants' habitations.[34]

To the Soviets, a man that "eats at a table and sleeps on a bed was considered 'bourgeoisie.'"[35]

---

[34] Swiss Legation Report of 1945.

[35] Montgomery, p. 210.

Yalta:
'Liberating' Central and Eastern Europe

While Soviet troops sieged Budapest, during the same time period of February 4-11, 1945, 'The Big Three'—U.S. President Franklin D. Roosevelt, British Prime Minister Winston Churchill, and Soviet Premier Joseph Stalin—met in the resort city of Yalta, located along the Black Sea coast of the Crimean Peninsula, to decide the fate of Germany and the hundreds of thousands of people in Poland, Hungary, Bulgaria, Romania, and Czechoslovakia. Roosevelt and Churchill wanted Soviet assistance to continue the war in the Pacific and defeat the Japanese, and Roosevelt wanted the Soviets to ratify the formation of the United Nations.

It had already been decided that Germany would be divided into four zones occupied by U.S., British, French, and Soviet forces; the remaining question was what to do with the defeated or 'liberated' countries of Eastern or Central Europe.

By the end of the war, the Soviet Union militarily occupied Eastern Europe. Under the Declaration of Liberated Europe, 'The Big Three' agreed to help those nations "liberated from the domination of Nazi Germany ... to destroy the last vestiges of nazism and fascism and to create democratic institutions of their own choice," based on principle eight from FDR and Churchill's Atlantic Charter: "The right of all peoples to choose the form of government under which they will live—the restoration of sovereign rights and self-government to those peoples who have been forcibly deprived to them by the aggressor nations."[36] How terribly and tragically ironic this principle must have seemed to the peoples of Soviet occupation.

The terms of the declaration specifically stated that in the 'liberated' European states, the Allies would work "to establish conditions of internal peace and ... interim governmental authorities broadly representative of all democratic elements in the population ... and the earliest possible establishment through free elections of governments responsive to the will of the people."[37] Stalin signed the agreement, though it was never his intention to keep it. Authentic democratic elections were never held in his satellite nations; Stalin had already decided that the popular front governments—coalitions of moderate, liberal, socialist, and communist parties united to protect democratic nations against fascism—would be fully taken over by his Communist Party.

In the final outcome, FDR and Churchill allowed Stalin to have Eastern Europe, thereby ratifying the provisions of the secret Hitler-Stalin pact of 1939. It is strange that Hungary, which at the time of the Yalta conference was being 'liberated' by the Soviet Union, through crushing defeat and destruction, was never mentioned in their declaration agreement. Montgomery concludes thus: "Hungary became an island in the Soviet sea after having been an oasis in Hitler's desert."[38]

---

[36] Yalta Conference Agreement, Declaration of a Liberated Europe. February 11, 1945 (2013, January 17). Wilson Center Digital Archive, National Archives. https://digitalarchive.wilsoncenter.org/document/116176

[37] *Ibid.*

[38] Montgomery, p. 209.

Chapter 8

THE SOVIETIZATION OF HUNGARY

The spread of dictatorship in no more than thirty years from a small area of a few square miles to almost two-fifths of the globe and to a dominant position on the Eurasian continent; its rise from an obscure heresy to a state religion commanding the observance of half a billion freeborn people; and the transformation of the apostles of this new despotism from inmates of police prisons into organizers of the most powerful and most oppressive police state the modern world has ever know are proof that the business of democracy has not been conducted with wisdom, circumspection, and diligence.[1]

[1] Strausz-Hupé, Robert, and Possony, Stefan T. (1950). *International Relations in the Age of the Conflict between Democracy and Dictatorship.* McGraw-Hill Book Co., Inc. p. vii.

Introduction: The Communists Take Absolute Control

In December 1944, a provisional government had been set up by the Soviets in Debrecen, Hungary, with a cross-party coalition led by the Smallholders Party. The coalition was center-left and co-ruled together with communists, social democrats, and others.[2] In theory, like the interim Soviet governments of Czechoslovakia and Eastern Germany, the objective of the coalition was democracy.[3] In reality, the coalition was a cobbled-together wreck of war-time political survivors, heavily under pressure from the Soviet Union. The Swiss Delegation to Hungary, upon leaving Hungary not long after the Soviets invaded, wrote in their official report that "The Hungarian government has no power whatsoever. It is simply tolerated by the Russians."[4]

Having been assured by the leftist bloc in Budapest that they would win, in November 1945, the Russians allowed free elections to be held in Hungary. The elections were accompanied by enormous parades and thousands of people waving red flags to express excitement for the Communist Party, who promised more food and economic and social progress. But the voters wanted a voice that year—voter participation was over 90%—and, despite the optics, they did not support the Left: the leftist bloc only received 40%, of which the Communist Party only re-

---

[2] Applebaum (2013). p. 74.

[3] *Ibid.*, p. 115.

[4] Swiss Legation Report of 1945.

ceived 17%.[5] In the provinces, similar election results followed. The loss must have come as a surprise to the Soviets, who nevertheless quickly took control of the three most important ministries—the Interior (which gave the party police control), Commerce, and Supplies—and they appointed Russians to head all three of the ministries.[6]

Following the failed elections, on February 4, 1946, the Soviets also named Mátyás Rákosi vice-premier (deputy prime minister) of Hungary, who at the time was the leader (secretary general) of the Hungarian Communist Party. The appointment gave him ultimate control. Historians from the museum of the House of Terror describe Hungary's political reality like this:

> Parliamentary government ceased to exist, as did political debates. Organs of the state were controlled by party bodies; real decision-making was in the hands of the party leadership, that is, the Political Committee. Mátyás Rákosi, "our father," "our wise leader," "Stalin's foremost Hungarian pupil," stood at the head of the Party.[7]

Rákosi was known as a Hungarian "renegade" who had helped found the Hungarian Communist Party in 1918 and collaborated with Béla Kun during Kun's communist takeover of the Hungarian government in 1919. After the collapse of the

---

[5] Tour at Terror Háza. June 1, 2023.

[6] Montgomery, pp. 212-213.

[7] Schmidt, Mária (Ed.). (2019). p. 18.

short-lived Hungarian Soviet Republic, Rákosi worked closely with Comintern, an organization that championed world-wide communism, and traveled on its behalf throughout Europe. Arrested in 1925 due to his work organizing the Communist Party in Hungary, he spent fifteen years in prison where he used his days to learn Russian and teach other prisoners the tenets of Marxism.[8] About Rákosi and his other Kun-collaborating cohorts, Montgomery declared "after more than twenty-five years' service with the Soviets they are again controlling the Hungarian people, and pretend to be Hungarian patriots."[9]

By 1948, the Communists had seized complete control of the country, nationalized private property, and declared Hungary's unconditional allegiance to the USSR. By 1949, Rákosi was the absolute ruler (and prime minister) under Soviet power. The Communists had also interned or executed the leadership of all other political organizations. Ferenc Szálasi had been executed on March 12, 1946, by hanging.

[8] Applebaum (2013). p. 48.
[9] Montgomery, pp. 210-13.

The Sovietization of Hungary: Retreating into Darkness

In *The Art of War* from the fifth century B.C., the great Chinese military strategist Sun Tzu wrote of the importance of destroying the enemy's will to resist using deception, treachery, surprise, and confusion; he stressed deception as the *key component* of warfare, one which could defeat the enemy, with the least cost to the aggressor.

In 1961, the Industrial College of the Armed Forces of the U.S. Department of Defense (now called The Eisenhower School) published an instructional manual on the global psychological conflict of the Cold War to "portray current analytical thought convening the psychological conflict between the East and the West." The manual *National Security Management: Global Psychological Conflict* stated: "The Sino-Soviet bloc, aiming to defeat the West with minimum cost to itself, and bidding to dominate the world, has refined Sun Tzu's simple prescriptions into a fine art."[10] This statement is vital to understanding what Hungary endured for decades—the Soviets' tireless chipping away at Hungarian identity, belief and values, and the will to resist; it also gives insight into the new Cold War being fought today by the advocates of true freedom and democracy against the deception of the communistic ideology taking precedence in the Western world.

---

[10] Sanders, Ralph & Brown, Fred R., Eds. (1961). p. 1.

Communism as an economic ideology envisions a classless, evenly distributed society (except for the ruling party, of course), and an economy where private property and the means of production are owned by the state. But in order to maintain control over the property and production of people, communism favors an authoritarian government—where strict obedience to the state is enforced at the cost of personal freedom. As we discussed in Chapter 1, "Imperialists, Globalists, and the United States: Claims Against Hungary," in the worldview from which communism derives, the state is sovereign and its citizens are subordinate. In order for the state to maintain subordination, especially against those who have an innate and inherent enthusiasm for liberty and autonomy, quite often extreme and inhumane means of control are required.

Stalin's expansion of Russia into Central and Eastern Europe was not just a territorial conquest. Driven by power, the Soviets were committed to do all in their power to strengthen the power of the Communist Party and spread communism worldwide; this reflected the vision of the Comintern—and was their greatest goal according to the tenets of Marxism, Leninism, and Stalinism. Values like life, liberty, and happiness were not part of their concern or ideology. And the Party's 'right' to do whatever it took to gain power—the morality that undergirded their decisions—was supposedly derived from their defense of the proletariat, or the "working-class people of the world."[11]

[11] Leites, Nathan (1951). *The Operational Code of the Politburo.* Rand Publications. p. 7.

Soviet Premier Joseph Stalin's technique in taking control over occupied nations was very strategic. He degraded human dignity by reappropriating people's minds (beliefs, thoughts, purposes, concepts of right and wrong, ideals) and their material or tangible resources (property, production of goods, physical selves, social interactions, careers, etc.).[12] These were to be replaced with the tenets of Marxism, a rote loyalty to the Party, a reverence for 'the workers', the fear of disobedience and non-conformity, and a soulless, pathetic compliance.

As the Industrial College of the Armed Forces instruction manual reveals, Stalin's goal was to completely dominate the souls of men and destroy their will to resist:

> There are many disquieting indications that the Communists may have developed, or stumbled upon, an all-inclusive or a totalitarian doctrine of psychological warfare ... the Communists do not at all aim to persuade the mind. Instead they seem to be orienting the *souls* of their audience ... Communist psychological-warfare techniques are revealed most dramatically in ... the activities commonly called "brainwashing" or "brain-changing."[13]

The process of 'Sovietization' is how Stalin attempted to 'capture souls' and mold their compliance. Through terror, de-

---

[12] Sabine, George H. (1955). Ideological Conflict and the Struggle for Power. In Sanders, Ralph & Brown, Fred R. (Eds.). (1961). *National Security Management: Global Psychological Conflict.* Industrial College of the Armed Forces, Washington, DC. pp. 3-21.

[13] Sanders, Ralph & Brown, Fred R. (Eds.). p. 49.

ception, and gaslighting, he imposed the Communist version of "*one* truth, one history, one party, one leader and one ideology."[14] The Industrial College manual explains "it was the dogmatism of Marx's philosophy, made vastly more dogmatic by Lenin, that engendered the belief that there can never be more than one right belief and that any dissent whatever is a threat to stable government. It was Marxian ideology, rather than the actual facts that induced in the Bolshevik leadership the belief that the world is its enemy and that international capitalism is a menace which justifies terrorism at home and aggression abroad."[15]

In her comprehensive account of Soviet occupation in Eastern Europe, *Iron Curtain: The Crushing of Eastern Europe 1944-1956*, Anne Applebaum describes the process of Sovietization in simple but depressing language. She writes that the Soviet Union imported "certain key elements of the Soviet system into every nation occupied by the Red Army, from the very beginning." These included: 1) The Soviet NKVD (secret police) in collaboration with local communist parties created a secret police force ("first and foremost"); 2) the Soviets put "trusted local communists in charge of the era's most powerful form of mass media: the radio;" 3) Soviets and their collaborators persecuted and banned independent organization of civil society; and 4) Soviet authorities "again in conjunction with local communist parties, carried out policies of mass ethnic cleansing."[16]

[14] Schmidt, Mária (2021). p. 20.
[15] Sabine, George H. (1955). pp. 11-12.
[16] Applebaum, pp. xxix-xxx.

Although the Communist Party in Hungary would have never gained power without the force of Soviet authority behind them, the party was now in control, at least as a puppet installation of Moscow. The Communist Party (though illegal) had been operating since 1919 but only had a few hundred members with a handful of activists. However, as the Red Army took over Hungary, the Communist Party of Hungary (MKP) began to reorganize and look for new members.[17] As they did, their network grew.

George Kennan, the Chief of Mission for the U.S. Embassy in Moscow in 1946, wrote to the U.S. Department of State detailing the Soviet post-war position. In his telegram, he warned of the "inner central core of Communist Parties in other countries" who placed people in "unrelated public capacities" but who are "in reality working closely together as an underground operating directorate of world communism, a concealed Comintern tightly coordinated and directed by Moscow."[18]

The Communists had a power-hungry Marxist worldview that did not agree with the freedom-loving majority in Hungary. How is it possible that with two diametrically opposed ideologies, the Hungarians could be dominated and controlled—for forty six years? Through terror, torture, fear, and deception, and through the systematic, strategic, Sovietization of Hungary.[19]

---

[17] Schmidt, Mária (Ed.). (2019). p. 15.

[18] Kennan, George (1946, February 22). *George Kennan's 'Long Telegram'.* U.S. State Department. https://nsarchive2.gwu.edu/coldwar/documents/episode-1/kennan.htm

[19] Sabine, George H. (1955). p. 3.

Sovietization Step One: Establish a Secret Police Force

In January 1945, the Hungarian Communist Party, arriving with the Soviet tanks, quickly took possession of the Arrow Cross headquarters at 60 Andrássy Road and installed their secret police. The Communists would now operate out of the same headquarters the Nazis had; both the Nazis and Soviets also used the basement cellars of 60 Andrássy Road as a prison to hold and torture those who opposed them, and whoever else they chose to punish.[20] The headquarters, which Arrow Cross leader Ferenc Szálasi had named 'The House of Loyalty' was renamed, as a warning to any opposition, the 'House of Horrors'.[21]

The secret police force was led by Péter Gábor, a member of the Communist Party since 1931 and a frequent visitor to Moscow. Gábor had remained in close contact with Béla Kun and his collaborators, and also with Mátyás Rákosi. Applebaum writes that the Soviet occupiers,

> immediately created a secret police force in its own image, often using people whom they had already trained in Moscow ... these newly minted secret policemen immediately began to use selective violence, carefully targeting their political enemies according to previously composed lists and criteria. In some cases, they targeted

[20] Applebaum, p. 76.
[21] Schmidt, Mária (Ed.). (2019). p. 55.

enemy ethnic groups as well. They also took control of the region's interior ministries, and in some cases the defense ministries as well, and participated in the immediate confiscation and redistribution of land.[22]

BOTH OF WHICH CHINA & B. GATES ARE DOING IN U.S.

Consistent with the process of Sovietization, Gábor's "Budapest Police" was completely controlled by the Communist Party, not by the Interior Ministry or the Hungarian government.[23, 24] Anne Applebaum writes "everywhere in Eastern Europe, their control over the secret police gave the minority communist parties an outsized influence over political events. Through the selective use of terror, they could send clear messages to their opponents, and to the general public, about what kinds of behavior and what kinds of people were no longer acceptable in the new regime."[25]

The main leaders of the Arrow Cross were executed. But some of the former Hungarian Nazis exchanged their Nazi uniforms for the uniform of the Soviet police. Since the Soviets early-on had seized control of the Ministry of the Interior and the political sections of the Department of Defense, they also had access to Arrow Cross membership records. There was, therefore, a rush of Arrow Cross members to join the Communist party.[26] From the Swiss Delegation Report of April-May 1945: "But not all of the pro-Nazis are being persecuted. It is known,

---

22 Applebaum (2013). p. xxix-xxx.

23 *Ibid.*, p. 75.

24 *Ibid.*, p. xxix-xxx.

25 *Ibid.*, p. 115.

26 Schmidt, Mária (Ed.). (2019). p. 15.

for instance, that a member of the guards of the general headquarters of the Hungarian Nazis, was arrested by the Russians, but was released very shortly after having joined the Communist Party."[27]

With ease, they exchanged the Nazi uniform for the one of the Communist police, and even continued working in the same building at Andrássy Road, though their loyalty was rightly questioned by the Soviets.[28]

Gabor's secret police had three different names over the years—first called the *Politikai Rendészeti Osztály* (the PRO, or 'Political Police Department'), later renamed *Államvédelmi Osztály* (ÁVO, the 'State Defense Department'), until it became *Államvédelmi Hatóság* (ÁVH, the 'State Security Department').[29]

And in the same way the Nazis had before them, the Communists used force "to classify people's political attitudes."[30] The security forces sought out anyone they believed might pose a threat to the regime. The 'guilty' and their conspirators would be jailed at the headquarters, and interrogations took place in the upstairs rooms of the headquarters, usually at night. The guilty would not be allowed to sleep for several days, and they often did not receive food or water. Some prisoners were made to stand with their noses rammed against a wall, arms stretched out horizontally for ten to twelve hours at a time. Daily beatings occurred, and other physical traumas, including burning prisoners with cigarettes and electrical current.

---

[27] Swiss Legation Report of 1945.

[28] Tour at Terror Háza. June 1, 2023.

[29] Schmidt, Mária (Ed.). (2019). p. 5.

[30] Vazsonyi, Balint (1998). *America's 30 Years War: Who is Winning?* Regnery Publishing, Inc. p. 8.

In my research trips to the House of Terror, I was particularly unnerved by the detention cell, where solitary punishment occurred. It is a cramped, dank cell of only about 20 inches by 24 inches where prisoners were made to stand for hours staring into two lightbulbs at eye level. In the "wet cell" prisoners were forced to sit in water in the dark for hours; the "fox hole" is a dark concrete cell with a low ceiling where a prisoner could not straighten up for hours, or for days.[31]

According to the historical accounts of the museum of the House of Terror: "The ÁVH officers were the masters of life and death ... Many victims died of the cruel ordeals suffered during their often week-long interrogations. Most of the prisoners, who survived the physical and psychological brutality, were eventually willing to sign any confession placed before them."[32] There were only two ways out of the prison—either sign the confession or commit suicide. Everyone knew that.[33]

The political trials held by the Communist Party were based on the Soviet model of show trials. These trials were a major tool used to manipulate society—used to give the public the impression that the 'defendant' was guilty—and facts regarding innocence or guilt did not matter. Since the Communists obviously had ultimate power, why put on a trial? Why have the 'guilty' sign confessions? The Party needed to legitimize themselves to society, to change public opinion, and to give the impression that regular citizens, leaders, or influencers were bad and cor-

---

[31] Tours at Terror Háza 2022 and 2023; and, Schmidt, Mária (Ed.). (2019). p. 56.

[32] Schmidt, Mária (Ed.). (2019). p. 5.

[33] Tour at Terror Háza. June 1, 2023.

rupt, the dregs of society. These were lies and gaslighting, to confuse people into thinking that what they knew to be true was not true.

It is estimated that during the relatively short period of time between 1949 and 1953, "at least three-quarters of a million Hungarians were charged with offences against the state; of those found guilty—about half—over 200,000 underwent imprisonment, internment or forced labour. The death toll included not only some two thousand sentenced to execution but many more who failed to survive torture at the hands of the ÁVH or the privations of the camps. A process of continuous purge.[34]

One of the first Hungarians to undergo the Communist show trials was Cardinal Jószef Mindszenty, who would be arrested and imprisoned for the third time in December 1948, this time for espionage and conspiracy against the Soviet-led state. He was also able to bear the torture and imprisonment of the secret police for the longest time on record. Mindszenty was not a stranger to political persecution, being a bold opponent against both communism and fascism (see Chapters 4 and 6). And in 1948 the Communist Party was cracking down on "clerical reactionism":[35]

> On December 26, 1948, an armed squad of the Communist secret police broke into the Cardinal's home and arrested him. There followed 40 days of day-and-night interrogation, hour after hour without any sleep, by brutal

[34] Cartledge, p. 425.
[35] Czókos, Gergely, p. 201.

> interrogators working in shifts. He was forced to stand with arms raised high for days at a time under blinding lights, during endless repetition of rapid-fire questions. When he was physically broken by three weeks of grueling interrogation, tormented with pain, and unable to say "no" any longer, the "treatment" with drugs began. He never signed any confession at all, and the alleged "confession" released by the Communist Government was a complete forgery, full of misspellings and errors, obviously prepared by uneducated interrogators. No other victim ever defied his tormentors for so long.[36]

Seeing what was in store for him, Mindszenty had written letters telling his fellow priests that any confession that might come from his imprisonment should be regarded as false. However, after being drugged and beaten for forty days he supposedly 'confessed' to these crimes and was sentenced to life imprisonment. His imprisonment, torture, and trial served at least one purpose: the world became aware of the conditions in Hungary, and even the United Nations General Assembly condemned his trial.[37] He would be released, after eight years of imprisonment, by the Hungarian Revolution of 1956. His freedom would only last a few days before the Soviet tanks rolled to crush the revolution and Mindszenty sought asylum at the American embassy. He stayed at the embassy for the next fifteen years.

36 Schlafly, p. 3
37 Czókos, Gergely, p. 201.

Sovietization Step Two: Establish Control Over the Media

Next, very early in Soviet occupation, the local Hungarian communists were placed in charge of the most powerful form of 'mass media' of that day—national radio. The radio could reach people far and wide in the city or the countryside, communicate to and educate the illiterate, and repeat communist doctrine until it infiltrated the minds and hearts of society.

In 1959, Stefan T. Possony, an international security strategist of the Cold War, defined the objectives of Communist psychological warfare in a list of eleven goals named the "Specific Goals of the Communist Effort." The Industrial College of the Armed Forces published these goals in their instructional manual in 1961. Goal two is the "creation of a larger group of oriented propagandists who spread Communist notions and are instrumental in creating and maintaining a suitable frame of reference imposed upon non-Communists."[38] In other words, goal two of communist psychological warfare is to create a state-controlled media to spread communist propaganda that will influence and control people's minds.

Under Sovietization in Hungary, the Hungarian Working People's Party (the Communist Party) was given control of the radio. On January 20, 1945, a decree was made by the interim

[38] Possony, Stefan, T. (1959). The Soviet Psychological Approach. First published in *SRI Journal,* Fourth Quarter, 1959. In Sanders, Ralph & Brown, Fred R. (Eds.). (1961). *National Security Management: Global Psychological Conflict,* Industrial College of the Armed Forces, Washington, DC. p. 58.

government that reestablished the Hungarian Press Agency and Magyar Radio to be led by a radio-experienced intellectual who was also a secret member of the Communist Party.[39] Magyar Radio's flagship Kossuth Radio station was now dominated by the Communist Party and "the people depended on state-controlled Radio Kossuth for news and believed little of what they heard."[40] The same was true for newspapers. Every day, factory workers had to arrive very early in the morning in order to be given a compulsory briefing on the newspaper of the Communist Party, *Szabad Nép* (Free People).[41]

Propaganda posters were also very popular with the Soviet Union. Hundreds of Soviet anti-religion posters were designed to create separation between people and religion, by either mocking religion as a superstition, or by holding religion up to be an enemy. Because religion *was* the enemy of Communism. The Christian religion contradicted communist ideology: while the regime persecuted and murdered victims based on their ideology, Christianity practiced temperance and forgiveness and taught individual responsibility. For the followers of Stalin, communism *was* their religion—and anything else was seen as disloyalty:

> The communists replaced God with their own leaders, whom they presented as infallible and omniscient. They swore allegiance to the leader, went into battle in his name, and surrounded his person with rituals befit-

39 Applebaum, p. 187.
40 Cartledge, p. 448.
41 *Ibid.*, p. 430.

> ting an idol. They proclaimed that they required men of a 'new type' in order to create a 'new world,' a special 'heaven on earth.' They persecuted religion, the faithful and the churches, because ethico-religious teaching was diametrically opposed to the ... communists' ideologies, which they wanted to elevate to the rank of creeds.[42]

The propaganda posters also attempted to separate children from their families and from the authority of their parents. In the posters, children were always presented as "bright, intelligent, and progressive" in contrast to their parents which were "always stupid and backward, eager to impose religious education." Juris Redevskis, who grew up in the 1980s under communist rule in formerly Soviet-annexed Latvia, wrote:

> Without exception, all totalitarian movements—whether they are the Soviet Bolsheviks of the last century or the Cultural Marxists and peddlers of the Critical Race Theory of our times—have sought to weaken the family by destroying the organic links between parents and children and substituting the natural authority of the parents with that of the state. Accordingly, parents' right to educate their children according to their own religious and philosophical convictions was a major target of the communist regime.[43]

---

[42] Schmidt, Mária (Ed.). (2019). p. 48.
[43] Redevski, Juris (2021, Winter). A Warning from the Past. *European Conservative*. (21). pp. 82-90.

Certainly, Redevskis is correct that parents today are also fighting against governmental authority and against public schools to educate their children according to their own beliefs. We see this especially in the determination of the U.S government, the European Union, and the international LGBT activists, to impose sexual orientation and gender ideology on young children. They also seem to want to firmly divide parents from their own children when they have expressed an interest in 'transitioning', or to separate children from parents who need guidance on sexual or identity issues.

Sovietization Step Three:
Ban Civil Society

Stalin's power to 'Sovietize' his newly acquired Central European satellites was greatly threatened by the intelligentsia—the highly educated and the socially and politically influential. Throughout Central and Eastern Europe, Stalin removed the established intelligentsia and banned most of the elements of civil society that gave the average citizen any influence--social and religious organizations, associations, books, universities, and channels of communication. After his invasion of Poland in 1940, the Soviet secret police, the NKVD, shot almost twenty-two thousand poles in the head—priests, business owners, military leaders, government officials, academics, and lawyers—and dumped them into pre-dug mass graves in the Katyn Forest. To Stalin, this was necessary to decapitate the strength of Polish society; these were the leaders who could have prevented the Sovietization and brainwashing underway in Poland.

In Hungary, János Kádár, the Minister of Home Affairs under the Rákosi government closed down five thousand civic associations in one year: "brass bands, choirs, theatre groups, boy scouts, reading societies, walking clubs, private schools, church institutions, charities for the relief of poverty, discussion societies, libraries, wine festivals, hunting and fishing clubs." Private, financial donations to charity became illegal, and the bank accounts set up for charity were seized for "the Party."[44]

Private homes were infiltrated, and letters and telephone communication were monitored. Gábor's secret police infiltrated the civil and religious organizations that were allowed to remain open and tried to destroy any national sentiment or allegiance other than to the Communist Party.

But why would all this matter? Sir Roger Scruton worried over whether the event of Sovietization would ever really be given due justice: "The extent of this evil is not widely known in the West, nor is its meaning often pondered."[45] Let's ponder it now—it is easy to understand why—because allegiance, collaboration and unity, or the 'agreement' between people can be a very powerful force on its own. Not only did banning and monitoring all forms of social interactions lead to the separation of people, but it also worked to destroy their identities and their purpose. Scruton, who between 1979 and 1989 supported the underground networks and their intellectual dissidents (at the cost of being arrested in 1985) wrote about his firsthand experience:

---

[44] Scruton, Roger (2014). *How to be a Conservative*. Bloomsbury Continuum. London. p. 120.
[45] *Ibid.*, p. 121.

> Free association is necessary to us, not only because "no man is an island," but because intrinsic values emerge from social cooperation. They are not imposed by some outside authority or instilled through fear. They grow from below, through relations of love, respect and accountability. The fallacy of thinking that we can plan for a society in which fulfillment is readily available, dispensed to all-comers by a benign bureaucracy, is not one that I need here attack. The important point is that what matters to us comes through our own efforts at constructing it, and seldom if ever from above.[46]

Goal Six of the Specific Goals of the Communist Effort describes this objective of communist psychological warfare as "the splitting of a society into many competing and mutually hostile groups and the sapping of the spirit of loyalty, community, mutual helpfulness, positive expectation, and willingness to take risks and to act."[47] It sought to atomize social groups through its own version of 'diversity' (forcing social units of "many competing and mutually hostile groups") to disable them from speaking as a cohesive unit to further their interests, to strip them of agency, and make them pliable tools of the state. Sir Roger Scruton put it more simply: "Everything is reduced to a means, and the ends of human life retreat into privacy and darkness."[48]

---

[46] *Ibid.*, p. 120.
[47] Possony, Stefan T. (1959). p. 58.
[48] Scruton, Roger (2014). p. 121.

Scruton organized secret lectures where his collaborators would fearfully but hopefully await information, learning, and outside news. In these meeting places, banned books of literature, philosophy, music, and theology were hidden and secretly studied.

> I would meet my contacts on street corners at prearranged times, to be taken by tram to some smoke-filled room in an outlying apartment, where a group of whispering "students" had gathered to meet me. Every knock on the door was followed by a frozen silence, and from time to time someone would lift a corner of the curtain and peer anxiously into the street. Books in many languages lined the walls and as often as not a crucifix would be fastened to the wall above the shelves.[49]

Scruton smuggled in books and printing materials, and he supported the underground messaging systems. His collaborators were professors, students, priests, rabbis, poets, and other would-be professionals, who for the sake of the Soviet worker's paradise had been relegated to menial jobs, like (for example) that of a "boiler stoker." Scruton recalls that "in all of them I saw the same marks of suffering tempered by hope; and the same eager desire for the sign that someone cared enough to help them.[50]

---

49 Scruton, Roger (2022). p. 20.
50 Scruton, Roger (2014). pp. 10-11.

There were no physical scars to mark this emotional bondage, but it internally struck at the worth and value of the human being. Jobs or careers that could express a person's character, or given meaning to their lives, were forbidden; for academics, publishing texts and books that could express their thoughts or ideas was forbidden; even the very thoughts and ideas, other than those of loyalty to the state, were forbidden. Scruton said, "the authorities had concealed their existence from the world, and had resolved to remove their traces from the book of history."[51] The Communists required the erasure of personal identity to the point of essentially rendering people invisible—as if they were not there and did not matter at all, except as servants of the state.

The Communist Party also wanted academia in Hungary to be aligned with Party ideology. You will recognize in the following quote the situation facing American universities and schools today: the lowering of academic standards, the 'canceling' of professors, and compulsory progressive education. Under Soviet-occupied Hungary,

> Large numbers of academics, including several scholars of international renown, lost their posts; would-be students who could not prove impeccably proletarian or peasant origins found that universities and colleges were closed to them. Lectures on Marxism and Leninism became compulsory for all students, translations of Soviet textbooks replaced their Hungarian equivalents,

[51] *Ibid.*

> and all Western books and journals were eliminated from university libraries; the magnificent library of the Academy of Sciences was purged of 4,000 volumes. The number of those admitted to higher education rocketed, reaching five times the level of attendance pre-war; but academic standards collapsed, both because a high proportion of the students admitted were ill-qualified to benefit from higher education and because many of their teachers were ill-qualified to dispense it.[52]

A Hungarian gentleman who was a child during the Soviet invasion of Hungary recalls that public education was "built around love for the Soviet Union, love of Stalin, and pressure to join the Communist youth movement. Yes, yes, if you wanted to go to higher education or to get a job after your education, or get a promotion, you had to join." When asked what he remembers most he says, "the atmosphere of fear." Every day more and more students disappeared from classrooms, sent to the Soviet labor camps.[53] Many young Hungarians learned to compartmentalize what they were taught in school—they seemed compliant, but at home parents taught religious adherence, love for country, and democratic ideals.

Even the history of occupied countries was 'erased' and replaced by the Communists, who would reinterpret the history of occupied states according to the Marxist belief of the inevitability of eventual world communism. As Hungary moved into

[52] Cartledge, p. 431.
[53] Interview-17_June 6, 2023.

the future, historian Mária Schmidt explains, "a more developed face of history would replace the period before."[54] Schmidt writes:

> History was expropriated by the Communists; nations subdued by them were deprived of the right to interpret their own pasts and assess their history from their own points of view. Their national heroes, holidays and symbols were replaced, they were expected to forget about their grievances, successes and achievements that could have made them feel proud.[55]

Instead of the Christian cross in public buildings, Hungarians were forced to replace them with pictures of Rákosi, Stalin, and Lenin.[56]

The national holidays of Soviet occupied countries were replaced with an official communist calendar of holidays, such as Stalin's birthday and the anniversary of the October Revolution (Bolshevik Revolution). In Hungary specifically, citizens were made to celebrate March 19 to mark the Hungarian Communist Revolution of 1919, and April 4 to mark the day the German troops withdrew from Hungary under the Soviet 'liberators'. The birthdays of Matyas Rákosi and subsequent leaders were also celebrated. These were all showcased with parades, performers, speeches, and special media announcements, requir-

[54] Interview-12_May 22, 2023.
[55] Schmidt, Mária (2021). p. 19.
[56] Tour at Terror Háza. June 1, 2023.

ing a lot of public attention and time. Applebaum writes that "Illegal celebrations of the 'wrong' holidays became a feature of public life and a form of low-level opposition ... [but] there were rewards for participation in the 'right' holidays."[57]

The Soviets forbade the public celebration of March 15 in Hungary, the anniversary of the beginning of the War of Independence against the Habsburgs, confining any remembrance of the day only to schools. Because this revolution had been crushed by the Russians, just like the Hungarian Revolution of 1956 would be (see Chapter 9, "Nationalism and Freedom"), the Soviets feared that celebrations might take on an anti-Russian nature. They also feared "any manifestation of national identity and belonging, because Communist ideology was based on internationalism and imagined a global Empire which would one day extend to the world as a whole."[58]

Sovietization was enforced through deception and gaslighting. It was very important to the Soviet Union to maintain their version of right and wrong, their version of who they were, and their version of history. They denied and distorted the truth about the Katyn Forest Massacre for decades. Their complicity in starting World War II was whitewashed. Hungarian historian Mária Schmidt makes us understand this in very simple, but visible terms:

57 Applebaum (2013). p. 322.
58 Schmidt, Mária (2021). p. 63.

> What was crucial was history. In other words, possessing the past. Communists claimed an exclusive right over it and clung to it tooth and nail. They imposed their Marxist-based view of history everywhere as compulsory, undisputed and unrivaled ... which laid a depressing burden on people's souls. It felt suffocating to be compelled to use doubletalk and be forced to repeat lies. Speaking the truth, especially about anti-Soviet resistance movements and anti-Communist rebellions, meant being persecuted with fire and sword and could entail imprisonment, dismissal from jobs, silencing and even execution.[59]

Possessing the narrative and propaganda of history was serious business to the Communists. Just like Communist Party newspaper, *Szabad Nép*, (Free People) declared of the torturing, murdering, perverted Communist secret police: "ÁVH's investigators and workers stem from the people, and love the abouring masses with all their heart."[60]

---

[59] *Ibid.*, p. 20.

[60] Schmidt, Mária (2019). p. 36. From *Szabad Nép*, 1950.

Sovietization Step 4: Internment in the Soviet GULAG

After the propaganda shock troops had left Hungary in the spring of 1945, thousands of Hungarians were abducted in the streets by soldiers without warning and dispersed (often without families' knowledge) to over a thousand different Soviet forced-labor camps throughout Russia,[61] commonly known as the Gulag, an acronym—'GULAG'—for *Glavnoye Upravleniye Ispravitelno-Trudovykh Lagerey,* which means 'Chief Administration of Corrective Labor Camps' in Russian.[62]

> The number of the accused was very high, and the nature of the charges very broad. ... In total, the Hungarian and Soviet security police interned some 40,000 Hungarians between 1945 and 1949. Around Budapest alone, the new regime built sixteen internment camps with a capacity to contain up to 23,000 prisoners.[63]

Goal Four of Communist psychological warfare is the "docility, discipline, and controllability of subject populations which must be commanded by the unopposed will of the party leadership."[64]

---

[61] Swiss Legation Report of 1945.
[62] Britannica, T. Editors of Encyclopaedia (2023, August 18). Gulag. *Encyclopedia Britannica.* https://www.britannica.com/place/Gulag.
[63] Applebaum (2013), p. 111.
[64] Possony, Stefan, T. (1959). p. 58.

The huge and intricate Gulag system of concentration and labor camps had been set up by the Soviet Union in 1919 to punish, weaken, and exploit the labor of its enemies. Inmates worked on dams, roads, and railways. It is estimated that many millions of people died in Gulag camps over the decades due to strenuous work, starvation, freezing temperatures and inhumane treatment.[65]

In a second wave of deportations, thousands of German residents in Hungary, and Hungarians of Germanic descent, from the age of two up to seventy, were abducted and sent "en masse" to the Gulag.[66] Political leaders, priests, officers, and schoolteachers, and anyone deemed a threat to the communist takeover were removed and sent to the Gulag.

Altogether, between 600,000 to 700,000 Hungarian citizens, including former soldiers, were captured and sent to Russian captivity. It is estimated that over 300,000 Hungarians lost their lives due to the Soviet forced labor camps. Some returned years later, severely undernourished, disconnected, and in search of their families.[67]

What about the Jews? The Swiss Delegation in Hungary at the time of the siege against Budapest reported: "Generally speaking, the Russians do not treat the Jews any better than the rest of the population."[68] Ironically, about 60% of the surviving Jews that had been deported by the Nazis returned to Hungary and had hoped life would begin again. Anne McCormick in a

[65] Schmidt, Mária (2019). pp. 13-14. Tour House of Terror.
[66] Swiss Legation Report of 1945.
[67] Schmidt, Mária (2019). pp. 13-14; Tour at Terror Háza. June 1, 2023.
[68] Swiss Legation Report of 1945.

November 1945 report from Budapest cabled to the NYT: "Only a small minority of Hungarian Jews are Zionists. The majority are loyal Hungarians who desire to remain in their country and help reconstruct it. It is estimated that about 60 percent are back and these are the hopeful citizens of Hungary. It is impossible not to admire their courage, energy and patriotism as they clear a little space among the ruins and begin over again."[69]

We have the writing of Aleksandr Solzhenitsyn, a Russian poet and outspoken critic of communism to understand the hopelessness and brutality of the Communist Party's Gulag, something hard to imagine today except perhaps in the case of the current Chinese Communist Party (CCP) and their 'reeducation' camps for Uyghur Muslims.[70] Solzhenitsyn was charged and sentenced in 1945 to eight years for writing letters that contained disparaging language against Stalin.[71]

The full extent of the horror endured by inmates of the Gulag will not be shared here, but can be understood by reading Solzhenitsyn's great work *The Gulag Archipelago*. These quotes will suffice to show the inhumanity of the thousands of prison camps that existed throughout the Soviet Union for decades:

---

[69] McCormick, Anne O'Hare (1945, November 25). Abroad: Jews Leaven of Commerce in Budapest. *New York Times*.

[70] Tour at Terror Háza. June 1, 2023.

[71] Frängsmyr, Tore, Editor-in-Charge; Allén, Sture, Editor (1993). *Nobel Lectures, Literature 1968-1980*, World Scientific Publishing Co., Singapore, Web accessed July 17, 2023 at: https://www.nobelprize.org/prizes/literature/1970/solzhenitsyn/biographical/

> Philosophers, psychologists, medical men, and writers could have observed in our camps, as nowhere else, in detail and on a large scale the special process of the narrowing of the intellectual and spiritual horizons of a human being, the reduction of the human being to an animal and the process of dying alive ... Hunger, which darkens the brain and refuses to allow it to be distracted by anything else at all, or to think about anything else at all, or to speak about anything else at all except food, food, and food ... bags of bones which are still joined together lying under blankets at the hospital, dying almost without movement—and then being carried out. And on the whole ... how simply a human being dies: He was speaking—and then he fell silent ... the various paths to death, which are sometimes called scurvy, sometimes pellagra, sometimes alimentary dystrophy. For instance, if there is blood on your bread after you have taken a bite—that is scurvy. From then on your teeth begin to fall out, your gums rot, ulcers appear on your legs, your flesh will begin to fall out. He is no longer afraid of death; he is wrapped in a submissive, rosy glow. If black astonished head lice are crawling on the face of your neighbor on the bunks, it is a sure sign of death.[72]

How can the inhumanity of man against another man—who bears the image of the same body, the same spirit, the same soul—be explained?

---

[72] Solzhenitsyn, A. The Way of Life and Customs of the Natives. *The Gulag*

Father Olofsson Károly Placid[73] (1916-2017) was a Hungarian Benedictine monk born in Budapest in 1916.[74] He was arrested in 1946 by the Soviet secret police because his participation in the 1945 election campaign for the Smallholders Party was considered an offense. The Soviet police tried to force him to confess a crime, but he refused and was sentenced to ten years in a Soviet Gulag. In the Gulag he took it upon himself to be the chief-encourager of the other prisoners, and secretly administered religious rites to those condemned to die. He often hid his communication to other prisoners by singing in Hungarian, which the guards did not understand. In Father Placid's words, he believed God had given him the task of "'awakening the minds' of his fellow prisoners, comforting them, so they might 'feel the presence of God' and feel human."[75] In an interview years after his release, he remembers:

> It was the sixth or eighth day, I was sweeping. I knew that at the end of one of the corridors there were six cells for those condemned to death. At that point, there were 32 condemned waiting there for their execution. ...

Archipelago Part III, Chapter 7. In Ericsson, Edward E., Jr.; Mahoney, Daniel J. (Eds.). (2006). *The Solzhenitsyn Reader. New and Essential Writings 1947-2005*. pp. 238-240.

[73] Tour at Terror Háza. June 1, 2023.

[74] Szigeti, Tom (2017, January 16). Placid Olofsson, the Hungarian "Monk of the Gulag," has Passed Away at 100. *Hungary Today*, Budapest. Https://hungarytoday.hu/placid-olofsson-hungarian-monk-gulag-passed-away-100/

[75] Losonczy, Anne-Marie, and Kara, David (2009). Biography: Placid Karoly Olofsson. *Mémoires Européenes du Goulag*. Archives Sonores. https://www.gulagmemories.eu/en/sound-archives/salle/placid-karoly-olofsson.

> My duty would be to comfort my fellow prisoners. Because, after all, that was easier for me: I had a spiritual training and no wife or children. But these young men had had to leave their young wives and little children behind. And the Soviet Union had succeeded, expertly, in giving us the feeling that our lives hung only by a thread. We never knew when they would shoot us in the back of the neck.[76]

Father Placid's servant's heart and outlook on life in the Gulag tells us much about how to cope and survive during the most difficult and darkest of times:

> The first rule for survival ... You must not dramatise your suffering because that weakens you. To stand up to suffering we need all our energy. In practice, we managed this by not letting any of the others complain. When someone moaned or expressed dissatisfaction or sadness, [we said] "Tell us about your job!" Everyone can talk about their job. During those ten years I learnt about so many jobs... turkey farming, bee keeping, mining, bookbinding and the like. We did not let anyone complain.[77]

He also tells of the importance of rejecting bitterness in order to survive:

[76] *Ibid.*
[77] *Ibid.*

> When the military court in Budapest sentenced us, we were nobodies, we were the vanquished and they were the victors. I'm not saying that the criterion of truth is the machine gun, but they were the victors and they crushed us ... so in these circumstances and this situation I must show that I am better, have more value and am nobler than them. That is what mobilises the necessary energy to survive, these small pleasures. So it was terribly important.[78]

Father Placid was released and returned to Hungary in 1955 where he took up his duties of priesthood in secret. He is reported to have said, prior to his death at 101 years old: "Remember this: God has a good sense of humor! The Soviet Union tried everything to ruin me for 10 years. But I'm still here, and where is the Soviet Union?"[79]

---

[78] *Ibid.*

[79] MacIntosh, Alex (2017, March 22). The Monk of the Gulag: 7 Inspirational Quotes from a Life Imprisoned. *Culture Trip*. https://theculturetrip.com/europe/hungary/articles/the-monk-of-the-gulag-7-inspirational-quotes-from-a-life-imprisoned.

Conclusion:
U.S. Prestige

The objectives of the Comintern reached their ultimate power through the soul-claiming appropriation of Hungary by the Soviet Union. It was the greatest irony that, though the Soviet Union had committed a clear act of war aggression by invading Poland in 1939, the Allies had ultimately approved the secret Hitler-Stalin pact by giving Poland, Hungary, and other 'satellite' countries over to the USSR to be Sovietized.

Colonel Dallas S. Townsend was the second in command at the American military mission in Hungary until the Spring of 1946. Townsend would go on to become the assistant U.S. attorney general in the Eisenhower administration. He criticized the U.S. for allowing the Soviets to take over Hungary—in direct defiance of the agreement at Yalta—the unfair elections; the lack of democratic governance; the destruction of Budapest; the rape and torture of civilians; and the worst inflation in history, caused by the Russians, to force Hungarians into poverty and submission. Townsend said that the U.S. had lost so much "prestige" in our decisions, that by the time he had left Budapest, we might as well "not have been there at all."[80]

[80] Montgomery relating Townsend's words to him. In Montgomery, p. 214.

Chapter 9

NATIONALISM AND FREEDOM: A SHINING LIGHT

We must see these strange events in their historical context. All the natural forms of social life—institutions, churches, clubs and companies—were oppressed or abolished by the communists. Politics and law were replaced by mock substitutes, and culture was driven underground. It is hardly surprising, therefore, that people cling to their national sentiments, because these were the only form of belonging that the communists could not extinguish.[1]

—Sir Roger Scruton (1991)

[1] Scruton, Roger (1991). pp. 82-84.

Introduction: The Hungarian *Virtus*

The Hungarians, though conquered, controlled, and robbed of their most precious rituals and traditions, who for decades had been the victims of brainwashing and terror, have never been willing to give up their freedom, nor their identity. Somehow, the unique Hungarian culture, and their emphatic embrace of freedom, continuously revives. János Csák, Hungarian Minister of Culture and Innovation, wrote in his insightful article "Where do we come from? What are we? Where are we going?" about the Hungarian spirit that survives:

> History has shown that the price of physical survival is often the loss of freedom and culture ... We Hungarians have never been able to give up either our culture or our freedom. The focus of the Hungarian mindset and way of life is intellectual and spiritual freedom. The desire for freedom and the competitive spirit that accompanies it can best be expressed in terms of the Latin *virtus*, i.e., virtue, courage, valour.[2]

Minister Csák, who could of course be excused for any bias toward the Hungarians, is objectively correct, as I, and many other foreigners to Hungary have observed. As Csák stated, the

[2] Csák, János (2022, April 22). Where Do We Come From? What are We? Where are we Going? *Hungarian Review*, 13 (1), Budapest.

Hungarian desire for freedom is accompanied by a "competitive spirit," that is (in my observation) courageous, fair, and fun, strives for moral excellence, and is especially brave in the face of battle. And in many ways, as one citizen from the town of Veszprém explains, the Hungarians have learned how to cope in the very best way they could—in the face of unbeatable odds:

> We Hungarians, we were very well trained by the time the Soviet occupation happened. The Hungarian nation was fighting for its existence for 500 years. We've lived through Ottomans, Habsburg, Treaty of Trianon, The Red Terror, German occupancy, and then we had the Soviet occupation. Hungarian people, Hungarian families, in order to survive, could create an instinctive kind of behavior in which they could preserve their identity and they could comply in a minimal level to the expectations of the power.[3]

But, as Csák points out, the patience of the Hungarian *virtus* can run out:

> The socio-psychological background of the Hungarian *virtus* [his virtue, courage, and valor] takes the following form: man suffers from injustices, but bears them, until finally he explodes. Zsigmond Móricz writes the following in his novel Sándor Rózsa (1941): 'such was his nature that he would not complain if a tree were hewn

[3] Focus Group 2-June 8, 2023.

> down upon him: he could not strike another without striking himself in the heart.' But only up to a certain point! Thanks to the Habsburgs, it came to be widely believed of the Hungarians that they were inherently unpredictable and rebellious. To Hungarian eyes, our hardships stem from the fact that we are a people alone, ringed around by more populous Germanic and Slavic (including Russian) peoples, with an added measure of Turkish pressure.[4]

It is the Hungarian spirit (or Hungarian *virtus*[5]), cultivated over many centuries and many different experiences, that has enabled the Hungarian people to endure cruel injustices, but only until the one day that the Hungarians finally 'explode against them. The 1956 Revolution is one example of this.

In the greater Soviet Union, following Stalin's death in 1953 and the rise of Soviet leader Nikita Khrushchev, there were some moderating influences or 'de-Stalinization' processes happening in Russia and in some of its satellites in Eastern Europe—but Hungary was not one of them.

The beginning of de-Stalinization was marked by Khrushchev's 'secret speech' at the twentieth Congress of the Communist Party of the Soviet Union, on February 25, 1956. In

---

4 Csák, János.

5 Virtusonline.org: "The word *virtus* derives from Latin, and means valor, moral strength, excellence, and worth. In ancient times, *virtus* denoted a way of life and manner of behavior that always aspired to the highest, most positive attributes of people and aspects of human interaction." https://www.virtusonline.org/virtus/virtus_description.cfm

his speech, also known as "On the Cult of Personality and Its Consequences," Khrushchev denounced Stalin as a murderer. His comments jarred and shocked his audience, some of whom were reported to literally have had heart attacks, and others went home to commit suicide.[6]

Krushchev wanted to moderate some of the most iron-fisted elements of Sovietization through political reforms and supposedly 'humanize' Communism. His denunciation of Stalin, though, was an attack on the man who had led Soviet Russia for twenty-nine years—from the end of their revolutionary in stability to victory in the "Great Patriotic War," as the Russians referred to WWII. For many Russians, there was no other leader but Stalin; with this perspective, it is easy to imagine how Khrushchev's new ideas and 'reforms' were not always well-received.[7]

On May 14, 1955, the Soviet Union created the Warsaw Pact, formally known as the Treaty of Friendship, Co-operation, and Mutual Assistance, which defined the Eastern bloc in contrast with the NATO-aligned countries of the Western bloc. This was an "alliance" and defense "treaty" between Russia and its seven Soviet satellite states in Central and Eastern Europe: Hungary, Albania, Bulgaria, Czechoslovakia, East Germany, Poland, and Romania. The treaty was a complement to the 1949 Council for Mutual Economic Assistance (Comecon), also set up by the So-

---

[6] Rettie, John (2009, January 22). Khrushchev, Secrets and Me. In Our Own Correspondent, *BBC 4 Radio*.

[7] Applebaum, Anne (2003). Thaw—and Release. *Gulag—A History*, Anchor Books, New York. p. 506-526.

viet Union, to strengthen economic cooperation with its satellite states. Both treaties further bound Hungary to Soviet control.[8]

And, while the Soviet Union grappled with 'moderating' changes at home, in Hungary dictator Mátyás Rákosi presided over an increasingly Stalinist, oppressive, regime that had brought the resentment of many Hungarians to a dangerous boiling point.[9]

Hungarian Revolution of 1956

Historian Márton Békécs describes the Hungarian Revolution of 1956 as a "unique act of history" and compares its brave spirit to America's fight for Independence in 1776.[10] This countrywide revolution against the Soviet-dominated Communist government of the Hungarian People's Republic lasted from October 23 to November 4, 1956, before being crushed by Soviet tanks and troops.

On October 22, 1956, a group of Hungarian university students compiled a list of sixteen points containing key national policy demands for the government. These demands were read

[8] North Atlantic Treaty Organization (NATO). The Cold War: Defense and Deterrence. What was the Warsaw Pact. https://www.nato.int/cps/en/natohq/declassified_138294.htm

[9] King, Harrison (2016, October). Remembering '56: The Hungarian Revolution. *Origins*. Ohio State University. https://origins.osu.edu/milestones/october-2016-remembering-56-hungarian-revolution-sixty?language_content_entity=en

[10] Interview-3_February 20, 2023.

at the foot of the General Bem statue, a Polish hero of the 1848 War of Liberation, to show solidarity with the parallel anti-communist demonstrations ongoing in Poznan, Poland.

The students' demands included: immediate withdrawal of all Soviet troops; a new and independent government; the trial of Rákosi before a people's tribunal; free and fair elections; freedom of the press and freedom of expression; a reorganization of the economy and industry; and the reestablishment of national symbols, holidays, and traditions.[11, 12]

The University students appealed to all Hungarians to join them at the Hungarian Parliament building to protest against the USSR's domination of Hungary through the unreformed Stalinist government of Mátyás Rákosi. Demonstrators headed for Parliament Square, tearing down Soviet flags, Red Stars, and Communist symbols from public buildings. Shouting "*Ruszkik haza!*" (Russkies go home!)—the protestors waved Hungarian flags that had been redesigned for the revolution—the Soviet-designed emblem in the center had been torn or cut out.[13]

Following an anti-Soviet protest march throughout Budapest, on October 23, the students attempted to enter Budapest's main broadcasting station to read their demands on air. However, they were detained by security guards. When crowds of people gathered outside the broadcasting station and called for

---

11 Applebaum (2013). pp. 457-458.

12 The American-Hungarian Federation. The 1956 Hungarian Revolution: 16 Points. http://www.americanhungarianfederation.org/news_1956_16Points.html

13 Colley, Rupert (2016). *The Hungarian Revolution, 1956*. CreateSpace Independent Publishing Platform, pp. 58-85.

their release, the ÁVH secret police opened fire on them. This was the defining event that ignited the Hungarian Revolution of 1956, as it was the first Soviet-initiated bloodshed against unarmed civilians.

All-out combat between the Hungarian revolutionaries and the Soviet Red Army soldiers began on October 25 in front of the Parliament, when ÁVH agents on the roof of the Agriculture Ministry fired on protesters. Confusion and panic set in. Soviet tanks, positioned around the Parliament for security purposes, began returning fire, believing they were the targets of rooftop fire from the revolutionaries. What was strange was that earlier in the day, Soviet soldiers had been engaging with and casually speaking to protestors, even allowing them to climb aboard their tanks. However, Budapest's relative peace had radically changed.[14]

Next, Hungarian revolutionaries began to organize into militias; local Hungarian communist leaders and ÁVH policemen were captured and summarily killed or lynched; political prisoners of the Communists were released and armed, including Cardinal József Mindzsenty, who after eight years of imprisonment made his way to the U.S. embassy for safety.[15]

Civilian armed fighters, waging an impromptu urban guerrilla campaign with small arms and Molotov cocktails, were highly effective against Soviet tanks and the occupation troops that had been called in from nearby barracks. Key intersections

---

[14] Ürményházi, Attila J. (2006, February). The Hungarian Revolution-Uprising, Budapest, 1956. *American-Hungarian Federation*, Washington, DC. p. 8.
[15] Colley.

of Budapest were barricaded and fortified to control access to the capital city and channel the responding Soviet forces. The vaunted Red Army was suffering an international humiliation at being totally dominated by some highly motivated Hungarian 'Freedom Fighters'.

The revolution was successful—but only initially. Euphoria swept over Budapest as Soviet forces withdrew and a ceasefire went into effect on October 28. Unimaginably, civilian revolutionaries had freed themselves from the Communist brutality of the Soviet Union! Images of joyous civilians, raising weapons and Hungarian tricolor flags (with holes in the centers where the communist symbols had been cut out), sitting atop the captured or destroyed Soviet tanks, stunned the world.[16]

Reformist politician Imre Nagy (who had been removed from office in 1953) was reinstated into government as Premier. Nagy promised, among a series of other democratic reforms, the establishment of a multiparty government system. On November 1, Nagy declared Hungarian neutrality and appealed to the United Nations for support.

Western powers were reluctant, however, to risk global confrontation and left the Hungarian freedom fighters to fend for themselves. The United States sent very conflicting messages. Radio Free Europe (RFE), the State Department's propaganda arm, encouraged the uprising and raised people's hopes—while the official statements from the Eisenhower White House expressed weak, half-hearted sentiments. U.S. President Dwight D. Eisenhower was purportedly concerned about the uncertain-

[16] King.

ties of the Suez Crisis and the forecasted probability of nuclear war.[17]

The U.S. government has struggled over the years to explain its schizophrenic, some might say blind, position towards Hungary's fight to free itself from communism. In one "Lessons Learned" analysis in the *International Journal of Intelligence and CounterIntelligence*, the excuse was offered that the RFE broadcasts had "contained emotional bombast" that Hungarian listeners may have merely misinterpreted as indicating "Western solidarity and support."[18] Such an explanation seems very cold solace.

For a handful of days, Hungary appeared to have freed itself. But by November 2, Nikita Khrushchev changed his mind about how to deal with the humiliation of the Red Army, which had gained international attention, and the repudiation of communist control in Hungary.

Late in the evening of November 3, in an operation code-named "Whirlwind," 150,000 Soviet troops and 2,500 tanks re-entered Hungary and drove towards Budapest. By Sunday, November 4, the Soviets seized all vital points of communication and transportation. The overnight "lightning" moves made by the Soviets paralyzed and out-gunned the revolutionary forces.

---

[17] National Security Archive (2017, May 10). Hungary, 1956: Reviving the Debate over (In)Action during the Revolution. George Washington University, Washington, DC. https://nsarchive.gwu.edu/briefing-book/openness-russia-eastern-europe/2017-05-10/hungary-1956-reviving-debate-over-us

[18] Johnson, A. Ross (2018). Managing Media Influence Operations: Lessons from Radio Free Europe/Radio Liberty. *International Journal of Intelligence and CounterIntelligence*, 31(4), 681-701, DOI: 10.1080/08850607.2018.1488498

Together with the Hungarian army, the revolutionaries fought back, but this time the Soviets were prepared with a combined arms effort—infantry, artillery, tanks, and even air strikes—that decimated the city. The Soviets rubbled every building that indicated signs of resistance.[19]

At 05:20 a.m. on November 4, Imre Nagy broadcast his final plea to the nation and the world, announcing that Soviet forces were attacking Budapest and that the revolutionary government was remaining at its post.[20] The last desperate cries of free Hungary went out over teletype and radio, repeated in English, German, and Russian:

> Please tell the world of the treacherous attack against our struggle for liberty .... Help! Help! Help! ... SOS! SOS! SOS! We have almost no weapons—only light machine guns, Russian-made long rifles and some carbines. We haven't any kind of heavy guns. The people are jumping at the tanks and throwing in hand grenades. ...The Hungarian people are not afraid of death. It is only a pity that we can't stand for long ....What is the United Nations doing? Give us a little encouragement. ... We hope the UN meeting won't be too late.[21]

---

[19] Colley.

[20] UN General Assembly (1957). *Report of the Special Committee on the Problem of Hungary*. Chapter VII. D (The Political Background of the Second Soviet Intervention). Para 291, p. 89.

[21] Schlafly.

The radio station, Free Kossuth Rádió, stopped broadcasting at 08:07 a.m.[22] As Cardinal Mindszenty related, "Freedom in Hungary had lasted only a few days. On November 4, 1956, a nation died while the United Nations talked and the United States played the role of Pontius Pilate."[23] American bestselling author James Michener termed it this way:

> At dawn on November 4, 1956, Russian communism showed its true character to the world. With the ferocity and barbarism unmatched in recent history, it moved its brutal tanks against the defenseless population, seeking escape from the terrors of communism and destroyed it.
>
> A city whose only offense was that it sought a decent life was shot to pieces. Dedicated Hungarian communists who had deviated slightly from the true Russian line were shot down ruthlessly and hunted from house to house. Even workers, on whom communism is supposed to be built, were rounded up like animals, and shipped in sealed boxcars to the USSR. A satellite country, which had dared to question Russian domination was annihilated.[24]

Imre Nagy was arrested, subjected to a secret trial for treason, and was eventually executed on June 16, 1958[25] on the orders of

[22] UN General Assembly (1957). Para 291, p. 89.

[23] Schlafly.

[24] Michener, James A. (1957). Foreward. In *The Bridge at Andau*, New York: Dial Press.

[25] Cartledge, p. 466-467.

the secretary general of the Hungarian Communist Party, János Kádár—the man who would rule Hungary for the next three decades.[26] The revolutionaries lost the battle, but their self-sacrifice, bravery, and lust for freedom would eventually lead to the ultimate victory:

> But I want to say something else, too, which little girls who were only four years old in 1956 could not have seen or understood: that people like Imre Nagy, Ferenc Jánosi, Mr. Szabó and István Angyal—with their heroic stance and at the cost of their lives—dealt a death blow to the communist behemoth, and it was they who launched the most important trend of the 20th century: humanity's common fight for the freedom of each individual human being.[27]

Thousands were killed and wounded during the revolution, and nearly a quarter-million Hungarians fled the country. Despite efforts to suppress Hungary with Stalinist-type domination and exploitation, the Hungarian people would not break. Instead, they developed their own slow evolution toward a "Goulash Communism,"[28] that permitted a hybrid system with some economic and cultural autonomy.

---

[26] Applebaum (2013). p. 460.

[27] Rice, Andrea Lauer, Edith K. Lauer (Eds.). (2006). *56 Stories: Personal Recollections of the 1956 Hungarian Revolution. A Hungarian American Perspective*. Kortárs Kiadó, Budapest, Hungary.

[28] A term commonly attributed to Nikita Khrushchev and understood as a unique form of Hungarian communism which blends regulated market economics with traditional or orthodox communism.

1991: The Catacombs Open

Until the 1980s, the Soviet Union had been successful in suppressing and destroying national movements in Eastern Europe. Nationalism in all its forms, or even the accusation of it, was dangerous and resulted in persecution or death, as the Hungarians experienced in 1956, and the Czechoslovakians in 1968.

But by the 1980s, nationalism, fed by anti-Russian sentiment and international pressure, was enthusiastically increasing in Soviet satellites all over the Soviet empire. The Soviet Union began to crumble: the economic burden of its satellite nations had become more than Russia could sustain as oil prices, an important source of its income, fell steeply; the nuclear power station at Chernobyl exploded; the threat of the U.S. Strategic Defense Initiative had become a reality—while Russia's nuclear arsenal had become outdated.[29]

Seeing no alternative, Mikhail Gorbachev, secretary general of the Communist Party of the Soviet Union (CPSU) from 1985-1991, passed laws that led to property privatization and took the USSR toward a market economy. Partly an effort to appear more democratic to international audiences, Gorbachev committed to transform Soviet socialism into what he called "democratic socialism," or socialism "with a human face." Gorbachev's policies of *Glasnost* (government openness and transparency) and *Perestroika* (restructuring) increased the confidence of the nationalistic revolutionaries and opened the door for popular uprisings:

---

[29] Schmidt (2021). pp. 44-48.

> As Communists started to become exhausted, nations under their yoke felt an ever-increasing urge to take possession of what belongs to them—their national pasts. At the very moment when that happened, countries that had been forced to become Communist shook off foreign occupation and the Communist ideology it had imposed on them. Beginning in the 1980s, people opposed to Communism started demanding the restitution of their national pasts and traditions with hitherto unseen energy and determination. The liberation of historical remembrance was accompanied by the resuscitation of national colours, symbols and banners whose use was now being imposed on the Communist regimes.[30]

At the same time, Russia began to admit to the atrocities they had kept hidden for decades –the historical facts they had denied and the false narratives they had created. Forty-seven years after George Earle's report to FDR blaming the Soviets for the massacre, Russia admitted its atrocities in the Katyn Forest.[31] In addition, Gorbachev allowed public confirmation of the existence of the 1939 Hitler-Stalin Pact. Solzhenitsyn's *Gulag Archipelago*, released in three volumes from 1973-1975, had already revealed to the world the terrors of the Soviet Gulag.

The façade of communism was slipping, and the Soviet Union began to lose its tight grip over Central and Eastern Europe. More to the point, Mária Schmidt writes that they lost their "monopoly over ideology":

[30] Schmidt, Mária (2021). pp. 19-20.
[31] Farrell, p. 107.

> As soon as they had lost control over history, Communists became incapable of controlling events. Countries under their occupation reconquered their national pasts and started working to take back control over their national histories, which amounted to depriving Communists of their monopoly over ideology. This process lasted officially until November 30, 1989, when CPSU General Secretary Mikhail Gorbachev declared at last that, "we have given up the claim to possess the monopoly of truth."[32]

Among the nationalist revolutionaries were Viktor Orbán, and other leaders of today's Fidesz party. Hungarian society began to revitalize, and new political parties were formed. In March 1988, several different political parties were created; the first was FIDESZ—the acronym for Fiatal Demokraták Szövetsége, (Alliance of Young Democrats)—created as an anti-communist opposition party made up of freedom fighters under the age of thirty-five. Viktor Orbán was one of the co-founders of Fidesz.

As became increasingly clear, Hungary was fed up with communism, in 1989 the Communists allowed a memorial ceremony and reburial of Imre Nagy to be held—in an effort to promote national reconciliation.[33] The ceremony was prepared by the communist ruling party but opposition parties were invited to speak. Though the ruling party kept tight control on the proceedings, Orbán, as spokesperson for Fidesz, thwarted the attending communists—at least one of whom had voted for Nagy's

[32] Schmidt, Mária (2021). p. 25.

[33] *Ibid.*, p. 71.

execution—and their plan of "pardoning each other with tears in their eyes and covering up each other's deeds." Calling out their hypocrisy, Orbán demanded an end to Soviet oppression in front of millions of people viewing the reburial on TV and radio:[34]

> If we believe in our own strength, we will be capable of bringing an end to the Communist dictatorship, if we are sufficiently resolute, we can force the ruling party to submit itself to free elections. If we do not lose sight of the principles of '56, we can elect for ourselves a government that will initiate immediate talks regarding the quick withdrawal of Soviet troops.[35]

In November 1989, the Berlin Wall fell; Estonia, Lithuania, and Latvia seceded in 1991; Ukraine proclaimed its independence, and the communist governments installed in Poland, Hungary, Czechoslovakia, Romania, and Bulgaria began to fall.[36] On December 25, 1991, the Soviet Union collapsed.

Balint Vazsonyi remembers "as soon as the Red Army departed, the historic qualities of Prague and Budapest reemerged."[37] Hungarians took back their culture and national holidays, starting with March 15, the anniversary of the beginning of the 1848 War of Independence against the Habsburgs. One Hungarian gentlemen who was a boy when the Red Army first took over Budapest, recalls that his first feeling after liberation was:

---

[34] *Ibid.*, pp. 82-83.
[35] *Ibid.*, pp. 82-83.
[36] NATO.
[37] Vazsonyi, p. 38.

> No more fear ... no more fear ... a big and good feeling, finally after 45 years the Soviets left. I was able to travel. To speak my mind freely. It was freedom. The whole system, the structure of the official Soviet world collapsed. I was happy for me. I was happy for my children.[38]

Freedom in Hungary! And the ability to control their own destinies. Scruton describes his network of intellectual and political dissidents: "In 1985 the secret police moved against me and I was arrested in Brno ... but our team kept going until 1989, when to our surprise, the catacombs were opened and our friends came pale, staggering and bewildered into the sunlight to be hailed by the people as the natural trustees of their restituted country. This was a wonderful moment."[39] Hungary, along with Poland and Czechoslovakia, were once again sovereign nations. Generations in Central Europe had lived under occupation and oppression—it was all they knew.

As the Soviet empire finally faded and new democracies were formed in Central Europe, the former underground resistance forces of Hungary, Poland, and Czechoslovakia began to meet to form a supportive network. Their initial goal was to dismantle the Soviet's institutionalized influence on their countries, primarily the Warsaw Pact and Comecon.[40] As Viktor Orbán said, "After the collapse of the communist regime, everything was about freedom."

---

[38] Interview 11-June 6, 2023.

[39] Scruton, Roger (2009). The flame that was snuffed out by freedom. *The Times*. In Dooley, Mark (Ed.) *Against the Tide* (2022). Bloomsbury Publishing. pp. 19-22.

[40] Orbán, Tamás (2021). Thirty Years of Visegrad Summits and the Themes of a Central European Cooperation. In Bendarzsevszkij, Anton (Ed.). *30 Years of The V4*. Danube Institute. pp. 10-20, p. 11.

A Vision for Central Europe

On February 15, 1991, the Visegrád Group[41] was officially established at Visegrád Castle, Hungary, where the newly declared leaders of each country—Hungarian Prime Minister József Antall, Czechoslovakian President Václav Havel, and Polish President Lech Wałęsa—signed the Visegrád Declaration. The common vision of the Visegrád Group (V3) for freedom, democracy, and free-market capitalism would later help to secure the three (at the time) nation's successful integration into the European Union and Euro-Atlantic alliance of NATO. The group was "widely regarded as a successful regional model for all post-communist countries to follow." The V3 establishment of CEFTA (Central European Free Trade Agreement) would "serve as a 'lobby' not only for them but for every other post-communist country to enter the EU in the future." [42]

The Warsaw Pact was officially declared at an end, in July 1991, by Czechoslovak President Vaclav Havel, about six months before the collapse of the Soviet Union in December and the withdrawal of Soviet troops. In 1992, Czechoslovakia was dissolved into the states of the Czech Republic and of Slovakia, and the V3 became known as the V4.[43]

However, many of the first officially-elected government leaders of the post-Soviet bloc were often 'reinvented' com-

---

[41] Visegrad Group. Visegrad Group Defence Cooperation. https://www.visegradgroup.eu/about/cooperation/defence
[42] Orbán, Tamás (2021). p. 10.
[43] *Ibid.*

munists of the Soviet era; the Freedom Fighters, the "natural trustees of their restituted country" who many expected to take leadership, were not invited to join in. Scruton's full account post-communism helps to explain:

> The catacombs were opened and our friends came pale, staggering and bewildered into the sunlight to be hailed by the people as the natural trustees of their restituted country. This was a wonderful moment, and for a while I believed that the public spirit that had reigned in the catacombs would now govern the state. It was not to be. Having been excluded for decades from the rewards of worldly advancement, our friends have failed to cultivate those arts—hypocrisy, treachery, and realpolitik—without which it is impossible to stay in government.[44]

Instead of the revolutionaries and proponents of freedom leading the newly freed countries, the former Soviet sympathizers carefully reinvented themselves and their resumes for the next elections. The citizens of Eastern Europe thought they had finally got what they wanted—freedom, democratic leadership, no more dictatorial pressures, but:

> Not since 1945 had so many records of party membership disappeared, or so many dissident biographies been invented. Within two years the real dissidents had returned to their studies, while the world outside was

[44] Scruton (2009). p. 20.

> racing on, led by a new political class that had learned to add a record of outspoken dissidence to all its other dissimulations.[45]

Suddenly, a new political class was formed: The former advocates and proponents of communism falsely redesigned themselves as advocates of freedom and rights during the Soviet occupation, and suddenly became 'politically correct'. This new political class was determined to "climb onto the European gravy train, which promised rewards of a kind that had been enjoyed, in previous years, only by the inner circle of the secret police."[46] They did not want a radical break with the former communist ways, and the *true* freedom fighters remained in opposition to this new political ruling class.

---

45 *Ibid.*
46 *Ibid.*

Conclusion: Hungarian Freedom, Old Persisting Problems

In 1998 Viktor Orbán was elected for the first time prime minister of Hungary; he was the first elected head of a central European government that had not been a member of the Soviet-era communist regime. Not long after, the goals of the V4 were realized: All four members of the V4 were admitted into the European Union on May 1, 2004; in 1999, Hungary, Czechia, and Poland all joined NATO, and Slovakia joined in 2004.[47]

In 2011, a sovereign and independent Hungary established a new constitution, known as the Hungarian Fundamental Law (See Chapter 2), based on the best traditions of Hungarian sovereign constitutional history, but focused on meeting the challenges of the twenty-first century. The vision of the people, (and of the Fidesz party), that saw a democratic Hungary based on the rule of law and a nation that provided freedom and security was finally being realized.

Unfortunately, as the European Union has grown in size, influence, and bureaucracy, Hungary's new-found freedom from Soviet oppression did not end its constant struggle for sovereignty. As Prime Minister Victor Orbán explained to the audience at the Conservative Political Action Conference (CPAC) Hungary 2022 in Budapest, Europe's reinvented political class of the early 1990s, which had claimed to uphold the values of freedom and democracy and who classified themselves as 'lib-

[47] Orbán, Tamás (2021). pp. 14-15.

eral', were actually natural allies with communist ideology. "American friends," Orban urged, "the time has come to start taking action":

> At all events we rose up, and in the late 1980s we decided that enough was enough. We wanted to regain our country and our freedom; we wanted to regain our country's freedom. The communists did not let this pass without response: police attacks, bans, wiretaps, infiltration by state agents, threats and blackmail. But we persevered, and we won. Soviets out, communists down. We thought we had finally got what we wanted, but we were wrong: under the dictatorship, liberals and conservatives entered into an anti-communist pact, but at the first subsequent opportunity the liberals sided with the communists. It turned out that in fact they were natural allies.[48]

Today, although free from the oppression of the Soviet Union, Hungarians have continued to struggle against Communism's legacy that has influenced government and leadership throughout Europe. They must continue to fight to ensure that their formal independence and decision-making power, now in the days of extensive globalization, international organizations, and arrogant 'woke' globalists, will remain firmly in their own hands.

---

[48] Visegrad Post (2022, May 24). Viktor Orbán's Speech at the CPAC on 19 May 2022. *Visegrad Post.* https://visegradpost.com/en/2022/05/24/viktor-orbans-speech-at-the-cpac-on-19-may-2022/

Chapter 10

A WARNING TO THE WEST: OUR NEW COLD WAR

Woe to those who call evil good, and good evil; who substitute darkness for light and light for darkness; who substitute bitter for sweet and sweet for bitter.

—Isaiah 5:20 NASB

Introduction:
Refusing To Go 'Woke'

The West may have defeated the Russians in the Cold War in terms of territorial expansion, but they did not win the Cold War of ideology. Instead, they perpetuated and enabled the spread of communism—and at the end of World War II, they gave the Communists the people, the land, and the power to reach this goal.

Recently on a trip to Budapest, I was startled by the number of Hungarians who told me (with confused looks on their faces) that the rhetoric currently coming out of the United States reminds them of their own "Soviet days." We should pay attention—our government, corporations, and our media and political elites find it way too easy to oppress freedom of thought and speech, to 'cancel' those who disagree with their ideological or political agenda, and to use regular deception, 'lawfare' and audacious lies to take away people's livelihoods and reputation.[1]

Political analyst and syndicated columnist Diana West observes

> the ideological war abroad, or more accurately, the anti-ideological war abroad ... was lost on all fronts in the battlespace at home: in the academy, in the media, in the

[1] Bradley-Farrell, Shea (2023, March 21). An American Perspective: Hungary's Fight for Sovereignty in the Russia-Ukraine War. Hungarian Conservative, Budapest. https://www.hungarianconservative.com/articles/opinion/american_perspective_bradley_farrell_hungary_orban_sovereignty_will_of_the_people/

> popular culture, in the arts, and in the zeitgeist up and down Main Street and even, or perhaps especially, along capitalism's main thoroughfare, Wall Street. It was as if we opposed an enemy Over There without noticing that great chunks of his ideology had taken root, flourished, and borne collectivist and thus anti-American fruit Over Here.[2]

The harvest of this anti-American fruit is evident today. A healthy fear of authoritarianism and utter rejection of communistic behavior have waned in the Western world.

> Forced obedience and conformity, a basic characteristic of Marxist communism, is showing up in Western governments, education, and social structures. At the same time, political and academic elites promote self-loathing of national sentiment, history, and the foundations of Western civilization. Do our citizens even realize it? And how long will we remain free?[3]

The 'progressivism' sweeping the Western World and denying our traditions seems to seek change for change's sake—not in order to arrive at a better place, and not for the progress of society. It is not based on ideas or concepts that are rooted and

---

[2] West, Diana. p. 35.

[3] Bradley-Farrell, Shea (2023, May 3). Nationalism and Freedom: 30 years After the Fall of the Berlin Wall. *The European Conservative*. https://europeanconservative.com/articles/commentary/nationalism-and-freedom-thirty-years-after-the-fall-of-the-berlin-wall/

grounded in sound wisdom. On the contrary, in many issues—open borders, surgical 'transitioning', abortion on demand, promoting racial divisiveness, embracing lawlessness, suppressing free speech, abhorring religiosity, and allowing the degradation of cities—'progressivism' actually seems to advocate for the destruction of society, and with it national pride and security. Many 'progressives', unable to show respect for the traditional values and identities that make them uncomfortable, often come across as angry and belligerent, petulant children. 'Progressivism' is not progressive at all.

Any nation, like Hungary or the United States, that continues to maintain Judeo-Christian values, with a respect for justice, equality, and rule of law, will sustain and preserve itself for future generations. But a nation that abandons the bedrock of Western values destroys itself from the inside and cannot stand.

During Nazi and Soviet occupation, Hungarians longingly dreamt of the life of freedom found in the Western world—they could not wait to be a part of it. Hungarians looked to the U.S. and to President Ronald Reagan's leadership as an example of a nation where family, freedom, and religious belief could flourish. At CPAC Hungary 2022, the first European-held CPAC, Prime Minister Orbán addressed his "American friends":

> I clearly remember well how we envied you back then: we envied your culture of democratic debate; the freedom in which you arranged public affairs in America; we envied your President Reagan for his charisma, his drive, his wit and his policies—and, of course, we rooted for him. All we had were the grey-suited communist functionaries and their political Newspeak, a stifling atmosphere and hopelessness.[4]

But Hungarians today see a United States that is now immersed in the 'woke' cultural Marxism that they fought so hard to destroy in their own country. According to Hungarians, it is the West that has left *them*, and *not* the other way around, as portrayed by European and American propaganda.

We must heed the words of Cardinal József Mindszenty, who fought against both fascism and Communism, spending years of his life in prison. On Christmas Day 1971, Cardinal Mindszenty reminded the world: "What I have previously condemned as evil and destructive, still is; and I will always be faithful to the principles which are necessary for the survival of Hungary and the freedom of its people."[5]

And that is the point—just because centuries have passed since our U.S. Constitution was formed, and decades have passed since the main whole of American and European societies revered the family unit and embraced traditional values—oppositional forces have not been eradicated. What was evil and destructive then, still is. And we must be faithful to the principles of truth.

[4] Visegrad Post (2002, May 24). Viktor Orbán's Speech at the CPAC on 19 May 2022. https://visegradpost.com/en/2022/05/24/viktor-orbans-speech-at-the-cpac-on-19-may-2022/

[5] Schlafly.

Transformation of the West: The New Cold War

The Comintern, according to the U.S. Library of Congress, was established in March 1919, two years after the Bolshevik Revolution to instigate a *world* revolution, and formally lasted until 1943. Its existence has been firmly denied, but today we see the footprint of its ideology spread throughout Europe and the United States.

Remember the warning of the Industrial College of the (U.S.) Armed Forces in 1961? "The Sino-Soviet bloc, aiming to defeat the West with minimum cost to itself, and bidding to dominate the world, has refined Sun Tzu's simple prescriptions into a fine art," a tireless chipping away at belief, identity, and the will to resist.[6] Similarly, there is a New Cold War being fought today in the Western world between the advocates of *real* freedom and democracy against the proponents of a controlling, communistic ideology.

Reagan's last bastion for freedom, the United States, "with no other source of power except the sovereign people,"[7] is led by the Biden administration and its 'state-controlled' media that rejects most American constitutional principles and the rule of

6 Sanders, Ralph & Brown Fred R. (Eds.). p. 1.

7 Reagan, Ronald (1964, October 27). A Time for Choosing Speech. *Ronald Reagan Presidential Library & Museum.* https://www.reaganlibrary.gov/reagans/ronald-reagan/time-choosing-speech-october-27-1964#:~:text=If%20we%20lose%20freedom%20here,of%20man%27s%20relation%20to%20man.

law, applying leftist illiberal ideologies—in gender, family, law, and civil liberties—as the only *one truth*.

In the U.S., civil liberties are trampled under vaccine mandates and selective FBI raids. Former U.S. President Donald J. Trump has been indicted *four times* in four and a half months, twice by U.S. President Joe Biden's Department of Justice, and twice by Democrat professional political operatives acting as state officials. Many Republican leaders (and a few Democrats) have described his treatment as flagrant election interference reminiscent of the persecution of political opponents in dictatorial regimes.

While Trump is tirelessly hounded over charges that stretch credibility, Biden, in spite of suspicious material evidence, remains beyond the reach of law. Each Trump indictment was made public immediately following new evidence in the Hunter Biden-Joe Biden financial scandals, as if to distract the public from the Bidens' criminal activities. In each indictment, according to unbiased legal analysis (not on mainstream media) such as that of well-known Democrat Alan Dershowitz, the rule of law has not been applied and each case promises to be overturned.

Attorney General Merrick Garland's willingness to label American parents as 'domestic terrorists' and to use the FBI for raiding the homes of law-abiding citizens is reminiscent of authoritarian-style 'justice'. The U.S. government has infiltrated private citizens on Facebook and Twitter to suppress freedom of speech and election results. January 6th protestors remain in jail for exercising their First Amendment right to dispute questionable and irregular election results. Yet BLM, Antifa, and repeat offense criminals ransack our cities and go unpunished. This is not progressive, it is insanity.

To the north of the U.S., Canada's Justin Trudeau rewrites history (reminding us of the Soviets) by claiming his vaccine mandates, that the majority of Canadians despised, were only "incentives" and "protections,"[8] a statement that makes his public admiration of the Chinese Communist Party's dictatorship more understandable. Across the Atlantic, European governments routinely label social and religious differences as "hate speech" and "discrimination," using legal force to control what people are allowed to say and do. In Europe and across the world, COVID-19 lockdowns smacked of totalitarianism.

> The European Union applies sanctions to punish sovereign nations like Hungary that promote traditional marriage, family roles, and parental rights. The U.S. ambassador to Hungary shuns diplomacy and antagonizes Hungary for this stance, and for protecting Hungarian prosperity and promoting peace to end the war in Ukraine. In many countries and in many ways, national sovereignty has been handed over to the EU, and member states have lost control over borders, economies, and communities.[9]

In 1959, Stefan T. Possony, international security strategist, warned about the insidious attack of communist ideology and its "paralysis" of Western society. In a strategy lesson republished by the U.S. Department of Defense, Possony wrote:

---

[8] Hays, Gabriel (2023, April 25). Justin Trudeau Accused of Rewriting History by Claiming He Never Forced Anyone to Get Vaccinated. *Fox News*. https://www.foxnews.com/media/justin-trudeau-accused-rewriting-history-claiming-never-forced-anyone-get-vaccinated

[9] Bradley-Farrell, Shea (2023, May 3).

> We would be foolish to ignore that the Communists have made great strides in the art of psychological manipulation. The West does not yet understand the nature of the psychological attack that has been launched. It does not comprehend the causes of its paralysis, and often does not even notice that its freedom to act has been impeded. Once the Free World will assess the conflict in its psychological dimension, the course of history will be reversed.[10]

The world is still waiting for this to happen. If we continue to wait, it will be too late.

Reagan's often-used speech bears repeating: "If we lose freedom here, there's no place to escape to. This is the last stand on earth. And this idea that government is beholden to the people, that it has no other source of power except the sovereign people, is still the newest and the most unique idea in all the long history of man's relation to man."[11]

Let's learn from the experiences of Hungary and its forty-seven years of darkness – forty-seven years yearning for freedom, yearning for the absence of fear in daily life, watching and longing to be like the countries of the "Free World." We have to learn and to act, before we no longer have what makes our lives worth living.

---

[10] Possony, Stefan T. (1959). p. 59.

[11] Reagan.

A Love Affair With Communism

Lies. Deception. Mind Control. This is what communistic ideology—Communist psychological warfare—is all about. With a large and deadly dose of *shame*, damning, guilt, and fear thrown in, people with the best intentions, who believe the best of mankind, are often confused and vulnerable. Shame and guilt are served up by those who want to manipulate and control, as they carefully deflect from the truth of who they really are.

Calling the 'progressive' Left's agenda 'communist' will most likely get you labeled as an extremist or conspiracy theorist. I judiciously avoided such labels for many years, content to stay out of the line of fire, believing that as an American my right to believe in God, family, country, and other traditional values could never be taken away. But we are slowly watching powerful progressive forces in our government, media, and society demand that we adhere to their version of truth, or become the targets of anger and shame, and risk losing livelihood, rights, and reputation if we don't. Staying silent just does not help. The many blatant similarities with Communism's totalitarianism cannot be ignored.

The "Specific Goals of the Communist Effort,"[12] outlined by Possany (see also Chapter 9), are shockingly like reading a description of current global social and political activities throughout the West. There is not one point, out of the eleven, that does not elucidate conditions applicable to descriptions of

[12] Sanders, Ralph & Brown, Fred R. (Eds.). p. 58.

the European Union and the United States, as currently run by a communistic political and media elite.[13] "Communist psychological warfare aims at the following objectives," the list begins. The goals are quoted in full:

> 1. The creation of a psychologically strong, obedient, disciplined, steadfast, and iron-willed leadership core which thinks and behaves in a certain way, in that way only, and in that way for a long time regardless of obstacles.

The first reflects the U.S. administration's 'deep state' reach, especially exemplified in the heavily George Soros-influenced State Department. It is also a description of the extensive bureaucratic and international organization network of the European Union: 'woke', iron-willed, and tolerating little compromise.

> 2. Creation of a larger group of oriented propagandists who spread Communist notions and are instrumental in creating and maintaining a suitable frame of reference imposed upon non-Communists.

The second is a description of the liberal Left's obedient and well-funded network of media, and also of their NGOs. Journalism and news reporting has become a thing of the past. In their place, media outlets develop narratives where conser-

[13] *Ibid.*

vatives are viewed as discriminatory; conspiracy theorists; guilty of hate speech; anti-semetic; etc., to shame the public into accepting leftist propaganda to make them more pliable to what their elitist leaders tell them.

> 3. The creation in both groups of a burning sense of hatred.

The third: Today, we often see anger and vitriol spewed at people who believe in traditional values. 'MAGA' Americans have been labeled "domestic terrorists" by their president, Joe Biden. Parents protecting kids from gender theories are labeled as hate mongers. Where is the debate, the discussion, the compromise?

> 4. Docility, discipline, and controllability of subject populations which must be commanded by the unopposed will of the party leadership.

The fourth issues the mandate of compliance. A friend told me recently that she would like to vote for Trump in 2024 and that she does not believe he has committed the crimes for which he's been indicted, but that for the sake of order and 'peace', he should just bow out of the election. Exactly what the 'party leadership' is trying to accomplish—docility and controllability.

> 5. The creation, in the ruling, upper, and intellectual classes of non-Communist societies, of frustration, confusion, pessimism, guilt, fear, defeatism, hopelessness, and neurosis, of lack of will, in essence the psychological destruction of anti-Communist leadership.

Whether or not you are a fan of Trump or Orbán, you must recognize the continual and strategic psychological attacks trying to destroy both them and their followers. In accord with the fifth goal of Communism, both leaders are labeled extremists and given monster-like attributes in the media that defy everyday common logic. Orbán and his country are repeatedly financially sanctioned and denigrated; Trump in particular (and as a former president) has endured relentless attacks in the form of legal indictments—four of them. When will Trump, Orbán, and their supporters feel enough hopelessness to just give up?

> 6. The splitting of a society into many competing and mutually hostile groups and the sapping of the spirit of loyalty, community, mutual helpfulness, positive expectation, and willingness to take risks and to act.

It may have been Barack Obama who first began to really divide America along the racial lines, but the progressives today have taken it to a new and destructive level. We find the sixth goal featured in the false teachings of 'Critical Race Theory', meant to shame Americans (and other westerners) into disloyalty to their origins and their country, and create racially tense communities, while denying the fact that we are all Americans, joined together into the greatest nation on earth.

> 7. The creation and stimulation of an all-pervading sense of fear and anxiety, whether it be fastened onto the dangers of nuclear war, or physical terror, or professional, social, and human ruin.

The seventh goal of the communist effort is conspicuous in the COVID-19 global pandemic. Those in leadership, often un-

elected officials, often used the pandemic to gain more power by systematically spreading fear, social exclusion and isolation, and false narratives. They deplatformed, 'canceled', and otherwise silenced those who dared challenge the official messaging.

> 8. The capture of the time dimension ... an expectation of cataclysm and no-progress under capitalism is established and paired with affirmed expectation that the future belongs to communism.

The eighth goal is evident in 'climate change', which acts like the cataclysmic bogeyman, invoked since Obama but fully sensationalized under the Biden administration.[14] *Now, it is officially branded an "existential threat" requiring sweeping, near-economic-suicide-levels of carbon cuts, making a mockery of the U.S. to the rest of the G-20 nations who make hollow, vague pledges towards "encouraging clean energy targets."*[15] *Furthermore, the Biden administration is committed to central economic planning and federal government mandates controlling all sectors of the economy including energy, transportation and commerce.*

> 9. The promise of relief from all troubles by means of an infallible as well as inevitable solution.[16]

---

[14] The White House (2021, January 21). National Climate Task Force. Washington DC. https://www.whitehouse.gov/climate/

[15] Shankleman, Jess (2023, September 7). World Leaders Head for Another Climate Cop-Out. *Bloomberg*, https://www.bloomberg.com/news/newsletters/2023-09-07/g-20-leaders-head-for-another-climate-cop-out

[16] Sanders, Ralph & Brown, Fred R. (Eds.). p. 58.

We have heard goal number nine in many forms: universal healthcare; free college education; university debt cancellation; social welfare of all types. Most recently, in 2021, government-mandated and supposedly infallible vaccines were going to save the world—so long as everyone 'did their part' and took the vaccine, whether they wanted to or not.

> 10. The semantic domination of intellectual, emotional, and sociopolitical life as well as the semantic control of all political life.[17]

There is no doubt that progressive control of language manifests the spirit of the tenth goal. We see a deliberate intent to use language to obfuscate meaning and disarm the general public. Words like 'gender' and 'sex' have been redefined, and progressive lawmakers and activists push to redefine them in law. Access to abortion is cloaked in terms like "sexual reproductive health and rights" or "healthcare"; "Bidenomics" is created to cover up historical inflation and debt in the U.S.; "End-of-life decision-making" is code for suicide.

> 11. The weakening and destruction of national consciences in the Free World and the inculcation of bad conscience about firm opposition to communism and the ideals usurped and distorted by it.[18]

[17] *Ibid.*
[18] *Ibid.*

Number eleven attempts to divest society of a national sense of purpose and meaning. Through shaming, labeling, canceling, and language distortion, progressives attempt to control the will of the people. These progressive tools destroy national pride and traditional values. Political and academic elites promote a self-loathing of national sentiment, history, and the foundations of Western civilization.

How did we get here? How, after fighting the Soviets in the Cold War, did we lose the Cold War of Ideology?

Aspects of Bolshevism from the very early 1900s became integrated into American society: legalized abortion-on-demand trumpeted as healthcare;[19] diminishment of parental rights and "the elevation of children's rights to the detriment of parental authority;"[20] the liberalization of marriage and divorce that led to the ultimate "withering away of the family."[21]

Even before the Soviet occupation of Eastern Europe, the Frankfurt School, a German educational institute that espoused Marxist philosophy, was relocated to the United States. Founded in 1923, the Frankfurt School, or Institute for Social Research, was dedicated to the study of socialism and labor; it was eventually driven out of Frankfurt, Germany, with the rise of the

---

[19] Rivkin-Fish, Michelle, Ph.D. (2017). Legacies of 1917 in Contemporary Russian Public Health: Addiction, HIV, and Abortion. *American Journal of Public Health*, 107(11), 1731–1735. https://doi.org/10.2105/AJPH.2017.304064 https://www.ncbi.nlm.nih.gov/pmc/articles/PMC5637678/

[20] West. p. 35.

[21] The Atlantic Report on the World Today (1952, February). The Soviet Family. *The Atlantic* https://www.theatlantic.com/magazine/archive/1952/02/the-soviet-family/640279/

Nazis in 1933 and found a new home at Columbia University in New York City.

Two of the principal philosophical products of the Frankfurt School were "political correctness" and critical theory. Critical theory—such as Critical Race Theory or Critical Gender Theory—is a way to deconstruct all the foundations and tenets of Western civilization with the goal of advancing Marxist ideology. The school greatly influenced the intellectual movements in the United States in the early 1900s, especially the New School for Social Research in New York City, founded by a group of 'progressive intellectuals' which promoted organized labor and Soviet-style thinking and objectives.

Some of the intellectuals of the Frankfurt School were also FDR's advisors and consultants, and quite a few were employed by General William "Wild Bill" Donovan in the U.S. Office of Strategic Services (OSS), the organization that would eventually become the CIA. Franz Neumann, chief of the OSS Central European Section of the Research Branch, was one—a Marxist theorist who also happened to be a Russian spy passing secret U.S. documents to the Soviets. Neumann's close friend Herbert Marcuse—a German-born Marxist and cofounder of the Frankfurt School—was another. Marcuse analyzed top secret American intelligence for the OSS and had close ties to the Communist party in Germany.[22]

Broken down into the most simplistic terms, the Soviet infiltration of FDR's administration and their denial of the truth of the Katyn Massacre; the blind eye the West gave at Yalta to Soviet occupation in Eastern Europe and the Hitler-Stalin pact; permission for the Frankfurt school to spread and thrive—all (among many others) are elements that contributed to the spread of communist ideology resulting in the progressively destructive policies of the West today.

Opposite Sides of the Same Coin: United by Socialism

Balint Vazsyoni (1936-2003), the Hungarian-American polymath, historian, and concert pianist, wrote that communism and fascism had the same philosophical roots.[23] He personally experienced the Nazi occupation of Hungary in 1944 as well as the rule of the Red Army of the Soviet Union and the Hungarian Communists. He knew and experienced the socialism at the heart of both philosophies, writing in 1998: "But all my experiences confirmed the perception that socialism in all its forms placed unlimited power in the hands of persons who were contemptuous of other humans, and who's basest instincts were unleashed in the process."[24] And this insight is a very important point to our discussion.

First, let us take a moment to be precise about Fascism and Communism:

- Fascism is based on the idea of a corporatist state, where different sectors of the economy, such as industry, agriculture, and labor, are organized into corporations that represent their own interests and collaborate with the government, at the imposed will of the government. This relationship is supposed to create a harmonious and efficient society that avoids class con-

[22] West, p. 287.
[23] Vazsonyi, p. 14.
[24] *Ibid.*, p. 10.

flict and promotes national unity. Fascism believes that the state is the highest expression of the collective will of the people, and that individual rights and freedoms are subordinate to the state's interests. Fascism advocates for a totalitarian system that controls all aspects of political, social, and cultural life.[25]

- Communist ideology aims to create a classless, egalitarian, and stateless society. It is based on the theories of Karl Marx and Friedrich Engels, who criticized capitalism for creating inequality and exploiting workers. Communists believe that the means of production, distribution, and exchange should be owned and controlled by the workers, which actually means these are owned and controlled by the state, and that wealth should be distributed according to the needs of each individual. Communism rejects religion, private property, and individual rights, believing these to be sources of oppression. Communism also advocates for a totalitarian system that controls all aspects of political, social, and cultural life.[26]

Key foundational similarities between Communism and Fascism are as follows:

[25] Soucy, R. (2023, August 25). Fascism. Encyclopedia Britannica. https://www.britannica.com/topic/fascism

[26] Ball, T. and Dagger, Richard (2023, August 9). Communism. Encyclopedia Britannica. https://www.britannica.com/topic/communism

- Both arose from social and economic crises caused by war and the Industrial Revolution.
- Both aim to create a 'new world order' based on their ideology and eliminate any alternative systems.
- Both are radical ideologies that require dictatorial control.
- Both use violence, terror, aggressive law enforcement tactics, and propaganda to suppress any opposition or dissent.
- Both engage in mass killings and genocide against all people they consider enemies or undesirables.
- At their root, and in practice, both deny a reverence for human dignity.

Nazism and Communism are both based on control and dictatorship, and though they are different systems, they are both based absolutely on socialism. The very term 'NAZI' is shorthand for the acronym (NSDAP) of the National Socialist German Workers' Party, though there is a concerted effort by contemporary advocates of socialism to disconnect the word "socialist" from the (literal) heart of the term. In 1947 Montgomery noted: "In reality, Hitlerism was mobocracy, it was national socialism, or the German brand of Stalinism."[27]

In Budapest, Vazsonyi's experience was that both the National Socialists (Nazis) and the Soviets began "to classify people's political attitudes," both using socialism "as a pretext for just

[27] Montgomery, pp. 89-90.

about anything—for the confiscation of people's belongings, for determining what could and could not be taught in the schools, for pronouncing what did or did not happen—and what should have happened—in the course of history."[28] And I know what Vazsonyi says is true. I have been in the basement of 60 Andrássy Road, House of Terror, and seen the cells, interrogation, and torture rooms used by Nazis and Communists alike.

György Gábori, of Hungarian Jewish descent, was one of many Hungarians who were held prisoner in both a Nazi concentration camp, and later, a Communist labor camp. With first-hand experience of the methods and cruelty of both extreme ideologies, Gábori concluded, "that apart from the uniforms, there was no real difference between the two totalitarian systems."[29] According to a report from the National Remembrance Project in Hungary, Gábori

> cherished no false illusions about socialism. This often brought him into conflict with his closest friends, but he always held fast to his convictions, as his words to his mentor, Pál Justus, make clear: "What we have gone through, my good Pál," he said, "is socialism itself, and in its most typical form. If I were to remain a socialist, it would mean kissing the hands of those who tortured me."

---

[28] Vazsonyi, p. 14.

[29] Czókos, Gergely; Kiss, Réka; Máthe, Áron; Szalai, Zoltán (Eds.). (2021). Heroes Among Us. 50 True Stories of Brave Hungarians in the 20th Century (Thomas Cooper, Trans.). Committee of National Remembrance. Open Books Publish, Budapest.

In our discussion, it is also important to address the 'secular religion' of both National Socialism and Communism. Socialism largely rejects traditional religion as the "opiate of the masses" and seeks to design its own liturgies and hagiographies in order to enshrine the ruling elite as authorities of divinity, and as a method of control. The House of Terror in Budapest describes it this way:

> Both Nazism—promoting racial war—and Communism—advocating class-war—regarded religion as their enemy. Whilst the totalitarian dictatorships persecuted and murdered their victims based on collective criteria, religion looks upon sin and practices forgiveness on the basis of individual responsibility. Both the Nazis and the communists replaced God with their own leaders, whom they presented as infallible and omniscient. They swore allegiance to the leader, went into battle in his name, and surrounded his person with rituals befitting an idol. They proclaimed that they required men of a "new type" in order to create a "new world," a special "heaven on earth." They persecuted religion, the faithful and the churches, because ethico-religious teaching was diametrically opposed to the Nazi's and communists' ideologies, which they wanted to elevate to the rank of creeds.[30]

Whatever the brand of socialism—national socialism or communism—both resulted in dictatorial control, violence, oppression, terror, and death. Like Fascism, Communism also sup-

[30] Schmidt, Mária (Ed.). (2019). p. 48.

ported a totalitarian system that suppressed any opposition or dissent, but it claimed to do so in the name of the proletariat or the working class, rather than in the nation or the leader—but this is a distinction without a difference. Pay very close attention to Ambassador Montgomery's explanation in 1947:

> Russian communism is practically the same system as German national socialism. As they used to say in Budapest, the only difference between Nazism and Bolshevism is that it is colder in Russia. Both envisioned world conquest and were not only perfectly ruthless, but used the same methods. Americans, being farther from Russia and more or less blinded by their hatred of Hitlerism, did not share this point of view with Europeans. This accounts for the fact that we did not make greater efforts to prevent pan-Slavism from succeeding pan-Germanism. The people of Central and Eastern Europe know only too well that if the Germans were locusts, the Russians were super-locusts, impoverished by a planned economy which had put guns before butter not since 1933, but since 1917.[31]

It is strange that over the past century, American leftists have decried Fascism, and at the same time felt very comfortable with Communism. FDR supported anti-fascist resistance or guerrilla groups operating against the Nazis, but not anti-communist groups. A blind eye was turned to the Soviet's oppression in

[31] Montgomery, p. 20.

Eastern Europe and their outright lie about democracy and free elections at the Yalta conference agreement. Nazis were put on trial at Nuremberg, and the Soviets showed up to judge them, although the Soviets also started WWII by invading Poland in collaboration with Hitler, and also committed atrocious war crimes.

And this, in large part, has contributed to the rise of communistic ideology in America. American media and intellectuals have refused to look upon the socialism that created communist societies—and their victims—the same way they look upon Nazi Germany and its victims. They have a willful blindness to a campaign of deception and manipulation. History be damned.

Mária Schmidt describes the Western efforts to rehabilitate the reputation of socialism's consequences when the true nature of the Soviet Gulags were revealed to the world: "When Solzhenitsyn's Gulag Archipelago was published in 1974, the way the West talked about Communism changed ... [but] Soviet operatives ... deployed a widespread campaign to discredit the writer ... joined by those Western left-liberal fellow traveller intellectuals ready to be mobilized."[32]

America's founding principles were established in our Constitution and Bill of Rights, with individual liberties endowed by our Creator, the rule of law, and freedom of speech among the most important. But some American political operatives have sought to invent new 'rights' to correct and improve what they see as America's failures. We now suffer under fundamental, socialist techniques meant to exert control over American soci-

---

[32] Schmidt, Mária (2021). p. 33.

ety—concepts like 'social justice' (a term Hitler used, a fact but that has been "air-brushed" out of history for American sensibilities);[33] group privileges based on race or boutique concepts of gender ideology; societal deconstruction; militant equity; and critical theory have all become features on the contemporary American political and social landscape.

Since 1991 and the supposed end of the Cold War, it has not been fashionable to use the proper label, 'Communism' to describe the end-state of socialism in its fullest expression of 'social justice'. This communism may not currently be the communism of the Soviet Gulag or the Chinese Laogai camps—but it is a form of justice based on controlling political agenda, and not objective standards. Unfortunately, many Americans find it convenient or attractive, and are drawn to its insidious appeal despite the documented history of brutality and cataclysm that has resulted from its implementation. Stefan T. Possony warned in 1959 against the draw of Communism's so-called system of social justice:

> Whenever the Communists succeed in convincing people that they are a sort of incarnation of humanity's social conscience and that they are history's anointed arbiters of any action undertaken by non-Communists, a person will tend to be apologetic about any doubts he harbors concerning communism. ...

---

[33] *Ibid.*, p. 103.

The purpose is to inculcate into the Free World guilt feelings about resistance to communism and at the same time immunize the 'Soviet peoples' with a sort of ideological vaccination against any notion that communist wars or even aggressions may be something less than emanations of an exalted sense of justice. The Free World has been infected to some degree by bad conscience and guilt feelings. Hence, partly at least, the often surprising paralysis of democratic will.[34]

Scruton noted that the reality of this fraud, committed in the name of 'socialism', initiated his decades-long connection with the underground networks in Poland, Czechoslovakia and Hungary. He said he quickly "learned to see socialism in another way—not as a dream of idealists, but as a real system of government imposed from above and maintained by force. I awoke to the fraud that had been committed in socialism's name, and felt an immediate obligation to do something about it."[35]

And this is the reality—Communism, like Fascism, is based on socialism, and represents a totalitarian ideology seeking to control all aspects of society, and to eliminate its opposition.

34 *Ibid.*, p. 52.
35 *Ibid.*, p. 52.

Awake to the Reality!

As we continue to fight the infiltration of Marxist ideology in the West and push against the strategies of communist psychological warfare, the full impact of our acceptance of Communism, or our neglect and complacency, has never been fully appreciated.

> Communist penetration existed—the historical record amply and redundantly confirms this—but endless wrangling even today wards off a comprehensive reckoning of the impact of that penetration.[36]

We are, sadly, experiencing the tragic and destructive impact today.

Why have we continued to allow Marxist principles to invade our Western institutions and our thinking? We have given universities, the media, and the political Western elites the power over our traditions and our values. Is the West about to repeat our version of Eastern Europe's horrid history? If so, it will be one from which the cost cannot be underestimated. Sir Roger Scruton wrote with honesty,

> I had not troubled myself to imagine, during those years of Thatcher's rise, what would happen to our still secure and comfortable world, were all basic freedoms to be taken away. I was cocooned in the false security of an

[36] West, p. 39.

> introspective island, with no knowledge of the realm of fear and negation that the communists had installed just a little way to the east of us. A visit to Poland and Czechoslovakia in 1979 awoke me to the reality. I encountered first-hand the thing that Orwell perceived when fighting alongside the communists in the Spanish Civil War and which he expressed in telling images in Nineteen Eighty-Four. I saw the translation into fact of the fictions that swam in the brains of my Marxist colleagues.[37]

We must awake to our present reality! In many respects, in our New Cold War against Communist ideology, we fight the philosophical and ideological descendants of the Communists who reinvented themselves in Eastern Europe after the fall of Communism. Their Marxism was handed down, infiltrating international organizations like the European Union, the United Nations, and the World Health Organization (WHO). For example, Director-General Adhanom Ghebreyesus Tedros, the head of WHO, has been accused of being one of the nine executive members of the TPLF, or the Tigray People's Liberation Front, a historically Marxist-Leninist revolutionary party. In addition, there is strong evidence to suggest that the Chinese Communist Party (CCP) helped get him elected.

Schmidt wrote that "as Roger Scruton sees it, (*Prospect* magazine, 15 July 2016), Eurocrats increasingly resemble Bolsheviks in having created a form of government which can only move forward—even on a road leading to a precipice."[38] It seems that

[37] Scruton, Roger (2014). p. 10.

as 'progressives' move forward, they have deconstructed the truth so much that they call for the normalization of pedophilia and of the mutilation of children. Through constant repetition of calling evil good, and good evil, they have worn society down and have begun to change our beliefs. They present darkness as light and light as darkness (Isaiah 5:20).

It bears repeating that when the façade of Communism slipped, the Soviet Union lost its "monopoly over ideology," leading, as Mária Schmidt points out, to their ultimate demise:

> Countries under their occupation reconquered their national pasts and started working to take back control over their national histories, which amounted to depriving Communists of their monopoly over ideology ... General Secretary Mikhail Gorbachev declared at last that, "We have given up the claim to possess the monopoly of truth."[39]

It is time for traditionalists and conservatives to no longer only be on the defense, but on the offense. We must speak and demand that the truth be upheld, and take back ideology, values, and the future, in the name of truth.

---

[38] Schmidt, Mária (2018). Language and Liberty. (Békés, Márton, ed.) (Betlen, J. and Bottyán, G., Trans.) Director General of the Public Endowment. p. 168.
[39] Schmidt, Mária (2021). p. 25.

Chapter 11

THE BIG THREE: LGBT, THE RUSSIA-UKRAINE WAR, AND ILLEGAL IMMIGRATION

We commit ourselves to promoting and safeguarding our heritage, our unique language, Hungarian culture and the languages and cultures of national minorities living in Hungary, along with all man-made and natural assets of the Carpathian Basin. We bear responsibility for our descendants and therefore we shall protect the living conditions of future generations by making prudent use of our material, intellectual and natural resources.

—The Fundamental Law of Hungary

Introduction: Protecting the Future

Despite the 'progressive' trend, Hungarians have not forgotten the value of their recently acquired freedom or their reclaimed national identity. Their constitution, established after the Soviet occupation, states: "We hold that the protection of our identity rooted in our historic constitution is a fundamental obligation of the State."[1]

Hungary's refusal to embrace a far-Left liberal social agenda has angered both the Biden administration, the EU, and their media elite, none of which have allowed truth, justice, or common sense to shape their behavior toward an ally member state of the EU and NATO. There are three main claims against Hungary: Hungary's position on child protection, illegal immigration, and the ongoing Russia-Ukraine War. As Orbán said in a 2023 speech in Transylvania: "If one is involved in European politics, as I am, then today 'Western values' mean three things: migration, LGBTQ, and war."

[1] Hungarian National Parliament (2011, April 25). The Fundamental Law of Hungary. National Avowal. p. 2. https://www.parlament.hu/documents/125505/138409/Fundamental+law/73811993-c377-428d-9808-ee03d6fb8178

LGBT:
The Child Protection Law and the EU Backlash

In June 2021, Hungary passed several amendments to previous legislation that protects the right of children to 'self-identify' with their *birth sex* and prohibit anyone from making content accessible to minors that is pornographic, overtly sexual, or promotes or portrays transgender ideology or homosexuality (this means rating media content that does not align with the amendment as "not appropriate for audiences under the age of eighteen").[2]

In addition, the amendments prohibit teaching gender theory in schools to minors and the use of materials that promote transitioning procedures such as 'gender reassignment' surgeries and hormone blocker therapies.[3] The law came as a result of Hungary's desire to protect children from the radical transgender movement and the leftist liberal oversexualization of children. Unlike some Western countries such as the U.S. and Canada, Hungary is not willing to allow minors to make life-altering decisions at a young age; in addition, Hungarians believe issues of sexuality are the sole right of parents to address.

---

[2] Hungarian National Parliament (2021, June 23). Act LXXIX, On taking more severe action against pedophile offenders and amending certain Acts for the protection of children. https://web.archive.org/web/20220103092634/https://njt.hu/translation/J2021T0079P_00000000_FIN.PDF

[3] Losonczi, Márton (2023, April 14). France, Germany Join EU In Effort to Strike Down Child Protection Law in Hungary. *Hungarian Conservative*, Budapest. https://www.hungarianconservative.com/articles/current/france_germany_join_eu_against_child_protection_law_hungary_karleskind_zoltan_kovacs/

The Child Protection Law also increased punitive measures against people who commit sex crimes against children and reinforced a commitment to "protect the institutions of family and marriage ... [and] the relationship between parents and children, in which the mother is a woman and the father is a man."[4]

The law was met with dismay and anger by the woke leftists of the EU who went to the extreme to spin Hungary's law as 'anti-LGBT'. Prime Minister Orbán's spokesman Zoltán Kovács plainly addressed the EU's intellectually-challenged, short-sighted (but purposeful) 'hate' propaganda saying: "Being pro-children and pro-family does not mean we're anti-gay."[5] In fact, the law does nothing to restrict or discriminate against LGBTQ+ adults.

Regardless, since then, Western politicians and their mainstream media have launched vicious attacks against Hungary, its laws, and the Orbán administration. But Prime Minister Orbán is settled on this position: "It is fixed in our constitutions that the family is a sacred institution; you cannot change it as you wish. Regardless of religious sentiments in society, this is still a very strong value."[6]

The Child Protection Law was clearly supported by Hungarians. But less than a year later, Hungarians—almost four million—voted overwhelming 'yes' to a child protection referen-

---

[4] Hungarian National Parliament (2021, June 23).

[5] Kovács, Zoltán (2023, March 24). Child Protection Law: They just don't get it, do they? *About Hungary*, Budapest. https://abouthungary.hu/blog/child-protection-law-they-just-dont-get-it-do-they

[6] Pinto, Jaime N. (2022). Forged by History: The Hungarian Struggle for Nationhood. *The European Conservative*. Spring 2 (22). pp 30-37.

dum which included these points: 1. protecting children against the teaching of gender ideology or sexual orientation in schools without parental consent; 2. prohibiting the promotion of gender-reassignment treatment to minors; 3. restricting exposure of sexually explicit media content to minors; and 4. discontinuance of media content that shows gender changing procedures to minors.[7]

In July 2021, the EU announced legal action against both Hungary and Poland "for violations of fundamental rights of LGBTIQ people."[8] Why would they do this? Had Hungary committed a serious act necessitating sanctions for going against the rule of law? No—Hungary's violation was for banning "access to content that portrays homosexuality for individuals under 18" and for requiring a disclaimer for a children's book that contained LGBTIQ content. It makes you wonder if the EU actually *hears* itself.

Under the treaties of the European Union, family and child protection laws are a matter of national competency[9] and not under Brussels' sphere of authority.[10] And as Judit Varga, at that time Hungary's Minister of Justice, said, Hungary's law is fully

---

[7] Kovács, Zoltán (2023, March 24).

[8] European Commission (2021, July 15). EU founding values: Commission starts legal action against Hungary and Poland for violations of fundamental rights of LGBTIQ people. Brussels. https://ec.europa.eu/commission/presscorner/detail/en/ip_21_3668.

[9] Kovács, Zoltán (2023, April 8). 01/03 @JuditVarga_EU: We stand firm in our commitment to protect our children, despite pressure from the liberal press and corrupt @Europarl_EN. The Hungarian reasoning is fully in line with the Charter of Fundamental Rights of the EU. *X*. https://tinyurl.com/ytwp2u8j.

in line with the EU Charter of Fundamental Rights. The law was clearly a decision made by the sovereign state of Hungary and supported by Hungarians.[11]

In late April of 2022, just a few weeks after the Child Protection Law was confirmed by the vote of Hungarian people in the referendum, the European Commission (EC) notified Hungary and Poland that the EC had activated the 'conditionality clause' against them. The EC applied the regulation to 750 billion euros set aside for COVID-19 pandemic funds, based on conditions contradictory to their interpretation of the "rule of law."[12]

Just a couple of months later in July 2022, the European Commission referred Hungary to the European Court of Justice (ECJ) for allegedly violating internal market rules and the fundamental rights of individuals, and included references to the child protection law.[13] Fifteen governments have joined in with the European Parliament to officially back the punitive procedures.[14] The ECJ sided with the European Parliament (EP), supporting the EU as it continues to overstep its purview and make national decisions for sovereign nations.

---

[10] Kovács, Zoltán (2022, Feb 16). The EU Court of Justice today made a political decision based on Hungary's Child Protection Act. *About Hungary*, Budapest. https://abouthungary.hu/blog/the-eu-court-of-justice-today-made-a-political-decision-based-on-hungarys-child-protection-act.

[11] Kovács, Zoltán (2023, March 24).

[12] *The Economist* (2022, November 24). The EU is withholding aid to press Hungary to reform. https://www.economist.com/europe/2022/11/24/the-eu-is-withholding-aid-to-press-hungary-to-reform

[13] Kovács, Zoltán (2023, March 24).

[14] Losonczi, Márton (2023, April 14).

On September 15, 2022, the EP adopted a report which found that fundamental rights "have further deteriorated" due to the "deliberate and systematic efforts of the Hungarian government." The European Parliament declared that Hungary had undermined European values and could no longer be considered a full democracy, but "a constitutional system in which elections occur, but respect for democratic norms and standards is absent."[15]

Let's do a fact check. Free and fair elections occur; Hungarians vote for parliamentary members and thus the administration and laws that they want in their own sovereign nation. How then are democratic standards absent? The EU appears to be engaged in lawfare—using, twisting, ambiguously stretching, and applying law to promote its own agenda. The EU uses 'Rule of Law' as a guise to repress countries that do not line up with its

> aggressively secularist anti-Christian ideology. ... The Conditionality Clause endorsed by the ECJ decision in February 2022 and now attached to the post-pandemic fund has little to do with macroeconomic stabilization. On the contrary, there is compelling evidence that its primary purpose is to empower the EU Establishment to exert financial pressure on the fiscal and structural policies of socially conservative countries. The net effect is to impose de facto sanctions on these members, undermining their economies and increasing their depen-

---

[15] European Parliament (2022, September 15). Press Release: MEPs: Hungary can no longer be considered a full democracy. Strasbourg. https://www.europarl.europa.eu/news/en/press-room/20220909IPR40137/meps-hungary-can-no-longer-be-considered-a-full-democracy.

dence on, and vulnerability to pressures from, 'false' Europe. This represents a worrying weaponization of the EU's policies, which more properly should be directed towards the general good.[16]

On December 12, 2022, the EU froze 6.3 billion euros of cohesion funds due to Hungary. Cohesion funds are meant to bolster countries with smaller economies in the EU and these were earmarked by Hungary for "education for disadvantaged children, rail transport upgrades, access to broadband and aid for regions affected by coal plant closures."[17] The EC said that Hungary had yet to comply with the EU Charter of Fundamental Rights and cash would not be distributed until Hungary complied. Hungary must meet "an even tougher set of 17 conditions also linked to the judiciary and dealing with corruption at high levels."

Spokesman Zoltán Kovács summed up Hungary's non-wavering position on protecting their children and their sovereignty: "In 2016, we did not give in to the attacks and called for a referendum on migration, in which 98 percent of Hungarians refused Brussels' migration policy. Since then, several other EU member states have adopted our migration policy. Time has proven us right. And it is exactly this course of action that we will follow regarding our law on child protection."[18]

---

16 Kinsella, Ray (2023). A 'Captured and Colonised' EU Threatens Europe. *The European Conservative*. Spring 2023, (26). 12-17.

17 Abnett, Kate; and Strupczewski (2022, December 22). EU holds back all of Hungary's cohesion funds over rights concerns. *Reuters*. https://www.reuters.com/world/europe/eu-holds-back-all-hungarys-cohesion-funds-over-rights-concerns-2022-12-22/

18 Kovács, Zoltán (2022, Feb 16).

Russia-Ukraine War: "Hungary First"

In March of 2023, the Hungarian parliament adopted a pro-peace resolution proposal, as submitted by FIDESZ-KDNP on the anniversary of the Russia-Ukraine war. The proposal expressed a commitment to peace, condemned Russia's military aggression against Ukraine, and recognized Ukraine's right to defense. The proposal also stated that Western sanctions had not stopped the war, but that Europe continues to finance the war due to high energy prices resulting from sanctions. Furthermore, the proposal emphasized that instead of weapons and sanctions, peace negotiations were needed immediately.[19]

Hungary has welcomed over three and a half million[20] Ukrainian refugees through their border–providing food, shelter, child and pet care, and paying travel fare for these refugees to settle in their place of preference. I have spent several hours in the Ukrainian refugee shelter in Hungary and saw the great lengths the Hungarian government and faith-based organizations have gone to in order to support the Ukrainian war ref-

[19] Magyar Nemzet (2023, April 11). Russians go home!—a counter-campaign was launched with American money. https://magyarnemzet.hu/belfold/2023/04/ruszkik-haza-ellenkampany-indult-amerikai-penzbol?utm_source=hirkereso&utm_medium=referral&utm_campaign=hiraggregator&fbclid=IwAR2S-w8PNWeBHNhtHip7kr_uLHFZ6k2271iVSt-JdSoNraPzyowutjqLOufo.

[20] United Nations High Commission for Refugees. Ukraine Refugee Situation. Operational Data Portal. https://data.unhcr.org/en/situations/ukraine

ugees. But these facts are rarely remembered in the media, instead they are buried under name-calling and blurring of facts. Kinga Gál, member of the European Parliament from Hungary explains:

> We really put in a lot of money for the refugees, but also in [aid to] Ukraine on the other side, and whatever they wanted, they got. The only thing [we said was] that we don't want to send weapons. We don't want to be involved in sending weapons ... anything else though, we can do. There is the [EU's] European Peace Facility where there is a lot of money put in by each member state, and Hungary does too. ...it is money that also helps Ukraine... we just said that we don't [want to] directly send tanks, weapons, whatever, to Ukraine. The other [problem] is that we don't see where this fighting and war will end.[21]

For steadfastly calling for peace and refusing to sanction Russian energy supply to Europe, Prime Minister Viktor Orbán has been labeled a "Putin sympathizer" by both the European Union and the U.S. administration. But Orbán's approach to the Russian-Ukraine war is not Russia-sympathetic, it is simply Hungarian-pragmatic. He has made it clear numerous times that Hungary condemns the Russian invasion into Ukraine and stands for Ukrainian sovereignty, but not to the point of agreeing to energy sanctions against Russia that would crush Hungary's economy.

---

[21] Interview 1-February 20, 2023.

On a visit to Budapest in early 2023, "97% NEM a szankciókra!" was one of the first billboard signs that greeted me. The phrase was on telephone poles and buildings everywhere and I soon translated it—"97% say no to sanctions!" I also realized its importance—it was not only the Orbán government that refused the West's energy sanctions against Russia—but the overwhelming majority of the Hungarian people. This is an example of national sovereignty in practice: the will of the people, within a sovereign member state of the European Union, spoke loudly and clearly. Former Minister of Justice Judit Varga (now member of Hungarian parliament) declared:

> We did not formulate this position on war just because we read it somewhere in the news. We actually measured the citizens' views. Hungarian citizens, 80%, or more, they hate war ... they have fears from war, and they just don't want to enter into wars, so this is the Hungarian citizens' position. I asked some of [the leaders of the U.S. government] at a dinner, "If you were in my shoes and there's a clear statistical data that 80% plus of your democracy does not want to have war, would this be a responsible behavior from the government to ask for war or to enter or to be involved?" This is the difference.[22]

Hungary (like the rest of Europe) has been reliant on Russian energy—85% of their natural gas, 65% of their oil, and 100 % of their nuclear fuel comes from Russia. Hungarian energy in-

[22] Interview 2-February 20, 2023.

frastructure is Soviet-era. And even though Hungary has made strides to diversify energy sources, it is a landlocked country with limited current options and therefore

> it is foolish for the EU to think Hungary (or any European country) can change energy reliance overnight in response to sanctions on Russia. Time, foreign investment, and financial support are all needed to change decades-old infrastructure and systems. Fortunately, Hungary's veto power in the foreign policy arena of the EU (as a sovereign member state) gave them the ability to negotiate and receive waivers for the sanctions which would have killed the Hungarian economy, and which *have* weakened Europe.[23]

Russia supplied about 40% of Europe's natural gas before Putin invaded Ukraine. In the first year of the war, this percentage continued to decrease until it had fallen almost 90% from a year before. For anyone paying attention, Putin's use of energy as a war weapon was a clue to how effective Western sanctions would be.

> Strategically decreased gas supply and the subsequent surge in global gas prices gave Gazprom, Russia's state-owned energy giant, record high profits of about $42 billion in the first half of 2022, a 20% increase in shares, and even a nice $10 billion dividend for the Kremlin.

[23] Bradley-Farrell, Shea (2023, March 21)

> Where then, were the "severe consequences" promised by President Biden and Western sanctions? According to analysts, Mr. Putin could reduce gas exports to Europe by 20% for up to three years and cut supplies completely for over a year "without adverse consequences" to his economy.[24]

China has also been a winner, securing Russian natural gas at a 50% discount throughout 2022, preceded by signing a ten-year, $80 billion oil deal with Russia in February 2022. And as Russian oil exports going to Europe, the U.S., Japan, and Korea have decreased, China has overtaken the EU as Russia's biggest buyer of oil products (June 2022). In spite of Western "severe" sanctions, Russia continues to circumvent the sanctions by selling to China and India, giving China the energy resources needed to fulfill its dream of economic hegemony over the U.S.[25]

The Great Power Competition (GPC) ramifications of a growing Sino-Russian partnership, and what this means for the future of the U.S. and its allies is also concerning. Although largely unreported by the media or the Biden administration, a global power shift towards Asia, spurred by Western sanctions "dismantling what's left of European economies" is happening, and is publicly flaunted by Putin.

---

[24] Bradley-Farrell, Shea (2022, September 19) Time to Negotiate Peace between Ukraine and Russia. *Washington Times*. https://www.washingtontimes.com/news/2022/sep/19/time-to-negotiate-peace-between-ukraine-and-russia/

[25] *Ibid.*

But Western leaders and U.S. War Hawks choose to fight this war by proxy—with inconsequential sanctions and by supplying Ukraine, a government rife with corruption, with billions of dollars in foreign aid with little accountability or oversight. What has this accomplished except an ongoing war, European economies in recession, and deeper American taxpayer debt?

Prime Minister Orbán's foreign policy approach is 'Hungary First', protecting the Hungarian economy, much like former U.S. President Donald Trump's campaign platform of 'America First'. Americans wish President Joe Biden would do the same. Biden flew half way around the world to Kyiv, but he never visited the devastated American town of East Palestine, Ohio, where chemical leakage from a train derailment in February continues to threaten the human and environmental health of that region. Biden has pledged U.S. weapons to Ukraine, ones the U.S. military needs; he has committed over $150 billion to secure Ukrainian borders and sovereignty, while protecting policies to keep the U.S. southern border open to mass illegal immigration, increasing the presence of Mexican cartels, deadly fentanyl, and the threat of terrorism in the U.S.

It is fruitless for the West to continue to enable the war. Even if Ukrainian soldiers have won a few tactical territorial victories, the truth is that the Russian Army will never simply pack up and go home. The Russians will no more quit Ukraine than they did in Crimea. The Russian military is ruthless—for anyone who doubts this, try Googling pictures of Grozny, Chechnya, following the second Chechnyan war. You will see the consequences of Russia's brutal, relentless army: thriving cities turned into lunar-landscape-like images of death and destruction. At the beginning of 2022, it was in the best interest of Ukraine for U.S. and EU leaders to step up and negotiate peace. But this was barely mentioned in 2022, and it is still not seriously discussed. In fact, the idea of peace is largely ignored.

These facts are not welcome in most circles, but to ignore them is unwise, most importantly for Ukrainian citizens, of whom 400,000 have been killed or injured, for Americans in economic stress with high oil prices and depleting oil reserves, and for Europe's weakening economy. Ukrainian President Zelensky, who turned average citizens into the militia, should be encouraged to seek armistice and concede Ukraine as a neutral non-NATO country. Geographical concessions to Russia are likely while gaining back monetary concessions for the loss of territory and life.

Peace will not come to Ukraine until the U.S. and Russia sit down face-to-face and negotiate specific terms and conditions of a peace treaty. Nothing short of that level of negotiation will be effective, respected, or guaranteed. No matter how much one might admire the bravery of Ukrainian citizens, they cannot continue to hold off Russia without bearing the deadly and costly penalties. Negotiating peace is all that is left. And Orbán continues to stand his ground on this issue.

Immigration: The EU and U.S. Imagine No Borders

In early 2023, the European Union Council of Interior Ministers imposed migrant quotas on each of the member states. Under the proposed quota regulation, Hungary would be obligated to accept 8,500 illegal migrants per year.[26] Hungary's government unequivocally said no.[27] So did its people—in a June 2023 poll, 77% of Hungarians rejected the mandatory quotas.[28]

The treaties of the European Union do not require unanimity for policies regarding migration,[29] but both Hungary and Poland object to the EU imposing a uniform migration and asylum policy without unanimous support from member states. As it stands, both Poland and Hungary oppose the proposed migration pact which will introduce a mandatory relocation system and impose a financial penalty of €20,000 per migrant for countries refusing to comply.

---

[26] About Hungary (2023, June 20). 77% of Hungarians reject the EU's migrant resettlement quota scheme. Budapest. https://abouthungary.hu/news-in-brief/77-of-hungarians-reject-eus-migrant-resettlement-quota-scheme.

[27] Kovács, Zoltán (2023, July 27). Gulyás Gergely: Any kind of migrant distribution mechanism is unacceptable. *About Hungary*, Budapest. https://abouthungary.hu/blog/gulyas-gergely-any-kind-of-migrant-distribution-mechanism-is-unacceptable.

[28] About Hungary (2023, June 20).

[29] Kovács, Zoltán (2023, July 26). Four reasons why the EU's budget amendment is absurd. *About Hungary*, Budapest. https://abouthungary.hu/blog/four-reasons-why-the-eus-budget-amendment-is-absurd-.

This too is nothing new. Beginning at least since 2015, EU bureaucracy in Brussels has pushed, prodded, and whined at Hungary to change its border protection policies and allow hundreds of thousands of illegal and undocumented migrants into the country, many of whom want to reach Germany and other Western European nations.

A misinformed concept of humanitarianism and demographic idealism has both European and American ruling parties recklessly pushing open border policies without considering the costs or long-term consequences—not just for the host country but also for the mass influx of immigrants. In Europe, the EU establishment says they want to ameliorate the demographic crisis—aging population and declining birth rates—through more migration; in America, the Left has been accused of encouraging reckless illegal immigration in order to change voting demographics.

But Hungary continues to protect its culture, economy, and borders in order to maintain its families, democracy, and way of life. Americans wish to do the same—not with closed borders and anti-immigration policies—but with controlled and lawful immigration.

The uprisings of the Arab Spring (beginning 2010-11) and ongoing civil war in Syria and Libya sparked what seemed like an unending flood of immigrants to Europe. In 2013, the numbers surged. Germany and other member states agreed to take in thousands of refugees. And Hungary did its part—registering about 20,000 asylum seekers in 2013 and 40,000 in 2014.[30]

---

30 Murray, Douglas (2018). *The Strange Death of Europe. Immigration, Identity, Islam.* Bloomsbury Publishing. p. 81.

In 2015, over a million migrants applied for asylum in Europe—with Hungary taking in more first-time asylum applicants per 100,000 people *than any other country in Europe.*[31]

These were mostly Syrian refugees fleeing the uprisings in the Middle East, but many others took advantage of the chaotic situation to enter Europe. Much like Biden's 'open border policies,' German Chancellor Angela Merkle's motivational words "*Wir schaffen das*" (We can do it) signaled to hundreds of thousands of would-be immigrants that the doors of Europe were open.

Europe was dragged along by Germany, some members were willing to take in mass numbers of refugees, and some were not. With the 'free movement' principle, a doctrinal principle in the 'borderless' European Union, refugees can just walk through neighboring states on their way north to Germany and to other destination countries. And a huge mass of people (mainly male) did exactly that, and moved through Europe.

By 2015, in only the first three months, more than 40,000 refugees had been registered in Hungary. In July, Hungary began constructing fences along the Serbian, Croatian, and Slovenian borders to control and get a handle on the mass flow of people. By September, Hungarian authorities announced that infrastructure was overwhelmed and declared a state of emergency, closing its border with Austria.

---

[31] Pew Research (August 2, 2016). Number of Refugees to Europe Surges to Record 1.3 Million in 2015. Pew Research Center. Web accessed at: https://www.pewresearch.org/global/2016/08/02/number-of-refugees-to-europe-surges-to-record-1-3-million-in-2015/#:~:text=By%20comparison%2C%20Hungary%20had%201%2C770,above%20the%20total%20European%20rate.

Meanwhile, George Soros' Open Society Foundations were spending millions of dollars in 2015 on pressure propaganda, groups, and institutions to keep borders open and migrants freely moving through Europe. Leaflets published by the Foundations informed migrants of their legal rights, equipped them with logistical information on how to get to their destination, and advocated "resistance against the European border regime."[32]

At the end of 2015, about 400,000 people total had been registered in Hungary, almost all heading toward Germany and Scandinavia, entering from Serbia or Croatia, at the rate of up to 10,000 people a day.[33] Hungary had tried to 'play ball' with the EU and go along with their migration schemes, but the policies were neither feasible nor safe.

To take pressure off of Germany, the European Commission tried to impose a quota for a temporary distribution of migrants among EU member states, but at that point, the EU member states refused. Under EU pressure, in 2016, Hungary called for a national referendum on migration, in which 98% of Hungarians also refused Brussels' migration policy.[34] A year later, the European Commission's migration commissioner announced a proposal for making the flow of migrants permanent.[35]

---

32 Murray, p. 81.

33 *Ibid.*

34 Kovács, Zoltán (2022, Feb 16).

35 About Hungary (2017, September 14). Hungary's struggles with Brussels over migrant crisis have only just begun, says state secretary. *About Hungary*, Budapest. https://abouthungary.hu/news-in-brief/hungarys-struggles-with-brussels-over-migrant-crisis-have-only-just-begun-says-minister

Neither the EU (who invited mass immigration during the Arab Spring) nor the U.S. (who lifted Trump-era policies and stopped enforcing U.S. immigration law), had a comprehensive plan in place to deal with a massive spike in population. In Europe, high migrant unemployment, poverty, cultural differences, differing worldviews, and a lack of civic integration contribute to riots, violence, and unrest in migrant communities, and to the creation of autonomous communities or bodies. These include the French banlieues, the 'no-go zones' in Germany and Sweden, where nationals and police are afraid to enter, and the Islamic Sharia councils in the UK.

In 2016, European Commission President Jean-Claude Juncker had stated, "borders are the worst invention ever made by politicians."[36] But the argument for why borders are necessary is completely obvious even to a simpleton—a nation provides a home for its people, and homes are places of comfort and security. Borders are the same as the walls that enclose our homes. In your home, you prioritize the protection of your family and your resources first. In your home you lock your doors at night and wisely choose who you allow to enter.

This logic flies in the face of those who blindly believe the liberal narrative that all people have an inherent desire to equally share resources and live peacefully together. Right now, ask the people of Ukraine, who have been invaded by Russian forces, if this naiveté is true.

---

[36] Hughes, David. Ferguson, Kate (2016, August 22). National Borders are 'the worst invention ever,' says EC chief Jean-Claude Juncker. *Independent. https://www.independent.co.uk/news/world/europe/national-borders-are-the-worst-invention-ever-says-ec-chief-jeanclaude-juncker-a7204006.html*

Hungary's stance on immigration (and that of U.S. conservatives, for that matter) is simple. The Hungarians want to secure their borders to protect their land and their citizens, they want to have the ability to decide who they invite into their countries, and to this end, they require asylum seekers to remain below the border and be officially accepted before coming into Hungary. Not knowing who illegally enters the country is a very serious matter of national security.

The world-altering terrorist attacks in the United States, Germany, and France, which were most likely avoidable, are clear evidence of that. In addition, Hungary cannot support—economically or infrastructurally—mass illegal migration.

> In the heart of conservative voters, social continuity and national identity take precedence over all other issues. Only now, when wave after wave of immigrants seek the benefit of our hard-won assets and freedoms, do the people fully grasp what loss of sovereignty means.[37]

Why do American and European leaders believe Ukrainian sovereignty is a fundamental and inviolate principle, while viewing the sovereignty of the U.S. and Hungary as unimportant, and the protection of our borders as inhumane? How has the U.S. Congress agreed to give Ukraine over $150 billion for its territorial fight, when it was unwilling to fund the $5 billion dollars needed to build a wall to protect the U.S. southern border?

---

[37] Scruton (2022). p. 52.

In the United States, the Biden administration's narrative of "humane, orderly, and safe" immigration is a disinformation campaign built on high levels of public deception by the administration and the media. Biden's open border policies have encouraged mass illegal immigration into the U.S., and it is common knowledge that no one comes across the U.S. border without collaborating and paying the Mexican cartels, brutal criminal organizations who have no regard for human life. As a retired border patrol agent told me on one of my trips to the U.S. southern border, illegal immigrants rarely decide to circumvent the Mexican cartels and 'freelance' their way across, because "the cartels will flat out kill them."

> Eighty percent of U.S. border patrol agents are currently processing illegal immigrants. They are not patrolling the border. National and local law enforcement have been called in to help respond to the overwhelming flood of immigrants and drugs and to rescue exhausted, dehydrated, abused, or dead immigrants—those raped, exploited, and shot by the cartels. I have personally seen stash houses where illegal immigrants are housed by 'coyotes' as they wait for transport into the interior of the U.S. and become victims of human trafficking. In the words of a senior border patrol agent, these are places "where bad things happen."[38]

[38] Bradley-Farrell, Shea (2022, May 26) The EU and US Imagine No Borders–Except for Ukraine. The European Conservative. https://europeanconservative.com/articles/commentary/the-u-s-and-eu-imagine-no-borders-except-for-ukraine/

In addition, the U.S. had seen (covered up by the Biden administration) a record number of illegal immigrants reported dying trying to cross into the United States. What is humanitarian, or even human, about this dangerous and illegal method of immigration?

A desire to preserve and protect our sovereign borders does not signal a lack of compassion, but of wisdom. Hungary, in fact, is a country that embraces Christian compassion and brotherhood, recently welcoming over three million Ukrainian refugees with shelter and food, giving funds for much-needed medical supplies. Hungary's humanitarian assistance to Christian minorities in the Nineveh region of Iraq is unmatched. What Hungary does not want is for its culture to be absorbed by those people, or to change its way of life, language, cultural beliefs, and traditions. Shouldn't their view be respected? In the same heart of compassion, the U.S. is the largest humanitarian assistance-provider in the world.

The majority of conservatives do not advocate for the total closing of borders, but only to secure them and stop the insanity of reckless border policies. Beyond the obvious economical strain, the cultural and social strain should not be ignored. In *The Strange Death of Europe*, Douglas Murray explains:

> We are confused over how this is meant to work. While generally agreeing that it is possible for an individual to absorb a particular culture (give the right degree of enthusiasm both from the individual and the culture) whatever the skin colour, we know that we Europeans cannot become whatever we like. We cannot become Indian or Chinese, for instance. And yet we are expected to believe that anyone in the world can move to Europe and become European. If being "European" is not about race—as we hope it is not—then it is even more impera-

> tive that it is about 'values'. This is what makes the question "What are European values?" so important. Yet this is another debate about which we are wholly confused.[39]

Hungarian Deputy Prime Minister Zsolt Semjén made sense in 2017 when he said that immigration into sovereign nations must only be allowed for those who can and will be assimilated, or at least, integrated, but "not those who have no respect for our way of life, our culture or our traditions; not those who break into our country from an alien, or even hostile, civilization—or from no civilization.[40] At the same time, Hungary has gladly embraced those coming legally from different nations and cultures that would assimilate into their way of life.

---

[39] Murray, p. 5

[40] Semjén, Zsolt (2017). *In The Future of Europe: Hungary: Brave and Free.* Békés, Márton (Ed.). p. 121.

Conclusion: The Will of the People

How is it that disagreement over policy decisions (most of them Hungarian domestic issues) has resulted in such vitriol from the EU and the United States? Even if the EU and the Biden administration disagree with the policies of the Hungarian conservative government and the citizens which elected Orbán's administration, surely treating a sovereign NATO ally and member of the European Union with the respect it deserves would be a better approach to effective diplomacy. Traditionally, American tools of diplomacy have included encouragement, persuasion, inducement, and incentives, relying on the positive aspects of commonality.

Hungary is fortunate to have a leader like Viktor Orbán who is brave enough to 'stick to his guns' in the face of extreme global pressure, wide-spread ridicule in the media, the withholding of EU funds, and an arrogant U.S. ambassador who has declared it his duty to stop Hungary's 'backslide' into authoritarianism as a (supposedly) human rights abuser of the LGBTIQ community. As Orbán said in his State of the Nation address in early 2022, "We do not care that the world has gone mad. We do not care what repellent aberrations some people indulge in. We do not care how Brussels excuses and explains the inexplicable. This is Hungary!"

In each of the widely publicized disagreements between the Orbán administration and the EU, in conjunction with the Biden administration, it isn't Orbán that speaks the loudest, it is Hungarian citizens. Whether it is the almost four million Hungarians who said no to the EU's gender ideology agenda (2022), the 97% who said no to Western energy sanctions (2023), or the 77% who said no to the EU's mandatory migrant relocation (2023), or the fourth consecutive landslide victory of Viktor Orbán and his party (2022)—Hungarian spirit, identity, and sovereignty remain. The will of the people of a sovereign EU member state has spoken.

Chapter 12

BALANCING BETWEEN THE EAST AND THE WEST

When we look at the map and find Europe a tiny appendix of the Asiatic mainland, we cannot help admiring the courage and tenacity of those who, through the centuries, prevented the submersion of Europe. One of the outposts holding out against immense pressure were the Magyars, though they had come from Asia themselves.[1]

— John Flournoy Montgomery,
U.S. Ambassador to Hungary (1933-1941)

[1] Montgomery, p. 16-17.

International relations have been very complicated for Hungary lately. While Hungary is often rejected and maligned by the major Western powers, the government is also routinely questioned or pressured about its relationship with Russia, and about its increasing economic ties to China.

As discussed in Chapter 3, "Origins and Battles: Fighting for Hungarian Identity," Hungarians were originally nomadic tribes from the East, yet they embraced Western European culture and Christianity over a thousand years ago. Today, remembering this historic distinctiveness—Hungary's political and economic balance, as well as their geographical location between the countries of the East and West—is key in understanding their motives and international relations, the main goal of which has been survival.

We must recall the Magyar conquest of the Carpathian Basin over 1100 years ago, two-thirds of which was lost after World War I, along with one third of the population. We remember the 1526 Battle of Mohács against the Ottoman Empire; the Revolution of 1848 against the Habsburgs; the dark months of the Nazi occupation, and the terror-filled decades of Soviet occupation. In spite of all this, and in spite of continually being surrounded by more powerful peoples and empires, the Hungarians have continued to rule over their territory. And survive.

Today, the Hungarians see their mission as the preservation of this territory, their nation, and their unique identity. As Prime Minister Orbán has publicly stated about Hungarian motivations: "It's not just about politics, it's about culture."[2] Histo-

---

[2] Orbán, Viktor (2014, July 26). XXV Bálványos Free Summer University and Youth Camp, Băile Tuşnad (Tusnádfürdő).

rian Márton Békés, Director of Research at the House of Terror in Budapest, explains:

> National identity, national pride to be Hungarian—this is for us, very important because we aren't in the (Western) European nation. We aren't Caucasian-type people in Europe. You look at me, I have blonde hair. My ancestors were German but in my heart, I am a semi-Asian type. This is a very strange situation, but the Hungarians are the most eastern part of Europe, and the most western part of Asia. We think about ourselves like that. During the Soviet occupation, Hungarian people were *forced* to learn Russian. Hungarian people weren't free to raise the [Hungarian] flag, and being proud to be Hungarian was forbidden.
>
> Our culture is not just about language, religion and social behavior, or the relationship between women and men. In Hungary, culture is about creating a model of survival as a nation not just as a people, but as a nation.[3]

The question for Hungary, especially since the fall of the Soviet Union, has been about what model to adopt to achieve prosperity and survival: Western, Eastern, or a model built specifically by Hungary, for Hungary? As the Soviet Union fell in the beginning of the 1990s, most believed a full assimilation into the Western world was the obvious approach for Hungary, and their process for assimilation should be to copy the Western model.

[3] Interview-3_February 20, 2023.

But in Orbán's 2014 speech in Transylvania, labeled his "Illiberal Democracy" speech (discussed in Chapter 1,"Imperialists, Globalists, and the U.S. Administration: Claims Against Hungary"), Orbán spoke of Hungary's desire to find its own model of competitiveness based on a policy of "Hungary first." Orbán's comments boiled down to a desire to find the best way to make Hungary competitive on the global stage.

Orbán noted that through the popularity of globalization, the modern world has mainly focused on understanding how a "major economic interest group, for example the European Union," is competitive or not. But he says there is more to learn about global competitiveness through the state:

> Yet there is an even more important race. I would articulate this as a race to invent a state that is most capable of making a nation successful. As the state is nothing else but a method of organizing a community ... the defining aspect of today's world can be articulated as a race to figure out a way of organizing communities, (and) a state that is most capable of making a nation competitive.[4]

Orbán continued by pointing out that some nations, whether liberal democracies or not, states such as China, India, Turkey, and Russia, have been economically successful, and that it is also important for us to understand how that came about. This issue, the search for 'new paradigms' of development is typically studied and researched in the field of international devel-

[4] Orbán, Viktor (2014, July 26). XXV Bálványos Free Summer University and Youth Camp, Băile Tuşnad (Tusnádfürdő).

opment, but not often considered from the outside, especially in a world obsessed with international alliances. In his speech, Orbán projected the path of Hungary over the next few years, similar to their path of years before:

> We are searching for (and we are doing our best to find, ways of parting with Western European dogmas, making ourselves independent from them) the form of organizing a community, that is capable of making us competitive in this great world-race.[5]

Consider his stated goal here: Independent from needing the support of the European Union, the support of America? If we take into account the costly EU economic sanctions applied against Hungary; the isolation and punishments placed on Hungary by the U.S.; the West's forced energy sanctions against the Russians, leading to the global energy crisis; and the West's determination to destroy the moral and traditional fabric of society, then the answer to the question of *why* Hungary feels the need to hedge its bets and strengthen relations with Eastern superpowers, becomes much clearer. Hungarian Member of Parliament Kinga Gál explains:

> I think what we have learned during these years is that it's in our interest to be open towards the West first of all, but also towards the East. This is also somehow a political and an economic strategy. Of course, you have

[5] *Ibid.*

> to be very careful with it. It's important to see the realities of the world and see how much share, for example, China has of the total GDP of the world. Where is Europe in relation to that, and where is the United States in relation to that? (China's economy) was totally different 10 years ago, or 20 years ago—a very different situation. So, we should see the realities (of the world economy). I think that is what is very important here, that we have a realistic approach to this issue.[6]

Unfortunately, as we have discussed at length, the U.S. and Europe are both on an all-out campaign to belittle, malign, sanction, and sabotage Hungary. And Orbán believes that the power and leadership of America (perhaps understandable based on the weakness of the Biden administration) will eventually come to an end. Let's pray not. Hungary also sees the center of the economic world shifting to Asia.[7] And as Orbán continued:

> the strength of American "soft power" is deteriorating, because liberal values today incorporate corruption, sex and violence, and with [these] liberal values discredit America and American modernization.[8]

---

[6] Interview 1-February 20, 2023.

[7] Horváth, Levente (2023, May 11). Beyond the bubble – introducing Eurasia Magazine. *About Hungary*, Budapest. https://abouthungary.hu/blog/beyond-the-bubble-introducing-eurasia-magazine

[8] Orbán, Viktor (2014, July 26). XXV Bálványos Free Summer University and Youth Camp, Băile Tuşnad (Tusnádfürdő).

He is right. Couple this with the fact that Hungary is a small country with a small economy, and geographically close to both of the Eastern superpowers of Russia (144 million people) and China (1.4 billion people), and you begin to see the actual sanity of the Hungarian policy they have named "Opening to the East." Minister János Csák wrote that: "To survive, we need to strike a balance and make agreements because we have never been stronger or more numerous than those who want to advance their interests to our detriment, or who simply find us an impediment."[9]

However, the fact is that both of these Eastern superpowers are ideologically opposed to individual freedom, traditionally a basic tenet of the West, and have dangerous authoritarian systems.

China's economy was a relatively small and isolated economy during the Maoist regime. But China began to reinsert itself into the global economy in the late 1970s with authoritarian state-led development. Under a system of socialism with central planning, China built the rudiments of an industrial base that eventually caused the growth of its successful consumer and export industry, unlocking the key to becoming a global economy, officially recognized as such in 2001 when it joined the World Trade Organization.

In 2007, China's manufacturing sector dramatically surged. Since then, China has become the second largest economy in the world (in terms of GDP) after the United States. However, China has only achieved a gross national income (GNI) per cap-

---

[9] Csák.

ita (income per person) of $21,250, far below that of the U.S. at $77,530 per person.[10] In addition, the state has nationalized property ownership and maintains tight control over the economy, with little transparency. Resistance to democracy enables a nation to repress labor, keep wages low, and gives the state a comparative advantage in global manufacturing.[11]

The Chinese government—the Chinese Communist Party (CCP)—has a constitution based on Marxist, Leninist, and Maoist ideology. Today, the CCP has been described as 'techno authoritarian', meaning it is an IT-backed dictatorship with innovations that allow mass facial recognition and biometric collection, for the ethnic profiling of Uyghur Muslims, and for drones that manage the Uyghurs' detention in 're-education' camps.[12]

In early 2023, President Xi Jinping literally re-wrote the government rulebook to solidify his own power and the power of the CCP, demanding that all cabinet-level decisions (the State Council) now defer to the highest-ranking members of the Communist party for major decisions and rely solely on the political

---

10 The World Bank (2022). International Comparison Program, World Bank | World Development Indicators database, World Bank | Eurostat-OECD PPP Programme. GNI Per Capita, PPP (current international $)—China. https://data.worldbank.org/indicator/NY.GNP.PCAP.PP.CD?locations=CN.

11 Rapley, John (2007). Understanding Development, Lynne Rienner Publishers, London. pp. 8-9.

12 Bateman, Jon (2022, April 25). U.S.-China Technological "Decoupling": A Strategy and Policy Framework. Carnegie Endowment for International Peace, Washington DC. https://carnegieendowment.org/2022/04/25/denying-support-for-chinese-and-china-enabled-authoritarianism-and-repression-pub-86924

thought of Xi himself.[13] This has been seen as a fundamental shift in policy to ensure loyalty to the party. Radio Free Asia reports that Xi's Central Committee of the Communist party recently,

> launched a nationwide disciplinary campaign that will inspect its 96 million members for loyalty to supreme leader Xi Jinping and weed out "black sheep" and "two-faced" officials from positions of power who were put there by rival political factions, under a "working group" run by the party's Central Commission for Discipline Inspection.[14]

Hungary sees China as a great source of income and as a good way to diversify their economic security. In addition, Hungary does not see America's security problems with China—stealing our technology, knowledge-base, and other resources—as problems that relate to them. Instead, it sees the hypocrisy of U.S. and Chinese economic interdependencies as a foil: China is the second largest foreign owner of U.S. debt (2020), and American companies have $107 billion invested in China, while China has only invested about $40 billion in the United States.[15] Former Hungarian Minister of Justice Judit Varga comments on another point:

---

[13] Ting, Gu (2023, March 29). China deletes Marxism, Leninism, Maoism, other ideologies from government rulebook. *Radio Free Asia*, Reed, Matt (Ed.), Mudie, Luisetta (Trans.). https://www.rfa.org/english/news/china/new-rulebook-03292023124017.html

[14] *Ibid.*

[15] The Heritage Foundation Solutions (2020, August). China Facts and Figure. *Heritage Foundation*, https://www.heritage.org/solutions/#China.

> There's a certain hypocrisy, because if in Germany a big mother company is sold to the Chinese, you do not read in the news that one hundred Chinese companies are now in Germany, because this is [typical of] the globalized world. But this is a double standard [against Hungary]. We think it's important that we cannot exclude [China] since we are a country in the Carpathian basin lying between East and West. You cannot exclude any communication in economic terms with other directions or other parts of the world. Hungary can be the point where the industries of West and the East can meet because we have no national resources.[16]

Orbán has been quoted as saying that the difference between Chinese and American foreign policy is that America and the West "feel morally superior and try to force others to conform to them. The Chinese never do that ... they are motivated by their own interests."[17]

It may be that Orbán's assertions are a bit naïve, or just wishful thinking. CCP interest, in the long term anyway, *is* conformity to its way of life; conformity is a basic tenet of Marxism. We often see this in the U.S., where American-based countries frequently feel the pressure from the CCP (because of the market size owned by China) to conform to their political values and foreign policy.[18] However, Orbán believes that a skillful politi-

---

[16] Interview 2-February 20, 2023.

[17] Pinto, Jaime N. (2022). Forged by History: The Hungarian Struggle for Nationhood. *The European Conservative*, (22). p. 35.

cian can cooperate with, and benefit from, Chinese business and still maintain Hungarian sovereignty and national interests. In addition, China is an economic superpower that Europe is heavily reliant upon for trade. As Orbán has said: "So China is here, whether we like it or not, and we have to compete."[19]

China is the largest exporter to the European Union and the third largest buyer of EU goods (2022).[20] Minister of Foreign Affairs and Trade Péter Szijjártó says "decoupling" from Chinese investments would "kill the European economy." Szijjártó also believes Chinese investments into Hungary are a way to maintain economic growth during a time when some Eurozone countries are in recession or close to it, including Germany, the European Union's largest economy.[21] The Russian-Ukraine war and the West's energy sanctions on Russia have caused gas prices to skyrocket and supported record-high inflation.

Germany has traditionally been Hungary's strongest economic partner. In August 2023, as part of a policy to ramp up the Hungarian defense industry, a new combat vehicle factory opened in southwest Hungary in Zalaegerszeg where Orbán an-

---

[18] House Foreign Affairs Committee (2020). Chinese Communist Party Coercion of US Companies. *United States House of Representatives.* Washington DC. https://foreignaffairs.house.gov/wp-content/uploads/2020/02/CCP-Coercion-of-U.S.-Companies.pdf

[19] Pinto.

[20] Gilchrist, Karen (2023, June 27). China decoupling would be an act of 'suicide' for Europe, Hungary's foreign minister says. *CNBC*, https://www.cnbc.com/2023/06/27/china-decoupling-would-be-suicide-for-europe-hungarys-pter-szijjrt.html.

[21] Ziady, Hannah (2023, August 23). Germany's economy hasn't looked this weak since the start of the pandemic, *CNN*. https://www.cnn.com/2023/08/23/economy/germany-economy-recession-pmi/index.html

nounced an agreement to manufacture combat drones in cooperation with Israeli and German companies. Germany owns the majority share of 51% of the new Rheinmetall factory in Zalaegerszeg and Hungary owns 49%.[22]

In 2022, foreign direct investment (FDI) into Hungary reached a new high of €6 billion with 48% coming from eastern countries and 42% from western. South Korea was the largest investor in terms of volume, and Germany's investments created more jobs. The majority of investments were made in the electric vehicle industry—to produce electric or hybrid vehicles and electric batteries.[23]

In 2022, the Chinese company Contemporary Amperex Technology made an investment of €7.4 billion[24] into Eastern Hungary with the building of a battery plant.[25] In July 2023 another Chinese company, Sunwoda Electronic, announced plans to build a power battery factory for electric vehicles with an initial investment of $275 million.[26] Hungary also hosts the largest

---

[22] Szandelszky, Bela. (2023, August 18). Hungary is to produce combat drones in cooperation with Israel and Germany, the prime minister says. *Associated Press*, Budapest. https://abcnews.go.com/International/wireStory/hungary-produce-combat-drones-cooperation-israel-germany-prime-102369250

[23] About Hungary (2022, December 29). FDI in Hungary reaches record 6 billion euros in 2022, Budapest. https://abouthungary.hu/news-in-brief/fdi-in-hungary-reaches-record-6-billion-euros-in-2022.

[24] Deme, Dániel (2022, August 12). EUR 7.4 BN Battery Plant to be Built in Debrecen, *Hungary Today*, Budapest. https://hungarytoday.hu/eur-7-4-bn-battery-plant-to-be-built-in-debrecen/

[25] Öry, Mariann (2022, September 23). Chinese Investment Contributes to Hungary's Growth, *Hungary Today*, Budapest. https://hungarytoday.hu/chinese-investment-contributes-to-hungarys-growth/

supply center of Huawei Technologies Co., outside of China. A Chinese-built rail line will connect Hungary to Serbia through the Belt and Road Initiative.[27] Minister Szijjártó, like Orbán, makes the point that China has never set any political criteria for their continued economic relationship with Hungary. About working with nations that hold differing worldviews, Minister Varga comments:

> We can be this kind of ... mediator. It does not mean that you have any kind of ideological sympathy, whatsoever, with what China is doing or Russia is doing. Why we are saying you cannot cut off all kind of economic ties with China or Russia because they will be always there. Russia is a country of 130 million (people). They will always exist. They will always have big national resources. You have to keep up communication, even if you condemn the war, and we condemn the aggression, it's crystal clear. For the sake of your own interest, you have to keep up the communication at least economically.[28]

[26] Wang, Ethan; Yan, Zhang; and Woo, Ryan (2023, July 27). China's Sunwoda plans $274.7 million Hungarian battery plant. *Reuters,* Christian Schmollinger and Emma Rumney (Eds.) https://www.reuters.com/technology/chinas-sunwoda-plans-2747-mln-hungarian-battery-plant-2023-07-27/

[27] Grove, Thomas; and, Hinshaw, Drew (2023, February 20). Hungary Extends Warm Welcome to Top Chinese Diplomat, *Wall Street Journal,* https://www.wsj.com/articles/hungary-extends-warm-welcome-to-top-chinese-diplomat-e79b9d8

[28] Interview-2_February 20, 2023.

However, social understanding and cultural ties with China have also been encouraged with the introduction of certain initiatives, and direct flights from Beijing to Budapest facilitate this. (Note: There are no direct flights between Washington DC and Budapest.) The number of university students from China has grown rapidly over the past ten years and there are five Confucius Institutes in a country with a population of less than 10 million (as comparison, the U.S. has about seven of these institutes, as some of them have been closed, in a population of 334 million). Other new initiatives, like the *Eurasia Magazine*, express obvious distaste for Western cooperation and promote a new international and political order with China as the dominant power.[29]

All in all, Hungary's economic alliance with China makes economic and national security sense, but a blind eye toward the influence of the dictatorial politics of the Chinese state is concerning. Even though I am quite positive the Orbán government and many Hungarians are aware of the dangers of the Chinese Communist Party—Orbán was quoted as saying that China would "never be a system of political individual freedom"[30]—I have been told by a few Hungarian citizens that the communism and authoritarianism of China has passed away; that China is "not really" authoritative, or it is "soft communism," and even, the most concerning, "just American propaganda."

[29] Horváth, Levente (2023, May 11). Beyond the bubble – introducing Eurasia Magazine. *About Hungary*, Budapest. https://abouthungary.hu/blog/beyond-the-bubble-introducing-eurasia-magazine

[30] Pinto.

Well, if that is true, we should tell that to the more than one million Uyghur Muslims held in CCP 're-education' camps to be cleansed from their faith, culture, language, and beliefs, and who have been subject to forced abortion, sterilization, and organ harvesting.[31]

The issue of how far to bring the CCP's influence into *America or Hungary* is not a matter of East versus West, but of right versus wrong, and of protecting national security.

---

[31] Garrison, Shea (2019, September 30). "How China 'is home to the worst human rights crises of our time'," *Washington Times*, Washington DC. https://www.washingtontimes.com/news/2019/sep/30/how-china-is-home-to-the-worst-human-rights-crises/.

Chapter 13

THE HUNGARIAN MODEL: CONCLUSIONS AND RECOMMENDATIONS

The people of Hungary are again the standard bearers of universal freedom in Europe today, just as they were in 1848; and this time in an era when the mere survival of mankind is at stake.[1]

—István Angyal,
Executed 1956 Revolutionary

---

[1] Schmidt, Mária (2021). p. 15. István Angyal was a 1956 Revolutionary. A Hungarian Jew and Auschwitz survivor, Angyal was a committed Leftist who became disaffected with the Hungarian regime not because of its Communism but because it failed to realize what he believed were the idealized democratic and egalitarian aspirations of that ideology.

A Successful Model

The world has heard a lot about the "Hungarian Model" of national success over the past few years. So, what *is* the Hungarian Model, and can we use it?

Simply put, Hungary is an excellent model of maintaining sovereignty and the foundational principles of God, family, and homeland, and especially of how to do so against a powerful, post-liberal, globalist order fighting against liberty in the New Cold War of today.

Remember goal five of the "Specific Goals of the Communist Effort" given to us by Possony in 1959 (see chapters 8 and 10): "The creation, in the ruling, upper, and intellectual classes of non-Communist societies, of frustration, confusion, pessimism, guilt, fear, defeatism, hopelessness, and neurosis, of lack of will, in essence the psychological destruction of anti-Communist leadership."[2]

The description above is certainly what the Soviets tried to do to the Hungarians for decades, but if so, the Hungarians have overcome it. My experience with the Hungarian "ruling and intellectual class" (a term that may slightly repel an American sensibility but is comfortably accepted in Hungary) is that they are far from defeated—they are forward thinking, deeply intellectual, proactive, confident, charming—all this done skillfully with a good and intact sense of humor. They do not exhibit signs of "psychological destruction." They follow the admoni-

---

[2] Sanders, Ralph & Brown, Fred R. (Eds.). p. 58.

tions of the Hungarian Benedictine Monk, Father Placid, who spent a decade in the Soviet Gulag and who declared himself "the happiest man in the whole Soviet Union:"[3]

> The first rule for survival. ... You must not dramatise your suffering because that weakens you. To stand up to suffering we need all our energy ..."Good Lord! Out of three and a half million prisoners, there will be hundreds, thousands, hundreds of thousands who will survive. I'm no worse than them; I'll survive too." So that will to survive, we passed it on to each other. We took care of each other. That meant a lot.[4]

It has occurred to me, in fact, that the Hungarians know how to remain calm and confident, while claiming their sovereignty and making their own decisions, controlling their destinies and teaching their children, because they spent decades *learning how* to deal with Communists—with an evil that tries to capture the soul of man.[5] Much like the Magyars of the tenth century who did not allow themselves to be absorbed by the tribes in the Carpathian Basin, so too the Hungarians of the last century did not allow themselves to become Soviet. Neither did they allow themselves to be absorbed by the Austrian Empire nor by the Ottoman Empire in the centuries before. They remained true to themselves.

[3] Magyar Nemzet (2016, December 25). Benedictine Monk Father Placid 100-years old today. Daily News Hungary, Budapest. https://dailynewshungary.com/benedictine-monk-father-placid-100-years-old-today/

[4] Losonczy.

[5] Sanders, Ralph & Brown, Fred R. (Eds.). (1961). p. 49.

In that regard, they are certainly a model for maintaining Western civilization, for those of us determined to reverse the woke destruction of our countries. The temper tantrums of petty German European parliamentarians or the undermining tactics of juvenile 'ambassadors' just do not derail the Hungarians. They laugh, smile, and remain pleasant. They are what we term in the U.S., "cheerful warriors." They don't take on the guilt or shame served to them, and they rarely get visibly upset. They just firmly remain constant in saying what is right, what is wrong, what they will tolerate, and what they will not. They are the adults in the room.

In 2017, Hungarian Prime Minister Viktor Orbán expressed the view held by so many in Central European conservative nations: "Twenty-seven years ago here in Central Europe we believed that Europe was our future; today we feel that we are the future of Europe." [6]

Hungary serves as an optimistic, successful model for cheerfully, yet firmly, advancing conservative principles in an often hostile environment. They have both a strong domestic and foreign policy agenda. The West has many lessons to learn from them—about border security and immigration, about protecting the innocence of children, about putting a nation first in foreign policy, and about strengthening the family, just to name a few.

Hungary's position on many issues should be an example to Europe. For example, its pro-family policies have steadily in-

---

[6] Orbán, Viktor (2017, July 22). Address to the 28th Bálványos Summer Open University and Student Camp. In *About Hungary*, Budapest. https://abouthungary.hu/speeches-and-remarks/viktor-orbans-speech-at-the-28th-balvanyos-summer-open-university-and-student-camp.

creased fertility rates in Hungary (see Chapter 2) and can speak to the demographic decline of Europe—the UN calls Europe a "shrinking and aging society." Europe, according to the United Nations Population Fund, can expect a -7% population growth between 2022 and 2050.[7] And this is *with* their open border policies on migration. The economic consequences of such a decline are numerous: Besides the national security implications, there are labor shortages, burdens on health and social care for the aging, and more.

During the Soviet regime, abortions hit an all-time high in Hungary in 1969, at more than 206,000 abortions.[8] Since the regime change in the early nineties, abortions have drastically declined. In 2021, there were less than 22,000 abortions,[9] the lowest on record.[10] Although Hungary's Fundamental Law defines life as beginning at conception, access to abortion is legal—and is broadly available up to twelve weeks (and in some cases up to twenty-four).

However, under a new Hungarian law implemented in September 2022, pregnant women seeking an abortion now have to present a document (issued by an obstetrician-gynecologist)

---

7 United Nations Population Fund (2023). The Problem with Too Few. In *United Nations*, New York. https://www.unfpa.org/swp2023/too-few.

8 Hungarian Central Statistical Office (2018). Induced Abortions. https://www.ksh.hu/docs/eng/xftp/idoszaki/eterhessegmegsz16.pdf.

9 Hungarian Central Statistical Office (2022). Number and rate of fetal losses. https://www.ksh.hu/stadat_files/nep/hu/nep0013.html.

10 Zemplényi, Lili (2022, September 14). Hungary's Heartbeat Bill: Hungarian Abortion Law Amended After 30 Years. In *Hungarian Conservative*, Budapest. https://www.hungarianconservative.com/articles/culture_society/hungarys-heartbeat-bill-hungarian-abortion-law-amended-after-30-years/.

certifying that they have been presented with "indications of the functioning of fetal vital functions," or the heartbeat of the fetus.[11]

It is deeply ironic, and sad, that this move has been fiercely attacked as "unnecessarily cruel"[12] by 'liberal' opponents across the world, the same people who have firmly denied the humanity and life of the fetus. If, as they claim, a fetus is not truly living nor human, why would listening to its heartbeat be cruel? The consequences of having an abortion, on the emotional health of the mother, should not be taken lightly. The "heartbeat law" gives women more truthful information based on simple life-affirming evidence in order to make a life-changing decision. This simple law is also a reflection of the Hungarian's desire to respect human dignity. The humanity and dignity of an unborn child, and the mother who gives the child life.

But perhaps the most important practical model for us is the Hungarian strategy for building the prosperous and peaceful nation that Viktor Orbán spoke of in his infamous "Illiberal Democracy" speech. It outlines a plan that is experienced and successful—one that took an offensive (not defensive) position—and played to win.

---

[11] Bene, Barbara (2022, September 14). New Rule: Women Should Listen to Fetal Heartbeat before Abortion. In *Hungary Today,* Budapest. https://hungarytoday.hu/new-rule-women-should-listen-to-fetal-heartbeat-before-abortion/.

[12] Komuves, Anita and Szakacs, Gergely (2022, September 14). Hungarian doctors, opposition protest 'cruel' change in abortion rules. In *Reuters.* https://www.reuters.com/world/europe/hungarian-doctors-opposition-protest-cruel-change-abortion-rules-2022-09-14/

Orbán's Twelve Points: Bringing Out the Best

Hungarian Prime Minister Viktor Orbán was a determined and fearless freedom fighter in the anti-communist movement. In his own words, he recounts growing up in what he describes as a "woke world," one in which critical race theory was called "scientific socialism," *wokeism* was taught at the university in the same way it is now in western nations, and the state worked to "entrench the power of the communists."[13] It was, according to him, an "everyday socialist dictatorship: That is what we grew up in. Political correctness, Orwellian Newspeak, state control of the public square, expropriation of private property and stigmatization of the Right."

Orbán knows the social consequences of communism, and at CPAC Hungary 2022, he offered Hungary's experience battling the "progressive Left" during the Communist era to the global leaders of today's conservative movement:

> This problem ... both in America and Western Europe—is the domination of public life by progressive liberals. The problem is the fact that they hold the most important positions in the most important institutions, that they occupy the dominant positions in the media, and

[13] Visegrad Post (2002, May 24). Viktor Orbaìn's Speech at the CPAC on 19 May 2022. https://visegradpost.com/en/2022/05/24/viktor-orbans-speech-at-the-cpac-on-19-may-2022/

> that they produce all the politically indoctrinating works of high and mass culture. They—the progressive left—tell us what is the truth and what is not, what is right and what is wrong. And as conservatives, our lot is to feel about our nations' public life as Sting felt in New York: like a 'legal alien'...
>
> I will tell you how fervent university students succeeded in dismantling a dictatorship, then in breaking the hegemony over opinions enjoyed by the returning communists and liberals, and how they managed to end the dominance of progressives in public life. I will tell you how Hungary became a bastion of conservative and Christian values in Europe ... We learned from General Patton that battle brings out all that is best and removes all that is base. This is also true on the political battlefield. Here, my friends, only the best remain standing—or, in short, the ultimate condition for victory is that we must become the best. You can win if you are the best.[14]

Perhaps even more importantly, Orbán offered his and the Fidesz party's defeat in 2002, and their process of strategy and rebuilding over the next eight years, as a further parallel to American current political and social atmosphere:

> When my friend Donald Trump won the U.S. presidential election in 2016, one of his main promises was about the need to "drain the swamp" ... nevertheless he was not

[14] *Ibid.*

> re-elected in 2020. He ended up like our first conservative, Christian government in 2002: we governed outstandingly ... but we were dragged down by the swamp of the Hungarian Left. And then, between 2002 and 2010, we saw what generally happens in such circumstances: the socialists spent the people's money. Hungary sank into debt, the economy fell into recession, inflation ran out of control, unemployment rose and people were unable to pay their bills. Street violence broke out and paramilitary groups were on the march ... The Left had cut back spending on the police so much that they were unable to maintain even the pretense of order, with the law protecting perpetrators rather than victims.

In speaking about the Hungarian government between 2002 and 2010, Orbán could have been describing the American experience between 2021 and 2024. But here was the hope, and the beginning of strategizing the Hungarian model:

> Dear Friends, in 2002 we organized a popular movement and intellectual resistance, with the troops left to us after our electoral defeat. We did not adopt a defensive attitude, and we did not resign ourselves to our minority status; we played to win and proclaimed the Reconquista. ... Dear Friends, the plan succeeded. In 2010 we came back. We had worked for eight years: step by step, brick by brick, we had fought and we had built. The formula is complete. Hungary is the laboratory in which we tested the antidote to dominance by progressives.

Orbán recognized the full worth of the Hungarian model in its curative powers, not only for crushing the liberal communists of the past but for arresting their progress in the future:

> How can I contribute to today's gathering? Perhaps if I tell you how we won: how we first defeated the communist regime; then how we defeated the liberals; and then, most recently, how we defeated the international liberal Left when they combined their forces against Hungary in the election. I will tell you now how we defeated them for the first, second, third, fourth and fifth time—and how we will defeat them again.

And Hungary has been rebuilding successfully ever since, under the leadership of Orbán and the Fidesz party. Which leads us directly to Prime Minister Viktor Orbán's Twelve Points. You will see that his twelve points make strategic yet practical sense, so much so that it would be hard for the Republican party today to miss recognizing or implementing them, (yet, even now, it frustratingly fails to see their value):

Point 1: Play by your own rules. We cannot win if we continue to accept the "solutions and paths offered by others" that we know are wrong. If we are continually defamed or "branded as deplorables" or troublemakers, we know that we must be doing something right! In fact, as Orbán commented "it is suspicious if none of this happens."

Point 2: Implement conservatism in domestic politics. Supporting religious freedom and families in policy and law is a matter of strengthening the nation. Securing borders and implementing (only) legal migration, is a matter of protecting the nation. This observation, recorded by Possony in 1950, was our warning to fight the spread of Communism with targeted domestic and foreign policy. It bears repeating, especially since it has been ignored by our government officials:

> [Communism's] rise from an obscure heresy to a state religion commanding the observance of half a billion freeborn people; and the transformation of the apostles of this new despotism from inmates of police prisons into organizers of the most powerful and most oppressive police state the modern world has ever know are proof that *the business of democracy has not been conducted with wisdom, circumspection, and diligence.*[15] (Emphasis mine)

Point 3: Keep national interests at the center of foreign policy. Putting "nation first," like the slogan "America First," in foreign policy and foreign aid continues to strengthen the nation while also building alliances and supporting other countries; it is not 'isolationism'—it encourages alliances and collaboration but not at the expense of the well-being of your own citizens. "After all, what else is the purpose of any country's foreign policy except to put its own interests, the interests of its citizens, first?"[16]

Point 4: We must have the media. As Orbán said in his CPAC Hungary 2022 speech, "Left-wing opinions only appear to be in the majority when the media helps to amplify them. The root of the problem is that the modern Western media aligns itself with the views of the Left." We need to support, and fund, media that promotes traditional, wise, and nation-building

[15] Strausz-Hupe & Possony (1950). p. vii.
[16] Anton, Michael (2019). The Trump Doctrine. *Foreign Policy,* Spring 2019. p. 42.

messages. The progressive Left certainly does support and fund the media that bears their messages, and as a result, they 'own' the media in America today.

Point 5: Expose your opponent's intentions. Reveal the underlying intentions of the progressive movement confidently and early. Expose it and do not vacillate. Force your opponent *to be on the defensive.* This is an important action that got President Trump elected, and it is the approach that Republican Congress members Dr. Paul Gosar and Marjorie Taylor Greene actively take. The majority of U.S. Congress, including the former Speaker of the House Kevin McCarthy, does not.

Point 6: Implement only economic policies that work. This would seem like a no-brainer, but socialist economic policies, many based on ideology and not economic theory, are implemented all around the world today and fail. Policies that promote job growth and better living standards are priority.

Point 7: Stay away from 'extreme' theories. Whether on the right side or the left, stay away from extreme political or social ideology. It alienates voters and supporters and skews society. This is a wise admonishment, yet today it often does not matter. Extreme theories get a lot of attention by an uneducated and shallowly-informed MSNBC-absorbing public, and those theories are sometimes—like the bizarre QAnon phenomenon—wrongly placed upon all proponents of conservatism.[17]

---

[17] Isaiah 7:9b New International Version.

Point 8: Read every day. Not too long ago, I had coffee and conversation with both President Trump and Prime Minister Orbán (on separate occasions) where we discussed world events, policy issues, and politics. Both men are extremely smart and able to analyze complicated issues while still seeing and handling the 'big picture'. You have to think fast to keep up with Trump in a conversation, as his mind analyzes information quickly and moves from topic to topic. He is very informed about the world on many and various subjects. Prime Minister Orbán is a thoughtful man who first planned on being an academic. He asks questions and considers your answers.

Orbán says "no invention has yet surpassed the book as a vehicle for understanding and conveying ideas" and I agree with him. He believes we need time set aside to read about and understand the increasingly complex world, how our opponents think, and "where their thinking is flawed. If we know that, the rest is mere technique. We must translate all this into the language of everyday action and political communication." I learned that he sets aside a day each week to read, gather knowledge, and broaden his mind—I have since followed his example.

Point 9: You gotta have faith. Encourage young conservatives to engage with faith and religion. If you do not believe "you will one day be held to account for your actions before God, you will think that you can do anything that is in your power." Faith keeps us grounded, and as Orbán quoted from the prophet Isaiah: "If you do not stand firm in your faith, you will not stand at all."

Point 10: Make friends. This is a major problem within the groups of the Right, at least in America. The GOP establishment works to destroy conservatives, MAGA believers, and

Trump supporters. Perhaps worse, most establishment Republicans are happy with the status quo. Mike Pence, hopeful as a presidential candidate, further creates division by publicly declaring there is no room in the Republican party for those who stand for peace in Ukraine. Insecure elbow-jabbing, while simultaneously smiling and feigning love, abounds in DC politics and coalitions. One organization goes this way, the other goes that way—support and collaboration are not elements of its high-level leaders.

But the other side, the one which we so loudly complain about, has an extensive network of collaboration and unity. And they have for decades. Why don't we? Orbán hit the nail on the head when he said:

> Our opponents, the progressive liberals and neo-Marxists, have unlimited unity: they have one another's backs. By contrast, we conservatives are capable of squabbling with one another over the smallest issue. And then we wonder at how our opponents corner us. We do indeed possess intellectual sophistication, and we care about intellectual nuance. But if we want to succeed in politics, we should never look at what we disagree on, but instead look for our common ground ... one should not look at the issues on which we can engage in heated disputes, but look for ways in which we can work together. Believe me, if we do not, our opponents will hunt us down one by one.[18]

[18] Orbán, Viktor (2022, May 19).

Point 11: Build communities and civil society. The stronger communities are, the more chance people will see the actual benefit of voting for conservative politicians. There has been a striking difference, especially in current times, of the differences in nations built by Leftism and those built by the *truly* progressive and protectionary policies of conservative nations. We blatantly see the differences in the declining democrat-led cities of San Francisco and prosperous republican-led cities in Florida under Governor Ron DeSantis. We see the lack of terrorist attacks in a strong border state such as Hungary and the terrorist attacks in cities such as Paris, Brussels, Nice, Berlin, Manchester, and Barcelona.

Point 12: Build Institutions. This is very important. Institutions are the vehicles through which change will come—by spreading the truth and changing the deceptive and lying narratives that have taken hold in the media, in academia, and in the minds of our youth. Building institutions that teach and spread the word about conservative principles are necessary, but rare. As Orbán said in his speech, these institutions—"whether they are think-tanks, education centers, talent workshops, foreign relations institutions, youth organizations or whatever, they should have a political aspect." Politics and politicians come and go, "but institutions stay with us for generations."

This is also a strategy that has been well-used by 'progressives' for decades. With institutions they have changed the fabric of Western society. Yet, proponents of the Right have yet to understand their significance.

Have you ever wondered why LGBT activists are so politically powerful? In large part, because the liberal Left funds nonprofit organizations as an integral part of their strategy—a strategy promoted by cultural Marxists for decades. Liberal leftists are great at this strategy and the Right has not yet realized the importance of funding NGOs to the same degree.

Tools, like the Corporate Equality Index[19] developed by activists at the Human Rights Campaign, an NGO funded by organizations like George Soros' Open Society Foundations, have fundamentally changed the fabric of American society. This group compels, threatens, and pressures corporations like Target,[20] Nike, Budweiser,[21] and many others into sexual and gender-identity obsession and compliance in order to achieve a 'perfect' index score. The fact that even the Fox News corporation offers employees a "workplace gender transition plan,"[22] allows transgender people their choice of bathrooms, and encourages 'proper' pronoun use—in the pursuit of a perfect Corporate Equality Index Score (which incidentally, Fox has achieved)[23]—should give us the final clue about the power of leftist NGOs in the United States.

---

[19] Human Rights Campaign Foundation (2023). 2023 Corporate Equality Index Criteria. At *Human Rights Campaign*, Washington DC. https://www.hrc.org/resources/corporate-equality-index-criteria.

[20] Target. A Bullseye View. LGBTQIA+ Team Members & Guests. In *Target Sustainability & ESG, Diversity Equity and Inclusion.* Web accessed October 10, 2023 at: https://corporate.target.com/sustainability-governance/our-team/diversity-equity-inclusion/team-members-guests/lgbtqia

[21] Kennedy, Dana (2023, April 7). Inside the CEI system pushing brands to endorse celebs like Dylan Mulvaney. In *The New York Post.* https://nypost.com/2023/04/07/inside-the-woke-scoring-system-guiding-american-companies/.

[22] Olohan, Mary Margaret (2023, May 22). Exclusive: Leaked Policy Exposes Fox News Stances on Woke Ideology. In *The Daily Signal*, Washington DC. https://www.dailysignal.com/2023/05/22/exclusive-leaked-policy-exposes-fox-news-stances-on-woke-ideology/.

Conclusion: Choosing the Future

All of Orbán's twelve points, if heeded, can instruct us on a future path and ameliorate strategies to build and protect our countries. Such a small country, but Hungary has been a leader in overcoming the pressures to go 'along with the crowd', a crowd which currently works against foundational values and just basic common sense, and which increasingly leads with authoritarian, totalitarian, and dictatorial behaviors.

It has only been a little more than thirty years since the fall of the Soviet Union, when Warsaw Pact countries became free to develop their own form of democratic government and to reclaim their history and national identity. Yet today, many Westerners have no sense of this history nor its importance, no memory of how desperately citizens of Soviet-occupied nations fought for freedom and the right to control their own destinies. Some chose death or imprisonment rather than bow under totalitarian control.

We need Hungary, their sense of history, and their understanding of the dangers of 'progressivism' that pull mankind back into the dark parts of history and threaten to erase Western identity. But similarly, I firmly believe that Hungary needs the (best of) the West and in particular, the American-inherent

---

[23] Fox Corporation (2022, January 27). News Release: Fox Corporation Recognized with Highest Rating in 2022 Human Rights Campaign Corporate Equality Index, New York. https://investor.foxcorporation.com/news-releases/news-release-details/fox-corporation-recognized-highest-rating-2022-human-rights.

attributes of friendship, strength, individualistic fierceness, and (according to several of my European friends) just plain American 'know-how' when it comes to getting things done.

The U.S. administration must realize that we cannot foster a mutually beneficial relationship with a foreign (NATO) ally using the sort of condemnation and condescension usually reserved for recently vanquished mortal enemies. President Biden and Ambassador Pressman have both used reckless language against the Hungarians.

A U.S. administration should seek to maximize the nobler aspects of our shared beliefs, values, and traditions in order to arrive at the best possible solutions and relationship between the U.S. and Hungary. We have strong economic ties to Hungary that must be preserved as well. The United States is the third largest investor into Hungary (2020), mainly within the automotive, software development, and life sciences sectors. According to the Department of State, about 450 U.S. companies are physically located in Hungary, and U.S. Foreign Direct Investment (FDI) produced more jobs for Hungary in 2020 than investment from any other country.[24]

The Commission of the European Union acts less like a unifying force and guardian of EU treaties and more like a ringleader of 'progressive' ideology—and one that must use undemocratic processes to achieve its goal. The European Union and its Commission have fostered a low-trust relationship with Hungary and other traditional-leaning states instead of nurturing col-

[24] U.S. Department of State (2021). 2021 Investment Climate Statements: Hungary. Washington DC. https://www.state.gov/reports/2021-investment-climate-statements/hungary/#:~:text=As%20a%20bloc%2C%20the%20EU,investor%20after%20Germany%20in%20201

laboration with respect to Hungary's (and all members') sovereignty. Yet it is crucial that the EU should do so. At the 2018 United Nations General Assembly, President Trump spoke to this point:

> We believe that when nations respect the rights of their neighbors and defend the interests of their people, they can better work together to secure the blessings of safety, prosperity, and peace. Each of us here today is the emissary of a distinct culture, a rich history, and a people bound together by ties of memory, tradition, and the values that make our homelands like nowhere else on earth. ... I honor the right of every nation in this room to pursue its own customs, beliefs, and traditions.

We all know the saying about repeating history—that if we do not learn from history, we will be forced to repeat it. Are we about to repeat a horrid chapter from history? One from which the cost cannot be overestimated?

The Hungarian-American pianist and political writer Balint Vazsonyi asked, "So, which one will *we* choose? As yet, our hands are on the controls. The tools are there, we still retain our national memory, and tens of millions remain in possession of their common sense."[25]

How true for us today! But we must awaken from the slumber of complacency, conformity, and ignorance, and choose the intellectual and physical freedom, liberty, and sovereignty that our Western nations, though never perfect and always perfecting, have been built upon. Our freedom, and the freedom of many generations after us, depends upon it.

---

25 Vazsonyi, p. 259.

BIBLIOGRAPHY

About Hungary (2017, September 14). Hungary's struggles with Brussels over migrant crisis have only just begun, says state secretary. *About Hungary*, Budapest. https://abouthungary.hu/news-in-brief/hungarys-struggles-with-brussels-over-migrant-crisis-have-only-just-begun-says-minister.

About Hungary (2022, December 29). FDI in Hungary reaches record 6 billion euros in 2022, Budapest. https://abouthungary.hu/news-in-brief/fdi-in-hungary-reaches-record-6-billion-euros-in-2022.

About Hungary (2023, May 17). Finance Ministry: Hungary's economy to avoid a recession in 2023 and return to steep growth next year. Web accessed at: https://abouthungary.hu/news-in-brief/finance-ministry-hungarys-economy-to-avoid-a-recession-in-2023-and-return-to-steep-growth-next-year.

About Hungary (2023, June 20). 77% of Hungarians reject the EU's migrant resettlement quota scheme. Budapest. https://abouthungary.hu/news-in-brief/77-of-hungarians-reject-eus-migrant-resettlement-quota-scheme.

About Hungary (2023, July 27). Gulyás Gergely: Any Kind of Migrant Distribution Mechanism is Unacceptable. Web accessed at: https://abouthungary.hu/blog/gulyas-gergely-any-kind-of-migrant-distribution-mechanism-is-unacceptable.

Ács, Pal (2019). .*Reformations in Hungary in the Age of the Ottoman Conquest.* Brown, Christopher B., *et al.*, Editors, V&R Academic; Aufl. ed. Edition.

Ágoston, Gábor. (1991) "Muslim Cultural Enclaves in Hungary Under Ottoman Rule." *Acta Orientalia Academiae Scientiarum Hungaricae,* 45 (2-3). pp. 181–204.

The American-Hungarian Federation. The 1956 Hungarian Revolution: 16 Points. http://www.americanhungarianfederation.org/news_1956_16Points.html.

Andelman, A. David (2007). *A Shattered Peace: Versailles 1919 and the Price We Pay Today.* Hoboken, NJ: John T. Wiley & Sons.

Anton, Michael (2019). The Trump Doctrine. *Foreign Policy,* Spring 2019.

Applebaum, Anne (2003). Thaw—and Release. *Gulag—A History,* Anchor Books, New York.

Applebaum, Anne (2013). *Iron Curtain: The Crushing of Eastern Europe.* Knopf Doubleday Publishing.

The Atlantic Report on the World Today (1952, February). The Soviet Family. *The Atlantic* https://www.theatlantic.com/magazine/archive/1952/02/the-soviet-family/640279/

Ball, T. and Dagger, Richard (2023, August 9). Communism. Encyclopedia Britannica. https://www.britannica.com/topic/communism.

Bandholtz, Harry Hill, Major General USA (1933). *An Undiplomatic Diary,* Kruger, Fitz-Conrad, Editor, New York: Columbia University Press.

Bateman, Jon (2022, April 25). U.S.-China Technological "Decoupling": A Strategy and Policy Framework. Carnegie Endowment for International Peace, Washington DC. https://carnegieendowment.org/2022/04/25/denying-support-for-chinese-and-china-enabled-authoritarianism-and-repression-pub-86924.

BBC (2020, November 16). EU budget blocked by Hungary and Poland over rule of law issue. *BBC News*. Web accessed at: https://www.bbc.com/news/world-europe-54964858.

Borsanyi, Gyorgy (1993). *The Life of a Communist Revolutionary, Béla Kun*. Boulder, CO: Social Science Monographs. pp. 146–7.

Brown, Anthony Cave (1975). *Bodyguard of Lies*, Guilford CT: The Lyon's Press.

Cartledge, Bryan (2011). *The Will to Survive: A History of Hungary*. C. Hurst & Co

Cartographia, Kft. (1997). *Történelmi világatlasz* [*World Atlas of History*], Budapest.

Central Intelligence Agency (1987). The Tangled Web. Studies in Intelligence. Spring, 1987: 10-13-3 National Archives and Records Administration. RG263-Records of the CIA.

Colley, Rupert (2016). *The Hungarian Revolution, 1956*. CreateSpace Independent Publishing Platform.

Csák, János (2022, April 22). Where Do We Come From? What are We? Where are we Going? *Hungarian Review*, 13 (1), Budapest.

Czókos, Gergely; Kiss, Réka; Máthe´, Áron; Szalai, Zoltán, Eds. (2021). *Heroes Among Us. 50 True Stories of Brave Hungarians in the 20th Century*. Trans. Thomas Cooper. *Committee of National Remembrance*. Open Books Publish, Budapest. Courtois, S., Werth, N., Panné, J-L., Paczkowski, A., Bartošek, K., Margolin, J-L. (1999). *The Black Book of Communism: Crimes, Terror, Repression*, Harvard University Press.

Detrez, Raymond; Segaert, Barbara (Eds.). (2008). Europe and the Historical Legacies in the Balkans. P.I.E- Peter Lang S.A., Éditions Scientifiques Internationales.

Dooley, Mark (Ed.). *Against the Tide*. (2022). Bloomsbury Publishing.

Dövényi, Zoltán (2021). Economic Activity. In *National Atlas of Hungary Society* (Kocsis, Károlyl; Kovács, Zoltán; Nemerkényi, Zsombor; Gercsák, Gábor; Kincses, Áron; Tóth, Géza Eds.). Research Centre for Astronomy and Earth Sciences. Geographical Institute. Budapest. pp. 88-95.

Dulles, Allen (1947). *Germany's Underground: The Plots to Kill Hilter and End the War.* Eumenes Publishing. p. 165. Originally published in 1947 by Macmillan Company, N.Y.

The Economist (2022, November 24). The EU is withholding aid to press Hungary to reform. https://www.economist.com/europe/2022/11/24/the-eu-is-withholding-aid-to-press-hungary-to-reform.

Eri, Gyöngyi (1989). *A Golden Age: Art and Society in Hungary (1896-1914).* Barbican Art Gallery.

Ertman, T. (2011). *Birth of the Leviathan: Building States and Regimes in Medieval and Early Modern Europe.* Cambridge University Press.

EUR-Lex Access to European Union Law. Unanimity. Glossary of summaries. https://eur-lex.europa.eu/EN/legal-content/glossary/unanimity.html.

European Commission (2021, July 15). EU founding values: Commission starts legal action against Hungary and Poland for violations of fundamental rights of LGBTIQ people. Brussels. https://ec.europa.eu/commission/presscorner/detail/en/ip_21_3668.

European Parliament (2021, December 16). Parliament approves the "rule of law conditionality" for access to EU funds. News. https://www.europarl.europa.eu/news/en/press-room/20201211IPR93622/parliament-approves- the-rule-of-law-conditionality-for-access-to-eu-funds.

European Parliament (2022, September 15). MEPs: Hungary can no longer be considered a full democracy. News. Web accessed at: https://www.europarl.europa.eu/news/en/press-room/20220909IPR40137/meps-hungary-can-no-longer-be-considered-a-full-democracy.

European Parliament (2022, October 03). Rule of Law conditionality: Commission must immediately initiate proceedings. https://www.europarl.europa.eu/news/en/press-room/20220304IPR24802/rule-of-law- conditionality-commission-must-immediately-initiate-proceedings.

European Parliament (2023, April). The Treaty of Lisbon. Fact Sheets on the European Union—2023. Web accessed at https://www.europarl.europa.eu/factsheets/en/sheet/5/the-treaty-of-lisbon.

Eurostat. An Official Website of the European Union. How many marriages and divorces took place. Web accessed at: https://ec.europa.eu/eurostat/web/products-eurostat-news/-/ddn-20220516-2.

Evans, M. Stanton (2013). *Stalin's Secret Agents: The Subversion of Roosevelt's Government*. Threshold Editions.

Family Policy of Hungary. Official Brochure. Maria Kopp Institute for Demography and Families (KINCS).

Farrell, Christopher J. (2021). *Exiled Emissary George H. Earle III. Soldier, Sailor, Diplomat, Governor, Spy*. Academica Press.

Fox Corporation (2022, January 27). News Release: Fox Corporation Recognized with Highest Rating in 2022 Human Rights Campaign Corporate Equality Index, New York. https://investor.foxcorporation.com/news- releases/news-release-details/fox-corporation-recognized-highest-rating-2022-human-rights.

Frängsmyr, Tore, Editor-in-Charge; Allén, Sture, Editor (1993). *Nobel Lectures, Literature 1968-1980*, World Scientific Publishing Co., Singapore, Web accessed July 17, 2023 at: https://www.nobelprize.org/prizes/literature/1970/solzhenitsyn/biographical/.

Füredi, Frank. (2021). Foreword. In Schmidt, Mária (2021). *From Country to Nation: Thirty Years of Freedom.* (János Betlen, Trans.). Director General of the Public Foundation (Original work published 2020) pp. 9-13.

Galántai, J. (1989). *Hungary in the First World War.* Budapest.

Goldberger, Samuel (1998, February). *Goldberger on Sakmyster: Hungary's Admiral on Horseback: Miklos Horthy, 1918-1944.* H-Net Reviews in the Humanities and Social Sciences. Habsburg.

Gulyás, Gergely (2023). Minister Gulyás on the Hungarian Day of National Unity, as translated by and posted on Twitter by Secretary of State for International Communication and International spokesman for the Cabinet Office of the Prime Minister, Zoltán Kovács. Web accessed at: https://twitter.com/zoltanspox/status/1665399054585528320?s=20.

Hazony, Yoram (2018). *The Virtue of Nationalism.* New York, NY: Basic Books, 2018.

Henderson, Sir Neville (1940). *Failure of a Mission.* New York: G.P. Putnam's Sons.

The Heritage Foundation Solutions (2020, August). China Facts and Figure. *Heritage Foundation,* https://www.heritage.org/solutions/#China.

Hevesi, Eugene (1944-1945). Review of the Year. IV. Southern Europe, Hungary, *American Jewish Yearbook.* American Jewish Committee. pp. 254-261.

Horthy, Nicholas (1957). *A Life for Hungary: Memoirs of Admiral Nicholas Horthy, Regent of Hungary.* Robert Speller & Sons.

Höttl, Wilhelm (1954). *The Secret Front: Nazi Political Espionage 1938-45.* New York: Enigma Books.

House Foreign Affairs Committee (2020). Chinese Communist Party Coercion of US Companies. *United States House of Representatives.* Washington DC. https://foreignaf-

fairs.house.gov/wp-content/uploads/2020/02/CCP-Coercion-of-U.S.-Companies.pdf.
Human Rights Campaign Foundation (2023). 2023 Corporate Equality Index Criteria. At *Human Rights Campaign*, Washington DC. https://www.hrc.org/resources/corporate-equality-index-criteria.
Human Rights Watch. World Report 2022: Hungary. web accessed September 27, 2023 at: https://www.hrw.org/world-report/2022/country-chapters/hungary.
Hungarian Central Statistical Office (2018). Induced Abortions. https://www.ksh.hu/docs/eng/xftp/idoszaki/eterhesseg-megsz16.pdf.
Hungarian Central Statistical Office (2022). Number and rate of fetal losses. https://www.ksh.hu/stadat_files/nep/hu/nep0013.html.
Hungarian National Parliament (2011, April 25). The Fundamental Law of Hungary. National Avowal. https://www.parlament.hu/documents/125505/138409/Fundamental+law/73811993-c377-428d-9808-ee03d6fb8178.
Hungarian National Parliament (2021, June 23). Act LXXIX, On taking more severe action against pedophile offenders and amending certain Acts for the protection of children. https://web.archive.org/web/20220103092634/https://njt.hu/translation/J2021T0079P_00000000_FIN.PDF.
International Military Tribunal (1945). *Trial of the Major War Criminals before the International Military Tribunal,* "Blue Series" (3). [Periodical] Retrieved from the Library of Congress, https://www.loc.gov/item/2011525338_NT_Vol-III/.
International Military Tribunal, Nuremberg (1949). Re-examination of Witness Weizsäcker. 21 May 1946. XIV. 228-286. *Trial of the Major War Criminals Before the International Military Tribunal, Nuremberg, 14 November 1945 - 1 October 1946 in 42 Volumes,* Nuremberg, Germany.

Judis, John B. (2018). *The Nationalist Revival: Trade, Immigration, and the Revolt Against Globalization.* Columbia Global Reports. New York, NY.

Johnson, A. Ross (2018). Managing Media Influence Operations: Lessons from Radio Free Europe/Radio Liberty. *International Journal of Intelligence and CounterIntelligence,* 31(4), 681-701, DOI: 10.1080/08850607.2018.1488498.

Judicial Watch (2022, April 12). Judicial Watch Election Monitoring Report: Firsthand Observations of the Hungarian National Elections of April 3, 2022.

Kállay, Nicholas (1954). *Hungarian Premier.* New York: Columbia University Press.

Kennan, George (1946, February 22). *George Kennan's 'Long Telegram'.* U.S. State Department. https://nsarchive2.gwu.edu/coldwar/documents/episode-1/kennan.htm.

Kertesz, Stephen D. (1953). *Diplomacy in a Whirlpool: Hungary between Nazi Germany and Soviet Russia.* University of Notre Dame Press.

King, Harrison (2016, October). Remembering '56: The Hungarian Revolution. *Origins.* Ohio State University. https://origins.osu.edu/milestones/october-2016-remembering-56-hungarian-revolution-sixty?language_content_entity=en.

Kinsella, Ray (2023). A 'Captured and Colonised' EU Threatens Europe. *The European Conservative.* Spring (26). pp 12-17.

Kovács, Zoltán (2023, April 8). 01/03 @JuditVarga_EU: We stand firm in our commitment to protect our children, despite pressure from the liberal press and corrupt @Europarl_EN. The Hungarian reasoning is fully in line with the Charter of Fundamental Rights of the EU. *X.* https://tinyurl.com/ytwp2u8j.

Leites, Nathan (1951). *The Operational Code of the Politburo.* Rand Publications.

Lendvai, Paul (2021). *The Hungarians: A Thousand Years of Victory in Defeat.* Princeton University Press.

Library of Congress. Research Guides. Communist International (Comintern). Archives at the Library of Congress. Web accessed at: https://guides.loc.gov/comintern-archives.

Losonczy, Anne-Marie, and Kara, David (2009). Biography: Placid Karoly Olofsson. *Mémoires Européenes du Goulag.* Archives Sonores. https://www.gulagmemories.eu/en/sound-archives/salle/placid-karoly-olofsson.

Macartney, C.A. (1956). *October Fifteenth, A History of Modern Hungary 1929-1945.* Part I, Edinburgh University Press.

Magyar Nemzet (2016, December 25). Benedictine Monk Father Placid 100-years old today. Daily News Hungary, Budapest. https://dailynewshungary.com/benedictine-monk-father-placid-100-years-old-today/.

Magyar Nemzet (2023, April 11). Russians go home!—a counter-campaign was launched with American money. https://magyarnemzet.hu/belfold/2023/04/ruszkik-haza-ellen-kampany-indult-amerikai-penzbol?utm_source=hirkereso&utm_medium=referral&utm_campaign=hiraggregator&fbclid=IwAR2S-w8PNWeBHNhtHip7kr_uLHFZ-6k2271iVStJdSoNraPzyowutjqLOufo.

Maria Kopp Institute for Demography and Families (KINCS). Family Policy of Hungary: Strong families make a strong nation. Source: Hungarian Statistical Office Budget Laws.

Maria Kopp Institute for Demography and Families (KINCS) (2022, May 3). 10+1 Facts About Mothers Who Gave Birth in the 2010s. Source: Hungarian Central Statistical Office.

Mayer, Arno J. (1967). *Politics and Diplomacy of Peacemaking. Containment and Counterrevolution at Versailles, 1918–1919.* New York: Knopf.

Michener, James A. (1957). Foreward. In *The Bridge at Andau,* New York: Dial Press.

Mee, Charles L., Jr. (1980). *The End of Order: Versailles 1919*. New York: E.P. Dutton.

Ministry of Justice (2021). The Fundamental Law of Hungary of 25 April 2011. Incorporating First -Ninth Amendments. National Avowal.

Minister of State. Ministry of Foreign Affairs of Hungary. The Fundamental Law. Official Document.

Montgomery, John F. (1947). *Hungary: The Unwilling Satellite*. The Devin-Adair Company.

Muir, Rory (2008). Cavalry Combat. *Tactics and the Experience of Battle in the Age of Napoleon*, New Haven: Yale University Press.

Murray, Douglas (2018). *The Strange Death of Europe. Immigration, Identity, Islam*. Bloomsbury Publishing.

National Election Office. (2010, April 25) Round 2 of the Parliamentary Election of 2010. Web accessed at: https://static.valasztas.hu//dyn/pv10/outroot/vdin2/en/l22.htm

National Security Archive (2017, May 10). Hungary, 1956: Reviving the Debate over (In)Action during the Revolution. George Washington University, Washington, DC. https://nsarchive.gwu.edu/briefing-book/openness-russia-eastern-europe/2017-05-10/hungary-1956-reviving-debate-over-us

North Atlantic Treaty Organization (NATO). The Cold War: Defense and Deterrence. What was the Warsaw Pact. https://www.nato.int/cps/en/natohq/declassified_138294.htm

Office for Democratic (2022, April 3). Institutions and Human Rights. Hungary. Parliamentary Elections and Referendum. Election Observation Mission Final Report. Web accessed at: https://www.valasztas.hu/web/national-election-office/parliamentary-elections-2022

Open Society Foundations Awarded Grants. Amnesty International. Web accessed at: https://www.opensocietyfoundations.org/grants/past?filter_keyword=amnesty+international

Open Society Foundations Awarded Grants. Freedom House. Web accessed at: https://www.opensocietyfoundations.org/grants/past?filter_keyword=freedom+house

Open Society Foundations Awarded Grants. Human Rights Watch. Web accessed at: https://www.opensocietyfoundations.org/grants/past?filter_keyword=human+rights+watch

Orbán, Tamás (2021). Thirty Years of Visegrad Summits and the Themes of a Central European Cooperation. In Bendarzsevszkij, Anton (Ed.). *30 Years of The V4*. Danube Institute. pp. 10-20.

Orban, Viktor (2014, July 26). XXV. Bálványos Free Summer University and Youth Camp, Băile Tuşnad (Tusnádfürdő).

Orbán, Viktor (2017, May 25). Prime Minister Viktor Orbán's opening speech at the Second Budapest World Congress of Families. Website of the Hungarian Government. Web accessed at: https://2015-2019.kormany.hu/en/the-prime-minister/the-prime-minister-s-speeches/prime-minister-viktor-orban-s-opening-speech-at-the-2nd-budapest-world-congress-of-families

Orbán, Viktor (2017, July 22). Address to the 28th Bálványos Summer Open University and Student Camp. In *About Hungary*, Budapest. https://abouthungary.hu/speeches-and-remarks/viktor-orbans-speech-at-the-28th-balvanyos-summer-open-university-and-student-camp.

Organisation for Economic Co-operation and Development (OECD) (2021, July). Hungary. OECD Economic Surveys. Executive Summary.

Organisation of Economic Co-operation and Development (OECD) (2022, November). Economic Outlook, Preliminary Version (2).

Pállfy, Géza (2001). "The Impact of the Ottoman Rule on Hungary," *Hungarian Studies Review,* Toronto, 26 (1-2). pp. 109–132.

Petersen, Neal H. (Ed.). (1996). *From Hitler's Doorstep:The Wartime Intelligence Reports of Allen Dulles,* University Park, PA: Pennsylvania State University Press.

Pew Research (August 2, 2016). Number of Refugees to Europe Surges to Record 1.3 Million in 2015. Pew Research Center. Web accessed at: https://www.pewresearch.org/global/2016/08/02/number-of-refugees-to-europe-surges-to-record-1-3-million-in-2015/#:~:text=By%20comparison%2C%20Hungary%20had%201%2C770,above%20the%20total%20European %20rate.

Pinto, Jaime N. (2022). Forged by History: The Hungarian Struggle for Nationhood. *The European Conservative,* Spring 2022, Issue 22, 30-37.

Planctus Destructionis Regni Hungariae Per Tartaros. The Latin Library, http://www.thelatinlibrary.com/planctus.html.

Possony, Stefan, T. (1959). The Soviet Psychological Approach. First published in *SRI Journal,* Fourth Quarter, 1959. In Sanders, Ralph & Brown, Fred R. (Eds.). (1961). *National Security Management: Global Psychological Conflict,* Industrial College of the Armed Forces, Washington, DC. p. 58.

Pritz, Pál (2003). Hungarian Foreign Policy in the Interwar Period. *Hungarian Academy of Sciences.* Budapest.

Rapley, John (2007). Understanding Development, Lynne Rienner Publishers, London.

Reagan, Ronald (1964, October 27). A Time for Choosing Speech. *Ronald Reagan Presidential Library & Museum.* https://www.reaganlibrary.gov/reagans/ronald-reagan/time-choosing-speech-october-27-1964#:~:text=If%20 we%20lose%20freedom%20here,of%20man%27s%20relation%20to%20man.

Redevski, Juris (2021, Winter). A Warning from the Past. *European Conservative.* (21). pp. 82-90.

Rettie, John (2009, January 22). Khrushchev, Secrets and Me. In Our Own Correspondent, *BBC 4 Radio.*

Reuters. (2021, October 12). Polish prime minister accuses opposition of lying about 'Polexit.' *Reuters.* https://www.reuters.com/world/europe/polish-prime-minister-accuses-opposition-lying-about-polexit-2021-10- 12/

Reuters (2022, July 9). U.S. Treasury To End 1979 Treaty With Global Minimum Tax Holdout Hungary. Europe. *Reuters.* Web accessed at: https://www.reuters.com/world/europe/us-treasury-end-1979-treaty-with-global-minimum-tax-holdout-hungary-2022-07-08/.

Rice, Andrea Lauer, Edith K. Lauer (Eds.). (2006). *56 Stories: Personal Recollections of the 1956 Hungarian Revolution. A Hungarian American Perspective.* Kortárs Kiado´, Budapest, Hungary.

Rivkin-Fish, Michelle, Ph.D. (2017). Legacies of 1917 in Contemporary Russian Public Health: Addiction, HIV, and Abortion. *American Journal of Public Health,* 107(11), 1731–1735. https://doi.org/10.2105/AJPH.2017.304064 https://www.ncbi.nlm.nih.gov/pmc/articles/PMC5637678/.

Sabine, George H. (1955). Ideological Conflict and the Struggle for Power. In Sanders, Ralph & Brown, Fred R. (Eds.). (1961). *National Security Management: Global Psychological Conflict.* Industrial College of the Armed Forces, Washington, DC. pp. 3-21.

Sakmyster, Thomas L. (1994). *Hungary's Admiral on Horseback: Miklós Horthy, 1918-1944.* East European Monographs.

Sanders, Ralph & Brown, Fred R., Eds. (1961). *National Security Management: Global Psychological Conflict*, Industrial College of the Armed Forces, Washington, D.C.,

Semjén, Zsolt (2017). In *the Future of Europe: Hungary: Brave and Free*. Békés, Márton (Ed.). p. 121.

Seton-Watson, H. and C. (1981). *The Making of a New Europe*, London.

Schlafly, Phyllis (1973, February 13). Mindszenty the Man. *The Phyllis Schlafly Report*. 6 (7). Section 1.

Schmidt, Mária (2018). Language and Liberty. (Békés, Márton, ed.) (Betlen, J. and Bottyán, G., Trans.) Director General of the Public Endowment.

Schmidt, Mária (Ed.). (2019). *Terror Háza*, Public Foundation for Research on Central and Eastern European History and Society, Budapest.

Schmidt, Mária (2021). *From Country to Nation: Thirty Years of Freedom*. (János Betlen, Trans.) Director General of the Public Foundation (Original work published 2020).

Scruton, Roger (2009). The Flame That Was Snuffed Out by Freedom. *The Times* In Dooley, Mark (Ed.) (2022). *Against the Tide*. Bloomsbury Publishing, pp. 19-22.

Scruton, Roger (2013). Identity, Marriage, Family: Our Core Conservative Values Have Been Betrayed. *The Guardian*. In Dooley, Mark (Ed.), *Against the Tide*. Bloomsbury Publishing. pp. 50-53.

Scruton, Roger (2014). *How to be a Conservative*. Bloomsbury Publishing. London.

Scruton, Roger (2019, December 21). My 2019. *Spectator*. In Dooley, Mark (Ed.). *Against the Tide*. (2022). Bloomsbury Publishing. pp. 224-231.

Solzhenitsyn, A. The Way of Life and Customs of the Natives. *The Gulag Archipelago Part III, Chapter 7*. In Ericsson, Edward E., Jr.; Mahoney, Daniel J. (Eds.). (2006). *The Solz-*

henitsyn Reader. New and Essential Writings 1947-2005. pp. 238-240.

Soucy, R. (2023, August 25). Fascism. Encyclopedia Britannica. https://www.britannica.com/topic/fascism.

Stoye, J. (2008). *The Siege of Vienna.* Pegasus.

Strausz-Hupé, Robert, and Possony, Stefan T. (1950). *International Relations in the Age of the Conflict between Democracy and Dictatorship.* McGraw-Hill Book Co., Inc.

Swiss Legation Report of the Russian Invasion of Hungary in the Spring of 1945, Appendix III. In Montgomery, p. 239.

Target. A Bullseye View. LGBTQIA+ Team Members & Guests. In *Target Sustainability & ESG, Diversity Equity and Inclusion.* Web accessed October 10, 2023 at: https://corporate.target.com/sustainability-governance/our-team/diversity-equity-inclusion/team-members-guests/lgbtqia.

Toynbee, Arnold (1973). *Constantine Porphyrogenitus and His World.* Oxford University Press.

Treaty of Lisbon (2007, December 17). Amending The Treaty on European Union and The Treaty Establishing the European Community. Declaration No. 17 Declaration Concerning Primacy.

UN General Assembly (1957). *Report of the Special Committee on the Problem of Hungary.* Chapter VII. D (The Political Background of the Second Soviet Intervention).

UNHCR Operational Data Portal. Ukraine Refugee Situation. Countries Featured in the Refugee Response Plan. Hungary. Web accessed August 26, 2023 at: https://data.unhcr.org/en/situations/ukraine.

United Nations Human Development Reports. Human Development Index (HDI) Web accessed at: https://hdr.undp.org/data-center/human-development-index#/indicies/HDI. Chart downloaded on Hungary HDI. GNI per capita 2017 PPP.

United Nations High Commission for Refugees. Ukraine Refugee Situation. Operational Data Portal. Web accessed October 28, 2023: https://data.unhcr.org/en/situations/ukraine.

United Nations Human Development Reports. Hungary. Data updates as of September 8, 2022. Web accessed at: https://hdr.undp.org/data-center/specific-country-data#/countries/HUN.

United Nations Population Fund (2023). The Problem with Too Few. In *United Nations*, New York. https://www.unfpa.org/swp2023/too-few.

U.S. Department of State (2021). 2021 Investment Climate Statements: Hungary. Washington DC. https://www.state.gov/reports/2021-investment-climate-statements/hungary/#:~:text=As%20a%20bloc%2C%20the%20EU,investor%20after%20Germany%20in%2020 1.

Ürményházi, Attila J. (2006, February). The Hungarian Revolution-Uprising, Budapest, 1956. *American- Hungarian Federation*, Washington, DC.

Ungváry, Krisztián (1995). The 'Second Stalingrad': The Destruction of Axis Forces at Budapest (February, 1945). In Dreisziger, Nandor (Ed.). *Hungary in the Age of Total War (1938-1948)*. (1998) Columbia University Press. p. 152.

VanBuren, Denise Doring (2022). Recalling the Life, Death and Courageous Example of Michael Kováts. *Daughters of the American Revolution*. https://tinyurl.com/3k39976j.

Várdy, Steven Béla (1998). The Impact of Trianon upon the Hungarian Mind: Irredentism and Hungary's Path to War. In Dreisziger, Nándor (Ed.). *Hungary in the Age of Total War*. New York: Columbia University Press. pp. 27-48; p. 28.

Vatican Archive. Admonition VI. Admonitions of St. Stephen, King of Hungary to his son Emeric. Based on translation from Message of John Paul II to the Hungarian Nation for the Millennium of St. Stephen Coronation. Vatican Archive.

https://www.vatican.va/content/john-paul-ii/en/speeches/2000/jul-sep/documents/hf_jp-ii_spe_20000821_santo-stefano.pdf.

Vecsey, Joseph. (1972) *Mindszenty the Man.* As told to Phyllis Schlafly. Cardinal Mindszenty Foundation. St. Louis.

Vermes, G. (1989). *István Tisza,* in Bödy, P. (Ed.). *Hungarian Statesmen of Destiny, 1860 – 1960.* Boulder, CO. p. 328.

Visegrad Group. Visegrad Group Defence Cooperation. https://www.visegradgroup.eu/about/cooperation/defence.

Visegrad Post (2002, May 24). Viktor Orbán's Speech at the CPAC on 19 May 2022. https://visegradpost.com/en/2022/05/24/viktor-orbans-speech-at-the-cpac-on-19-may-2022/

West, Diana (2013). *American Betrayal. The Secret Assault on our Nation's Character.* St. Martin's Press.

The White House (2021, January 21). National Climate Task Force. Washington DC. https://www.whitehouse.gov/climate/.

The World Bank World Development Indicators Online Web accessed 2023 at: https://databank.worldbank.org/reports.aspx?source=2&series=SH.XPD.CHEX.GD.ZS&country=.

The World Bank World Development Indicators Online. Web accessed August 2023 at: https://databank.worldbank.org/reports.aspx?source=2&series=SH.XPD.CHEX.GD.ZS&country=.

The World Bank. Fertility rate, total (births per woman) Hungary. Web accessed at: https://data.worldbank.org/indicator/SP.DYN.TFRT.IN?locations=HU

The World Bank. Hungary. Web accessed August 2023 at: https://data.worldbank.org/country/HU

The World Bank (2022). International Comparison Program, World Bank | World Development Indicators database, World Bank | Eurostat-OECD PPP Programme. GNI

Per Capita, PPP (current international $)—China. https://data.worldbank.org/indicator/NY.GNP.PCAP.PP.CD?locations=CN.

Yalta Conference Agreement, Declaration of a Liberated Europe. February 11, 1945 (2013, January 17). Wilson Center Digital Archive, National Archives. https://digitalarchive.wilsoncenter.org/document/116176.

THE CENTER FOR FUNDAMENTAL RIGHTS

It is among the primary aims of the Center for Fundamental Rights to re-discover books written from a conservative perspective that have previously been unjustly overlooked, or whose publication faced obstacles due to their courageous, straight language. Be they in Hungarian, or foreign languages, we consider it our duty to support the work of intellectually honest thinkers. For us, the most important task is to bring those books to the readers, that help expand the toolset of "common sense".

We hope you'll enjoy our books.

ALAPJOGOKÉRT KÖZPONT
CENTER FOR FUNDAMENTAL RIGHTS

The publication of
the **Last Warning to the West**
was greatly inspired by and
its research was strongly supported by:

István Kovács - Balázs Molnár - Miklós Szánthó

MAKING HUNGARY GREAT AGAIN

2010-2022

INTEGRITY, COURAGE, DIGNITY

We recommend this book, detailing the first decade of conservative government, by the Center for Fundamental Rights to those readers who wish to attain a wider understanding of the practical achievements of Hungary's government between 2010 and 2020, and who wish to gain insight into the intellectual background and the strategic thinking behind those results.

Gergely Szilvay

A CRITIQUE OF GENDER THEORY

THOUGHTS ON THE REVOLUTION IN ANTHROPOLOGY FROM FEMINISM TO TRANS

This book explores gender theory, why it is possible to deal with its various branches as a single phenomenon, the real-life consequences of this approach, and why it is utterly wrong. The reader can find out what "gender mainstreaming" means, if there is such a thing as "gay propaganda", if gender theory qualifies as an ideology, why it's a bad idea to re-write our fairy tales, or subject those of our fellow human beings who feel severe discomfort over their genders to sex change surgery. The author delves into the mistakes of the feminists, and demonstrates the distorted trends that appear in universities due to these mistakes. The book makes it clear that gender roles are far from being a pure social construct and have deep biological roots.

Áron Máthé

THE UKRAINIAN PUZZLE

HUNGARY'S PERSPECTIVE ON A CHANGING NEIGHBOR

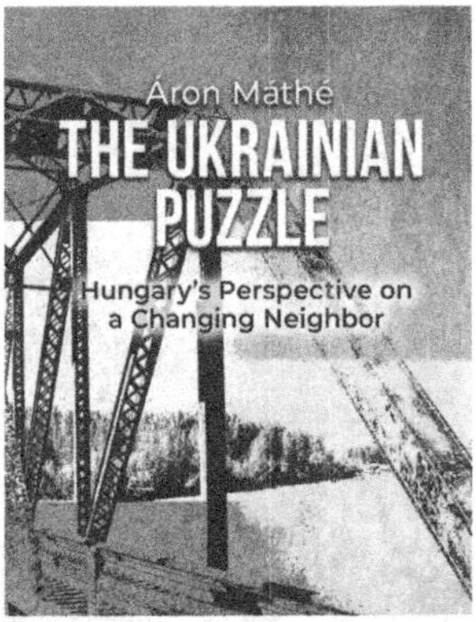

There is a perception in both Ukraine and Hungary, fuelled by atrocious reporting in the major liberal international media, that the two countries are hostile to each other. The post-Maidan laws passed by the new government in Kiev on official language and education were aimed at the Russian minority, but Hungarians who have lived in Subcarpathia for over a millennium are collateral damage. A survey conducted in the spring of 2023 found that 42 percent of Ukrainian respondents considered Hungary an "enemy country." We believe that bad blood is not only the product of propaganda that maliciously misrepresents or simply misunderstands Hungary's pro-peace foreign policy position. It may also be due to the fact that over the past three decades Hungary has not devoted sufficient energy to demonstrating to Ukrainians - and indeed to all of Europe - the efforts it has made on behalf of our eastern neighbor since the end of the Cold War and the fall of communism. This book is primarily a collection of facts, along with some historical background.

Tilo Schabert

BOSTON POLITICS

THE CREATIVITY OF POWER

The book, as its title suggests, deals with politics and creative strategies of using political power. Those who successfully deploy good political power need to display such intellectual and intuitive prowess, along with such mental and physical resilience, that "politics" could justifiably be identified as a form of art, in the old-fashioned, noble sense of the word. In Boston Politics, Tilo Schabert dissects the political operation of the American city of Boston, which works as a great model for understanding everything we need to know about using political power. Local politics revolves around a single person, the main character of the book, Kevin H. White, the city mayor. Mr. White is the originator of every political event, he is also where the buck stops, he is the sole actor capable of seeing the forest among all the myriad branches of the many trees. Boston Politics is much more a than foundational text on the history of modern politics. It's a book for all those who want to understand what lies behind effective governance and the use of political power.

Michael J. Knowles's famous best-seller,
the **REASONS TO VOTE FOR DEMOCRATS - A COMPREHENSIVE GUIDE** published in Hungarian:

Michael J. Knowles

MIÉRT IS SZAVAZZUNK A LIBERNYÁKOKRA?

ÁTFOGÓ, KIMERÍTŐ SZAKMAI ÚTMUTATÓ

Michael J. Knowles is one of the best-known conservative political commentators in the United States and host of The Michael Knowles Show. Six years ago, the writer-actor Knowles did something few have dared to do before: he wrote a cold but honest critique of liberal mainstream politics in his own unique form. "Reasons to Vote for Democrats is the author's take on the values he believes liberal politics should embody. The book is 245 pages, but only the chapter headings are written by the author, the book is mainly blank pages. The reason for this is that, in Knowles's view, the Liberals are very poor at what they do. It is a memorial to liberalism as an outdated ideology which, in his view, has become a mere mechanism of power.

Made in the USA
Las Vegas, NV
22 December 2023

83452415R00197